ŽIŽEK'S POLITICS

ŽIŽEK'S POLITICS

Jodi Dean

Routledge
Taylor & Francis Group
New York London

Routledge is an imprint of the
Taylor & Francis Group, an informa business

Routledge
Taylor & Francis Group
270 Madison Avenue
New York, NY 10016

Routledge
Taylor & Francis Group
2 Park Square
Milton Park, Abingdon
Oxon OX14 4RN

International Standard Book Number-10: 0-415-95176-3 (Softcover) 0-415-95175-5 (Hardcover)
International Standard Book Number-13: 978-0-415-95176-0 (Softcover) 978-0-415-95175-3 (Hardcover)

Library of Congress Cataloging-in-Publication Data

Dean, Jodi, 1962-
    Zizek's politics / by Jodi Dean.
      p. cm.
    ISBN 0-415-95175-5 (hardcover) -- ISBN 0-415-95176-3 (pbk.)
    1. Žižek, Slavoj. 2. Political science--Philosophy. 3. Radicalism. I. Title.

JA71.D433 2006
320.092--dc22
                                                    2006004542

Visit the Taylor & Francis Web site at
http://www.taylorandfrancis.com

and the Routledge Web site at
http://www.routledge-ny.com

For Kian, the first

Contents

Acknowledgments   ix

Introduction   xi

Chapter 1   Enjoyment as a Category of Political Theory   1

Chapter 2   Fascism and Stalinism   47

Chapter 3   Democratic Fundamentalism   95

Chapter 4   Law: From Superego to Love   135

Conclusion: Revolution Today   179

Notes   205

Index   231

ACKNOWLEDGMENTS

Nearly a decade ago, Van Zimmerman's perverse enjoyment in the oscillations between the positions of the fool and the knave incited my interest in Žižek. I'm still not sure whether to thank Van, curse him, or recognize that in academic work one thanks those whom one has in a certain sense already cursed. Among the accursed who've shared in my efforts to work through Žižek's thought are those who have taken the time to read and comment on my blog, I Cite. I was surprised and delighted to be in conversation with a variety of people from whom I likely would not have learned had my thinking been confined to the institutional settings typical of the academy. Blogging the trials and errors constitutive of thinking and writing enabled me to think with others and in so doing confront possibilities I would not have imagined alone. I am indebted to these often anonymous (or known to me only by first names or avatars) interlocutors for their daily provocations, particularly to those who engaged the posts on Žižek. Fortunately, some have not remained anonymous so I can thank them by name: P. E. Bird, Matt Calarco, Marc E. Goodman, Doug Johnson, Adam Kotsko, Marc Lombardo, Amish Lovelock, Peter Milat, John Reeve, Charles Rozier, Kenneth Rufo, Steven Shaviro, Hugh Thomas, Adam Thurschwell, and George Wolfe. I am also indebted to my cocontributors to the group blog, Long

Sunday, and those who have joined us in discussion. A very special thanks goes to Alain Wittman, invaluable to both I Cite and Long Sunday, who has commented most helpfully on numerous portions of this book. I am uncomfortably aware of the too many places where I have not been able to do justice to his criticisms and concerns. So I thank and curse Alain for this awareness.

I thank and curse other readers who have given their time to this project, offering valuable (if unheeded) suggestions on various sections of the manuscript: Anna Creadick, Tom Dumm, Peter Fitzpatrick (and the students in his discussion group on law and social theory at Birkbeck School of Law), Bob Gooding-Williams, Bill MacNeil, Andrew Norris, and Mark Reinhardt. I am particularly indebted to Lee Quinby's generous readings of each chapter. Our continuing conversations inspire me as I find myself comforted yet mystified by Lee's unending optimism.

Finally, I am indebted without reservation to the one who has endured (and likely cursed) this project on numerous levels over the years. Paul Passavant read and commented on numerous drafts of the manuscript. He listened and responded as I worked through various arguments. And, fortunately, he held onto the steering wheel of a car with threadbare tires, during a torrential downpour on the New York State Thruway, as he drove to the airport a manically vocal Slavoj Žižek (who was enthusiastically praising Paul's triumphal masculinity in weathering the storm).

Chapters three and four were published, respectively as "Žižek against Democracy," *Law, Culture and the Humanities* (2005) 1: 154-177 and "Žižek on Law," *Law and Critique* (2004) 15: 1-24. Each has been substantially updated and revised.

Geneva, New York
February 2006

INTRODUCTION

A few years ago, I interviewed Slovenian philosopher Slavoj Žižek for the Abercrombie and Fitch catalog. The catalog was well known in the United States for selling clothes by featuring barely clad teenage bodies in highly charged homoerotic photographs by Bruce Weber. It also ran interviews with academics, writers, musicians, and more or less alternative celebrities. That Abercrombie wanted to feature this philosopher (who later supplied text for a particularly beautiful and risqué edition of the catalog) testifies to his near pop-star status. So do the massive crowds attending his lectures across the globe and the fact that he is the subject of a feature length documentary film directed by Astra Taylor. Be that as it may, when I told Žižek that I would show him the interview in advance, he cheerily replied, "Oh that's not necessary. Whatever I say, you can make me say the opposite!"

Žižek is not an analytically formal or traditional political philosopher. What Ernesto Laclau says of Žižek's early tour de force, *The Sublime Object of Ideology*, also applies to Žižek's work more generally: rather than "a systematic structure in which an argument is developed according to a predetermined plan," Žižek provides "a series of theoretical interventions which shed mutual light on each other, not in terms of the *progression* of the argument, but in terms of what we could call the *reiteration* of the latter in different discursive contexts."[1] Žižek might begin an article or book chapter with a question or observation, something along the lines of "have you ever noticed the difference between French, German, and British toilets?" He will offer an explanation for the difference and then he might suggest a second explanation that is diametrically opposed to the first one. He will likely conclude by observing how the first and second explanations are "two sides of the same coin," how in these two seemingly opposed interpretations we in fact encounter a certain unity. Saying the opposite can be just another way of saying the same thing—if we push the idea far enough.

After undertaking such a dialectical reversal or confronting a parallax gap Žižek may, in what appears at first glance to be a rather stunning non sequitur, turn to a Hitchcock film (a discussion of *Vertigo* appears in almost every one of his books) or perhaps to an idea first developed by the French psychoanalytic philosopher Jacques Lacan. Yet these moves are not arbitrary jumps. They are, in fact, extensions of the initial idea into a different domain, a domain that may have previously seemed clear, a domain that Žižek now shows to contain an unsettling paradox, an excess that our previous understanding cannot account for.

Žižek's arguments are compelling because they open up and enliven what has become fixed and stale. The strength of a given conceptualization thus becomes manifest through repeated applications and expressions. A remarkable aspect of this repetition is the way it proceeds through error. That is, Žižek's applications demonstrate how getting the right answer, getting to truth, is a process of trial and error, or, more precisely, a process of discerning what was missing from our previous way of thinking. If a problem is important enough to think through, then this thinking through will necessarily involve mistakes and omissions. Such mistakes can create new spaces for thought; the errors can incite more thinking, new directions. As my father once told me, anything worth doing is worth doing badly. An idea that is perfect and whole does not provide any space for further thought. Nothing is left to say. Žižek's mode of thinking, one that draws heavily from the philosopher G. W. F. Hegel, extends out of the insight that such perfect wholes are illusions. There is always something left out, a remainder or excess the very exclusion of which was necessary for the production of the "whole" in the first place. Locating this excess and disrupting the whole, working with negativity—the force of negation—is thus a central component of Žižek's approach.

Of course, most readers first become interested in Žižek because of the sheer liveliness of his writing.[2] I was initially stunned and intrigued by his recounting of a joke about a monkey who goes into a bar and washes his testicles in a customer's whiskey (this little story is in *The Plague of Fantasies*). Žižek combines dense philosophical discussions with dirty jokes, odd anecdotes, and commentaries on popular culture. Commentators and critics alike tend to emphasize this style, sometimes treating it as the key to his thought, sometimes treating it as grounds for dismissing Žižek altogether.[3] To my mind, jokes about monkey testicles make reading about Hegel just a little bit more fun; a couple of paragraphs on alien films are a reward for plowing through a long discussion of Jacques Lacan.

At any rate, those less enamored of Žižek's unique combination of high and low culture often combine their criticism with an emphasis on how much Žižek writes. Not only has he published over twenty books in English alone, but he also writes for the popular press, that is for periodicals such as the *New York Times*, the *London Review of Books*, the *Frankfurter Rundschau*, *In These Times*, *The Guardian*, and more. He also speaks to large audiences all over the world, is frequently interviewed, and, over all, seems to have attained a popularity or cult status exceedingly rare for a philosopher.

A second oft-emphasized aspect of Žižek's writing is the extent and difficulty of his archive. He develops his thought through critical dialogue with a vast array of formidable thinkers, including, but not limited to, Giorgio Agamben, Louis Althusser, Alain Badiou, Judith Butler, Gilles Deleuze, Jacques Derrida, Rene Descartes, Sigmund Freud, G.W. F. Hegel, Martin Heidegger, Immanuel Kant, Soren Kierkegaard, Jacques Lacan, Ernesto Laclau, V. I. Lenin, Nicolas Malebranche, Karl Marx, Blaise Pascal, Saint Paul, Jacques Ranciere, and F. W. J. Schelling. In light of this challenging and extensive archive, as well as of the singular importance of Hegel and Lacan for Žižek's working through of the philosophical tradition, Ian Parker takes the view that there is no "theoretical system as such in Žižek's work."[4] Instead, there are only the concepts that he borrows from these thinkers, concepts distorted in different ways depending on the context, audience, or deadlock that needs to be avoided. I disagree. I think it is absolutely nonsensical to claim that someone who relies so heavily on Hegelian dialectics and Lacanian formalism is unsystematic. Accordingly, this book presents Žižek's specific, systematic, approach to political theory.

If one's goal is to understand Žižek, then a systematic approach has distinct advantages over the emphasis on style and the emphasis on difficulty. These advantages start to appear when we recognize the paradoxical way that these two emphases clash, how each excludes the other. One says that Žižek is too popular, the other that he is too elite (so elite that only someone well versed in each of the thinkers I listed above could ever hope to understand him!). Together these emphases express a sense that Žižek is, somehow, too much.

The emphasis on style often reflects a prior conception of serious thinking as necessarily detached from popular culture. According to this conception, the true philosopher should not be sullied by such earthy matters as toilet design and trends in women's pubic hair. Neither should the true philosopher be so *out there*, so present in popular media. Žižek is himself so present that in 2004 the *Chronicle of Higher Education* ran a regular column by Scott McLemee entitled "Žižek Watch." McLemee's articles treated Žižek as a pop phenomenon, someone with fans, someone providing "wide eyed" readers with addictive concoctions of Hitchcock, "fisting," and Hollywood features. Indeed, in his last column, McLemee writes, "there is something about reading Mr. Žižek that calls to mind certain remarks by Andy Warhol on the reassuring consistency of Coke and Campbell's soup. No matter which can you open, it's going to be the same as the last one you tasted."[5] McLemee's column thus highlights the blurriness between Žižek's writing about popular culture and his status as a figure in pop culture.

It's important, though, to keep this status in perspective. A quick glance at Amazon Bookseller's sales rankings shows that not one of Žižek's books is among the top 25,000 books sold. There are other public intellectuals—Elaine Scarry, Cornell West (who appeared in *The Matrix Reloaded*), bell hooks—with much greater name recognition and broader popular appeal. Why then the preoccupation with Žižek's popularity? To my mind, it is because his enthusiasm for popular culture seems to some to be antagonistic to serious thought. His enjoyment of mainstream movies, his delight in shocking audiences with ethnic and sexual jokes, suggests to many an excess incompatible with rigorous, systematic thought.

This is not my view. In fact, I argue in this book that Žižek presents a systematic theory of politics. The key component of this system is the category of enjoyment. As I explain in Chapter One, Žižek's thinking about enjoyment relies on the work of psychoanalyst Jacques Lacan. Enjoyment, *jouissance*, is a kind of ambiguous excess, an object that sets off desire, that transforms an everyday item or acquaintance into something more, something special, the

"One." What is important at this point, though, is that this very notion of enjoyment can shed light on the place of popular culture in Žižek's thought.

In *For They Know Not What They Do*, Žižek says that at the center of the theoretical space of that book (and its predecessor, *The Sublime Object of Ideology*) is "of course the author's (and as the author hopes, also the reader's) enjoyment of popular culture."[6] At the center of his thinking, then, is enjoyment—his and others'. Enjoyment, for Žižek, is a term of art, a technical, Lacanian concept that denotes an intense, excessive, pleasure-pain. Enjoyment by its very nature is excessive, something that can lure us into a kind of idiotic stupor or ecstatic state. Moreover, as I hope to make clear in this book, our relationship to enjoyment is never easy, never innocent. Enjoyment can be that extra kick *on behalf of which* we do our duty: "Sorry about that extra twenty dollars I tacked onto your ticket, ma'm, but, well, it's the law" or "These comments I wrote on your paper may seem cruel, but, well, it's really for your own good." So when Žižek says that his enjoyment of popular culture and ours is at the center of these books, he is not simply referring to the pleasures of Hollywood films. Rather, he is calling our attention to the way that we all, in contemporary consumer-driven entertainment society, enjoy popular culture and the way this enjoyment binds us into the ideological formation that supports global capital.

Here is an example. I read celebrity tabloids—the really awful kinds that focus on diets, clothes, romance, and scandal. These tabloids are my reward for going to the gym. Now, one might say that, as an academic, I am not the typical tabloid reader, that somehow I have a critical, intellectual distance from these stories. What Žižek makes clear is how this kind of distance is in fact the *sine qua non* of ideology. As I explain in the first chapter, Žižek reworks the Marxist category of ideology to conceive it in terms of the fantasy that attaches us to a formation and thus supplies us with enjoyment. For Žižek, ideology is manifest not in what we know, but in what we do, in the practices and behaviors in which we persist even as we know better. When I distance myself from other tabloid readers, then, I feel special, important (not like those poor unfortunates who really care who Brad Pitt marries or how much Lindsay Lohan weighs). This distance, moreover, relieves me of responsibility for the fact that at the level of what I am doing, buying and reading the magazine, my acts are exactly the same as those of anyone else who purchases tabloids. By emphasizing the category of enjoyment, then, Žižek challenges us to recognize, and take responsibility for, our own enjoyment.

By inserting popular culture into his writing, and himself into popular culture, Žižek enacts the way enjoyment colors or stains *all thinking and acting*. What this means, as I set out in detail in Chapter Three, is that there is a deep nonrational and libidinal nugget in even the most rational, formal ways of thinking. Again, it is not simply that popular culture is at the core of the theoretical enterprise of his books—it is that enjoyment is. Enjoyment is an unavoidable component of *any* philosophical effort (though many try to deny it). Žižek thus emphasizes the inevitable stain on philosophy, on thought, as he tries to demonstrate a way of thinking that breaks with (Žižek often uses Lacan's term *traverses*) the fantasy of "pure reason."

This leads to another key element of Žižek's thought: the possibility of taking the position of the excess. As I explain in discussions of his readings of St. Paul and Lenin, Žižek theorizes revolutionary politics as occurring through the occupation of this excessive place. Paul endeavors to put the Christian message to work, to establish new collectives beyond old oppositions between Greeks and Jews. Lenin also breaks with the given, arguing against all around him and against Marxist orthodoxy that the time for revolution is now, that it cannot be predicted, awaited, but must be accomplished with no assurances of success. Like Paul, he puts truth to work, organizing it in the form of a revolutionary political Party.

Žižek emphasizes that Lacan conceptualized this excessive place, this place without guarantees, in his formula for "the discourse of the analyst" (which I set out in Chapter Two). In psychoanalysis, the analyst just sits there, asking questions from time to time. She is some kind of object or cipher onto which the analysand transfers love, desire, aggression, and knowledge. The analysand, in other words, proceeds through analysis by positing the analyst as someone who knows exactly what is wrong with him and exactly what he should do to get rid of his symptom and get better. But, really, the analyst does not know. Moreover, the analyst steadfastly refuses to provide the analysand with any answers whatsoever. No ideals, no moral certainty, no goals, no choices. Nothing. This is what makes the analyst so traumatic, Žižek explains, the fact that she refuses to establish a law or set a limit, that she does not function as some kind of new master.[7] Analysis is over when the analysand accepts that the analyst does not know, that there is not any secret meaning or explanation, and then takes responsibility for getting on with his life. The challenge for the analysand, then, is freedom, autonomously determining his own limits, directly assuming his own enjoyment. So, again, the position of the analyst is in this excessive place as an object through which the analysand works through the analytical process.

Why is the analyst necessary in the first place? If she is not going to tell the analysand what to do, how he should be living, then why does he not save his money, skip the whole process, and figure out things for himself? There are two basic answers. First, the analysand is not self-transparent. He is a stranger to himself, a decentered agent "struggling with a foreign kernel."[8] What is more likely than self-understanding, is self-misunderstanding, that is, one's fundamental misperception of one's own condition. Becoming aware of this misperception, grappling with it, is the work of analysis. Accordingly, second, the analyst is that external agent or position that gives a new form to our activity. Saying things out loud, presenting them to another, and confronting them in front of this external position concretizes and arranges our thoughts and activities in a different way, a way that is more difficult to escape or avoid. The analyst then provides a form through which we acquire a perspective on and a relation to our selves.

Paul's Christian collectives and Lenin's revolutionary Party are, for Žižek, similarly formal arrangements, forms "for a new type of knowledge linked to a collective political subject."[9] Each provides an external perspective on our activities, a way to concretize and organize our spontaneous experiences. More strongly put, a political Party is necessary precisely because politics is not given; it does not arise naturally or organically out of the multiplicity of immanent flows and affects but has to be produced, arranged, and constructed out of these flows in light of something larger.

In my view, when Žižek draws on popular culture and inserts himself into this culture, he is taking the position of an object of enjoyment, an excessive object that cannot easily be recuperated or assimilated. This excessive position is that of the analyst as well as that of the Party. Reading Žižek as occupying the position of the analyst tells us that it is wrong to expect Žižek to tell us what to do, to provide an ultimate solution or direction through which to solve all the world's problems. The analyst does not provide the analysand with ideals and goals; instead, he occupies the place of an object in relation to which we work these out for ourselves. In adopting the position of the analyst, Žižek is also practicing what he refers to as "Bartleby politics," a politics rooted in a kind of refusal wherein the subject turns itself into a disruptive (of our peace of mind!) violently passive object who says, "I would prefer not to."[10] Thus, to my mind, becoming preoccupied with Žižek's style is like becoming preoccupied with what one's analyst is wearing. Why such a preoccupation? How is this preoccupation enabling us to avoid confronting the truth of our desire, our own investments in enjoyment? How is complaining that Žižek (or the analyst) will not tell us what to do a way that we avoid trying to figure this out for ourselves?[11]

Reading Žižek in terms of an excessive object also means seeing his position as analogous to the formal position of the Party. Here it tells us that rather than a set of answers or dictates, Žižek is providing an intervention that cuts through the multiplicity of affects and experiences in which we find ourselves and organizes them from a specific perspective. As we shall see, for Žižek, this perspective is anchored in class struggle as the fundamental antagonism rupturing and constituting the social. So again, he does not give us an answer; he does not know what we should do, but his thought provides an external point in relation to which we can organize, consider, and formalize our experiences as ideological subjects.

I turn now, much more briefly, to the emphasis on difficulty. It is true—Žižek engages a wide range of challenging thinkers. These engagements drive his argumentation, and it makes sense that scholars will want to debate his interpretations, to say that he gets Hegel wrong or misunderstands Kierkegaard. This is a legitimate approach, but it is not the one I take. Rather, I am interested in the way Žižek fits his insights and concepts together, how his engagements are elements of a larger way of thinking. Admittedly, discerning the system is not easy. Žižek does not lay it out; he puts it to work.[12] In this book, I lay it out, presenting Žižek's political thought in terms of this underlying system.[13]

To this end, I have adopted several methodological guidelines. First, I do not debate Žižek's interpretations of other philosophers. Instead, I treat these interpretations as aspects of his thought. This approach accords with Žižek's rendering of the entire history of philosophy as a series of misunderstandings—productive misreadings, that displace one another, introducing gaps into thinking.[14]

Second, I try to avoid Lacanian jargon. This is not always possible, but I try. Third, I place Žižek into the context of some of the problems and concerns presently occupying contemporary American political theorists working out of critical, Left, traditions. To that end, I compare his position to other positions prominent in radical political thought, demonstrating how his approach both resembles those of others and has certain advantages that they lack. Additionally, as a way of facilitating this effort, I draw most of my examples from the American political context. In sum, my goal is to present Žižek's ideas in ways useful to political theorists trying to break out of the present political impasse.

Let me specify somewhat this impasse. Dominant voices in political theory today tend to emphasize diversity and tolerance. Some approach diversity from the perspective of democratic debate, presenting a conception of politics premised on ideals of participation, inclusion, equality, and mutual respect. Others emphasize the multiplicity of ways of being in the world and the importance of an ethos of generosity toward those ways that may differ, radically, from our own. Neither of these approaches, however, provides an adequate response to right wing fundamentalists, nationalist ideologues, and neoliberal capitalist globalizers. In fact, as long as Left intellectuals reject anything that smacks of dogmatism, as long as we reject a politics of conviction, as long as we refuse to draw a line in the sand and say enough is enough, then the Right can continue in its exploitation and repression of most of the world's peoples. Differently put, Left political theorists today seem to want a politics that includes everything and everyone. In my view, this is not politics. Politics involves division, saying "yes" to some options and "no" to others. A willingness to accept this division and take responsibility for it seems to have been lost, or relegated to small, local struggles.

To my mind, Žižek's political theory both demonstrates this willingness and provides a compelling argument for why it is necessary today. His emphasis on the impossibility of pure forms of the subject, thought, democracy, and law draws out the enjoyment that stains and enables these forms, calling upon us to take responsibility for this enjoyment rather than seeking to excuse ourselves with recourse to some big Other of History, Law, Tradition, or Religion. At the same time, precisely insofar as he conceptualizes these nonexistent big Others as incomplete, as non-all, he neither rejects nor abandons them for some fantasy of being outside or beyond them, but recognizes instead how freedom may be possible within them.

Žižek is an engaging thinker. His work is engaging as enjoyment—ours and his—an enjoyment that enables thought and that we should acknowledge and take responsibility for. His work is engaging in its conviction, its willingness to confront academic orthodoxies from a standpoint of truth. And, his work is engaging in the hard work of meeting diverse audiences and constituencies, responding to political events as they unfold, and acting in a broad, mediatized arena. Rarely has philosophy been so engaging.

1
ENJOYMENT AS A CATEGORY OF POLITICAL THEORY

Introduction

In an interview with Glyn Daly, Slavoj Žižek says that "all politics relies upon, and even manipulates, a certain economy of enjoyment."[1] Throughout his work, not only *For They Know Not What They Do*, which is subtitled, *Enjoyment as a Political Factor*, Žižek draws out the workings of enjoyment (what Jacques Lacan calls *jouissance*) in racist and ethnic ideological fantasies, in socialism's bureaucratic excesses, and in the cynicism of the narcissistic subjects of late capitalism. Žižek frequently invokes the seemingly nonsensical ceremonies and redundancies that accompany political institutions: extravagant pomp and rhetoric, advice from committees of experts on ethics, the officiousness of paperwork, and the sanctimonious righteousness of perpetually ineffectual radicals. As he writes in *The Parallax View*, "our politics is more and more directly the politics of *jouissance*, concerned with ways of soliciting, or controlling and regulating, *jouissance*."[2] In this chapter, I introduce the category of enjoyment as the key to understanding Žižek's political thought. In so doing, I hope to demonstrate as well the importance of enjoyment as a category of political theory.

The category is not a magic bullet or golden ticket. It is not a pill we can take or a practice we can adopt that will revolutionize current political action and thought. Nonetheless, it contributes to thinking about our attachment to and investment in violent, destructive, and authoritarian modes of being. Žižek's use of the notion of enjoyment helps clarify how the accomplishments of new social movements associated with feminism, gay activism, and antiracism—their successes in challenging the patriarchal family and the disciplined society—have not ushered in a new world of freely self-creating identities, but rather interconnect with expansions and intensifications of global corporate capitalism to generate new forms of guilt, anxiety, and dependency.[3] For political theorists, then, his work is indispensable to understanding the deep libidinal attraction of domination, that is, the passion of our attachments to the objects constitutive of our subjectivities, however contingent these objects may be, and hence to the challenge of freedom under communicative capitalism.[4]

I can approach these matters from a different direction. The present is marked by a bizarre opposition between speed and fixity. Everything in the global capitalist consumer–entertainment economy moves quickly (except, of course, those horrid computerized answering systems that entrap us when we call companies and offices), but little changes; or, better, the idea of effecting change—making a difference—seems extraordinarily difficult, even naïve. The truly committed appear as fanatics or fundamentalists, or, more mildly, as quaint throwbacks refusing to accept the fact that the sixties are over. Contributions to global financial and information spheres circulate rapidly, yet few think it possible to change the course and conditions of this circulation. The global capitalist economy presents itself as the only game in town, as the condition of politics, struggle, and action. So, there are swarms of activities, of interpretations, transgressions, and interventions, but with remarkably little impact; most fail to register at all.[5] In this context, the contingencies of everyday life present themselves less as openings to immense possibility than they do as nuggets of fixity.

Pluralization, or the deterritorializing and reterritorializing force of capitalist intensification, generates leftovers and remainders. Even as migrations of people, capital, and information challenge and exceed previously congealed formations, they produce new sites and objects of attachment, new economies and arrangements of enjoyment. As William Connolly points out, the very push to pluralize can become marked by its own excessive demand to eliminate all attachment to fundamentals.[6] Insofar as Žižek's political theory posits enjoyment as an irreducible component of human being, as that which enables and ruptures the subject, it can contribute to our thinking about these nuggets of fixity and our deep attachment to them.

In considering enjoyment as a category of political theory, I begin with a general discussion of the concept in psychoanalysis. I then turn specifically to Žižek's work, taking up the role of enjoyment and fantasy in his reworking of the theory of ideology. After attending to the place of enjoyment in ideological interpellation and addressing more specifically Žižek's use of the concept for understanding racism and ethnic nationalism, I analyze some of the specific, formal features of the concept. Here I emphasize enjoyment as it fixes the place of the subject, enjoyment and our relation to others, and the superego support of enjoyment. With these elements in place, I argue for Žižek's account of the challenges of freedom in communicative capitalism as a compelling alternative to current emphases on multiplicity and pluralization. Žižek's emphasis on enjoyment enables us to confront the excesses generated by global capitalism as they fix and attach contemporary subjects into relations of domination and exploitation.

What Is Enjoyment?

Most simply, *enjoyment* (*jouissance*) refers to an excessive pleasure and pain, to that something extra that twists pleasure into a fascinating, even unbearable intensity. We might think here of the difference between friendship and passionate love. Whereas spending time with friends may be pleasurable, falling in love can be agonizing. Yet it is a special kind of agony, an agony that makes us feel more alive, more fully present, more in tune with what makes life worth living, and dying for, than anything else. Enjoyment, then, is this extra, this excess beyond the given, measurable, rational, and useful.[7] It cannot be reduced to the seemingly rational terms of a cost/benefit analysis. Nor can enjoyment be allocated through the weighing of pros and cons. Instead, enjoyment is that "something extra" for the sake of which we do what might otherwise seem irrational, counter productive, or even wrong.

The basic psychoanalytic account of enjoyment tells a story of the infant's primary connection with its mother. This story begins by positing an ideal oneness that was never fully realized, but whose loss helps make sense of human psychic life.[8] At one with the mother, the infant does not separate itself from her; her breast, her body, are the infant's own. Once the infant can distinguish between itself and its mother, once the breast is something separate, that connection is lost forever. The child will of course try to regain or recover a sense of oneness. It will work to fill in the missing piece, typically by trying to please the mother, to be what she wants. The child will also attempt to overlap its desire with the mother's desire. Her desire, something powerful, overwhelming, and mysterious, becomes the cause of the child's desire. So not only will it try to be what she wants, but also it will try to want what she wants. Yet insofar as the mother, as desiring, is incomplete, the child has a kind of breathing room; it is not fully taken over into her as if she were closed, total. The child then has some sense that both it and its mother are lacking; they both desire. It covers over this lack with a fantasy that tells it what she wants, that tells it something about the mother's desire, that gives the child a way to be what she wants or explains to it its failure. The fantasy is attached to a little nugget (what Lacan designates as *objet petit a*)—in Bruce Fink's terms, a remainder and a reminder—of originary enjoyment.[9]

Another version of this story emphasizes our entry into the symbolic order of language. We are born into language, into its rules, into structures of meaning and expectation that precede us. As infants and young children, our pleasures and pains, wants and needs, are given to us, projected onto us as our parents try to figure out why we will not stop crying and settle down. Words are provided that distinguish us from our environment, from animals, from other people. Words break us into parts: nose, chin, ear, eye. We are taught to read faces for their moods: happy, sad, angry, surprised. Yet again, enjoyment is the price of our entry into language. We sacrifice primordial interconnectedness (something we imagine as direct, unmediated bodily communion with an other) when we enter the symbolic order of language. More precisely, the fantasy of this originary communion inhabits our experience of language, our sense of not being able to say it all as well as the enjoyment that provides our speaking with extra dimensions of which we may only be obliquely aware.[10] Enjoyment cannot be signified directly. It exceeds symbolization and, indeed, can only be signified through inconsistencies, holes, and slippages in the symbolic order.[11]

To be sure, in the same way that the mother is incomplete, so is the symbolic order of language. That is, we do not go into it fully. There is always a surplus or leftover that resists symbolic integration (Žižek follows Lacan in referring to this surplus as Real).[12] Not everything can be said. The very act of saying something opens up questions and effects irreducible to the content of what is said. Meanings escape words; intensities and excitements exceed meaning.

Meaning itself comes not with a transcendental guarantee or refer-ent but relies on some kind of contingent, inert signifier as a stand-in for the stupid fact that a name refers to an object simply because that is what we call it.[13] Our bodily experiences, although inscribed by language, are irreducible to it. Nuggets of enjoyment remain.

These stories of the loss of something we never had are not hypotheses to be proven through extensive baby-watching. Rather, the story has the status of something that must be presupposed if we are to make sense of experiences of desire and longing, of drive and frustration, of our odd tendencies to persist in habits of being and interaction that are profoundly destructive to ourselves and others. Lacanian psychoanalysis thus takes the view that this story is Real in the sense that it informs psychoanalytic understanding of desire, drive, and the fundamental, traumatic separation consti-tutive of what it is to be human. For example, positing the loss of a primary connection or enjoyment accounts for the openness of desire, for the way we can desire something but upon getting it feel "that's not it," "that's not what I really wanted." When we intro-duce additional elements of the story, moreover, and emphasize the intrusion of the symbolic law that both bars access to enjoyment and frees the subject from enjoyment's overwhelming proximity, we can better grasp the paradoxical functioning of prohibition, the way that prohibition can both incite desire and provide relief from the compulsion to enjoy.

Likewise, insofar as the Lacanian account of drive holds that drives are not to be understood in terms of direct bodily needs but rather as byproducts of the body's ensnarement in the symbolic order, the very failure to satisfy desire can become itself a source of enjoyment.[14] The circular movement of drive is enjoyable; enjoyment, in other words, is the pleasure provided by the pain-ful experience of repeatedly missing one's goal.[15] With respect to drive, then, the nugget of enjoyment is not what one is trying to reach but cannot; rather, it is that little extra that adheres to the process of trying. To this extent, the inescapability of enjoyment equals drive. Enjoyment results when focus shifts from the end to the means, when processes and procedures themselves provide libidinal satisfaction.

Overall, the two versions of the story that posits an impossible originary enjoyment set out an important underlying supposition of Žižek's thought: neither the subject nor the structure of language and law in which it finds itself is complete; both are ruptured by a gap, by an excess and a lack. Žižek follows Lacan in thinking of this excess and lack in terms of enjoyment, an irrational remainder or reminder to which the subject is forever tied in a complex push–pull dynamic: in drive the subject pushes enjoyment away (but still gets it); in desire the subject pulls enjoyment toward (but continues to miss it).

As Žižek frequently observes, Lacan changes his account of enjoyment in the course of his teaching. What the earlier Lacan theorizes as an imaginary fullness becomes the mesmerizing, terrifying presence of the Real (the Thing, something Žižek compares to the alien in Ridley Scott's *Alien* movie) and shifts yet again to become the multiplicity of nuggets of enjoyment (*lichettes*) through which late capitalism reproduces itself.[16] Although Žižek draws most extensively from the later Lacan, he does not proceed as if the final account of enjoyment is necessarily the best or proper one. Instead, he treats the stages in Lacan's teaching as ways of thinking about political order, resistance, revolt, and the recuperation of transgression in late capitalism. Thus, Žižek maps Lacan's stages onto political–theoretical shifts from absolute authority, to the democratic invention, to the emergence of the totalitarian leader, to today's generalized perversity (a mapping we encounter in subsequent chapters in the form of Žižek's discussion of different ideological formations in terms of Lacan's four discourses). Nevertheless, Žižek emphasizes that these shifts are not total: previous arrangements of enjoyment persist, adding to the challenge

of theorizing the present. Today we encounter longings for fullness, fear of traumatic destruction, hatred of others who threaten
our enjoyment, and the idiotic, momentary *jouissance* of popular
culture. How a society arranges its enjoyment, in other words, is
not uniform or singular. Differing economies of enjoyment—capitalist, socialist, nationalist, racist, sexist—can and do coexist. A
key task for political theorists, then, is to discern how these differing arrangements of enjoyment reproduce contemporary arrangements of domination.

Enjoyment in Ideology

Žižek's reworking of the category of ideology extends the notion
of enjoyment into the political field. To this end, he concerns himself with the ways that ideological formations work as economies
of enjoyment to forbid, permit, direct, and command enjoyment.
Žižek argues that an ideological formation is more than a set of
different elements constituted as a set by virtue of a certain nodal
point (such as the "empty signifier" in Ernesto Laclau and Chantal
Mouffe's theory of hegemony).[17] Likewise, ideology is more than
a discursive formation that covers over the fundamental incompleteness and impossibility of society. Rather, what is crucial to
an ideological formation is the fantasy that supports it, that is,
the point of excessive, irrational enjoyment that accounts for the
hold of an ideological edifice on the subject. Fantasy explains the
incompleteness of society (that is, it accounts for the antagonism
rupturing society) in a way that promises and produces enjoyment.[18] Discourse analysis and ideology critique, then, can do little
in and of themselves to change society. Real substantive change
has to confront (Žižek uses the Lacanian term *traverse*) ideology's
underlying fantasy. To set out Žižek's notion of ideology in more
detail, I focus on (1) the role of enjoyment in ideological interpellation and (2) the way fantasy structures our enjoyment.

Among the many problems that have plagued the Marxist concept of ideology is its connotation of false consciousness.[19] The very idea of ideology critique seems to place the scientific, intelligent, or enlightened critic on a plane high above the poor duped masses. Žižek's account avoids this difficulty by shifting attention from what people *know* to what they *do*, that is, to the way people persist in actions despite what they know to be true.[20] For example, I know that tabloids are scandalous rags, delivering my attention to advertisers and the entertainment industry, feeding the celebrity–consumer machine, but I read them anyway. I may even read them critically, ironically, as if I were different from the typical tabloid reader, but I am still buying and reading them. For Žižek, this continued activity is a mark of belief, a belief that is exteriorized in a variety of institutionalized practices.

One might think that with this emphasis on practices, Žižek's account resembles less a theory of ideology than it does Michel Foucault's theory of the emergence of individuals out of normalizing practices. The difference between Žižek and Foucault is that Žižek is concerned with the way these practices are subjectivized, the way they are experienced by the subject, or, more precisely, the way the subject emerges as the failure of these practices to be subjectivized or internalized completely, without remainder.

Drawing from Louis Althusser's theory of ideological interpellation, Žižek asks how the effect of belief in a cause arises—how, in other words, a subject comes to recognize himself as hailed by an ideological institution (such as the state in the form of the policeman saying, "Hey, you!" or God's call as made manifest through the practices, texts, and institutions of the church). The subject may go about specific activities related to a cause, but why does the subject recognize this particular cause as his own? Why does he respond to the hail? Why is it he who is hailed, addressed, or called? Žižek's surprising answer is *not* that the subject has a preexisting good reason for responding and *not* that the cause in some way corresponds to the subject's deep or true interests. Rather, the subject responds to a certain irrational injunction, that is, to the very fact of the groundless command.

We might think here of the word of God, binding because it is God's word, or of the fundamental authority of law grounded in the fact that it is law. In each case, if we point to something beyond God or law as the grounds for their authority, we are positing something higher, something by which to judge God or law, say, reason or morality. If we then say that reason or morality is the ultimate authority, we get stuck in the same tautology: reason authorizes because it is reasonable; morality authorizes because it is moral. Žižek conceives of this tautology as an object, a sticking point, a residue of irrationality (*objet petit a*) that serves as the very condition for the subject's submission to the ideological hail. Hence, he offers a play on words—*jouis*-sense, enjoyment-in-sense (enjoy-meant)—to capture the conjunction of the meaning offered by ideology with its ultimate core of meaninglessness, or irrational enjoyment.[21]

Thus, unlike Foucault, Žižek emphasizes the subjectivization of the practices constitutive of belief: belief in an ideological cause results from an excessive, traumatic kernel that resists symbolization or incorporation into a signifying economy. The excess of the subject with respect to its practices, then, is not the result of a multiplicity of competing hails (although this is not excluded). It is more fundamental: the subject is the very failure of interpellation and symbolization, an absence that is marked (embodied or positivized) by the irrational injunction.[22]

Žižek also differs from Foucault with respect to the status or place of the subjectivized practices. Whereas Foucault accounts for the unity of disciplinary practices by referring to the dispersion of specific logics of power (for example, logics around confession and speaking, observation and surveillance, examination and judgment as they take material form in architectures, urban planning, and designs for education and punishment), Žižek addresses a peculiar fact about the subject's performance of its practices: the gaze before which it imagines itself performing. This gaze constitutes "the Other who registers my acts in the symbolic network."[23]

Following Lacan, Žižek understands this gaze as the ego ideal, as a point of symbolic identification. The gaze is more than the product of a particular architecture intended to install normalizing judgment and discipline the behavior of the observed (as with, for example, the panopticon introduced by Jeremy Bentham and elaborated by Foucault). Instead, for Žižek, the gaze is a crucial supposition for the very capacity to act at all. Identifying with the gaze enables the subject to be active. The gaze is the point from which one sees one's actions as valuable and worthwhile, as making sense. Absent that gaze, one may feel trapped, passive, or unsure as to the point of doing anything at all.

This gaze, then, structures our relation to our practices. Instead of experiencing the state as myriad forms and organizations, branches and edicts, presences and regulations, say, in our daily activities, we posit the state as a kind of entity, an other, aware of what we are doing (a positing that, unfortunately, makes ever more sense as it materializes in surveillance technologies). Similarly, we may posit an enemy assessing our every action. The point, then, is that through symbolic identification the subject posits the very entity it understands itself as responding to. How it imagines this other will be crucial to the kinds of activities the subject can undertake.[24]

Symbolic identification, positing the gaze before which one acts, is a primary mechanism by which the subject is integrated into the socio-ideological field. Of course, insofar as ideological interpellation is never complete, insofar as there is always a remainder, the subject never knows for sure what the other wants—what exactly it as a subject is to the other and what it should be doing. This uncertainty is comparable to the uncertainty of the child in the face of the mother's desire: what does she really want? Is it me? How can it be me? Am I what she wants? Thus, as in the example of the child, so in ideological interpellation does the subject fill in these gaps with fantasy. Fantasy answers the question of who and what I am to the other. It provides a screen to cover the lack in the other and a frame or set of coordinates for our desire. Through fantasy, for example, we may identify or overlap an ideological edifice's irrational excess (the nugget of enjoyment escaping meaning, *objet petit a*) with the gaze before which we imagine ourselves acting. In this way, we may posit a powerful, knowing, enjoying other or we may posit the excess as somehow eluding the gaze, as something the gaze might condemn or something we should hide from the gaze. At any rate, fantasy tells us how to desire.[25]

Desire depends on a missing enjoyment—on its lack. Fantasy is the framework through which some empirical content, an object, person, experience, or practice, comes to function for us as "it," as what we desire. Although we are accustomed to thinking about fantasies as the stories we tell ourselves about getting what we want, say, having it all or achieving our goals, Žižek follows Lacan in emphasizing the operation of fantasy at a more fundamental level. This more fundamental fantasy, insofar as it tells us how to desire, keeps our desire alive, unfulfilled, and intact as *desire*. Thus, fantasy provides us with an explanation for why our enjoyment is missing, how we would have, could have, really enjoyed *if only*.... Such fantasmic explanations may posit another who has stolen our enjoyment or who has concentrated all the enjoyment in his hands, preventing the rest of us from enjoying (as in Freud's account of the primal father in *Totem and Taboo*). What is crucial, though, is the way the fantasy keeps open the possibility of enjoyment by telling us why we are not really enjoying.

Here are a few examples. I would have had all of my mother's love if it had not been for my father or my sister. I would have had complete freedom in the state of nature if it had not been for all those insecure others worried about their own self-preservation and having a right to all things, including my body (as Hobbes theorizes in *Leviathan*). I would have had a great day working at McDonald's if it had not been for my mean manager and the rude customers. I would have acted kindly, generously, and responsively, had I not had to do my duty and follow the rules.

In each example, fantasy binds me to a certain set of relations. It structures and confines my thinking and acting such that my desires attach me to seemingly inescapable hierarchical relations or patterns of domination. The possibility of enjoyment that the fantasy holds open makes it very difficult for me to resist or break out of the situation in which I find myself. In the familial relation, there is competition and jealousy. I can get little bits of enjoyment, perhaps, by undermining my sister or amusing my mother when she is disappointed with my father. Much more difficult is finding a way to persist within this family outside of the economy of enjoyment that has structured my desire. In the Hobbesian example, there is a war of all against all. I can get enjoyment only by renouncing it, by concentrating it in a sovereign. The possibility of acknowledging that I never had an initial freedom to enjoy is foreclosed from the outset. In the McDonald's example, I get enjoyment by snatching little bits of it away from those I fantasize as taking it from me. Sure, nothing really changes. I am still stuck working at McDonald's, but there is nothing like the thrill of making impatient customers wait or even spitting in their food. Finally, in the example of duty, I find enjoyment in my very compliance, gaining satisfaction in the fullness of its exercise.[26]

Žižek's account of the fantasmic organization of enjoyment provides a particularly compelling way to think about contemporary ethnic nationalism. Since at least the 1980s, questions of race and ethnicity have generally coalesced into two opposing approaches. On one side are appeals to ethnic and racial identity. Groups argue for rights, such as rights to self-determination or for the preservation of their linguistic and cultural heritage, on the basis of a certain essential difference. Even as race has been exposed for its lack of a scientific or biological foundation, people who have been discriminated against on the basis of race find categories of racial and ethnic identity useful as grounds for claims for inclusion, recognition, and redress. For some, particularly those endeavoring to establish or maintain ethnically pure homelands, these efforts at ethnic preservation lead to ethnic cleansing and genocide. On the other side, many, particularly among leftist activists and academics, rightly reject racial essentialism, precisely because race has no biological basis.[27] From this side, arguments that rely on the reassertion of race risk reinstalling precisely the racial logic that antiracism contests.

Considering ethnic nationalism in terms of enjoyment provides a way to escape this stand-off. Žižek argues that enjoyment is what holds a community together. Following Lacan, he refers to this shared enjoyment as the Thing.[28] The national Thing is not simply a collection of features, our specific traditions, foods, or myths, for example (it is not simply the elements of a set). Rather, our Thing is our belief that these features make us who we are. Even more powerfully, this Thing is more than an effect of the practices carried out in its name: it is the added enjoyment that results from these practices. "A nation *exists*," Žižek writes, "only as long as its specific *enjoyment* continues to be materialized in a set of social practices and transmitted through national myths or fantasies that secure these practices."[29] The Thing is contingent but Real.

This idea of enjoyment enables us to distinguish between countries recognized as nation states that do not work as nations or that are traversed and ruptured by different nationalities (differing organizations of enjoyment). Similarly, we are well placed to consider the collapse, disintegration, or transformation of nations in terms of changes in their enjoyment. A community may no longer be a community when there is no belief in a shared enjoyment, whether shared in a fantasmic past or an idealized future.

Since a community's enjoyment consists in no positive attribute, it comes to the fore in myths and fantasies—myths that generally explain the ways our enjoyment is threatened by others who want to steal it, who want to ruin our way of life by corrupting it with their own peculiar enjoyment. Žižek writes, "what 'bothers' us in the 'other' (Jew, Japanese, African, Turk) is that he appears to entertain a privileged relationship to the object—the other either possesses the object-treasure, having snatched it away from us (which is why we don't have it), or he poses a threat to our possession of the object."[30] In turn, we find enjoyment in fantasizing about *their* enjoyment, in positing an enjoyment beyond what we imagine for ourselves. We do not like the excess of others' ways of life (their music, the way they smell, their relation to their bodies). Their way of life seems immediately intrusive, an assault, like they are flaunting it, daring us, blatantly refusing to sacrifice their enjoyment and come under a common symbolic order. Why do their lives seem so authentic, so real? Why are they so much more in tune with their sexuality, able to eat and drink and live while I am hard at work? The very excessiveness of their enjoyment makes them "them," other, foreign.

We are also captivated by their excesses, hating the others' for enjoying in ways barred to us. In a sense, when we hate them, we hate our own excess enjoyment, whether it is the enjoyment we presuppose we have sacrificed (but actually never had) or whether it is enjoyment that we cannot escape, that stains our endeavors despite (because of) our best efforts.[31] We hate their enjoyment and see them as foreign and threatening and thus acquire a sense of the special quality of *our* way of life. Our enjoyment becomes real to us as ours to the extent that we are already deprived of it, that it is threatened or stolen.[32] Examples include the eternal feminine stolen by the Catholic Church in the best-seller, *The Da Vinci*

Code, or the powerful maternal, feminine essence appropriated by patriarchy in some versions of cultural feminism; the anti-Semitic vision of wealth to be had if not for the Jews; the sexual access to white women posited by white American racism toward black men; the fulfillment and sanctity that straight marriage would provide were it not under threat by same-sex couples; the prosperity, security, and freedom Americans would be enjoying had it not been stolen by fanatical Islamic fundamentalists according to the terms of the so-called war on terror.

These examples highlight the way the fantasy organization of desire underpins the ideological formation of a community. An ideological formation is more than a set of meanings or images and more than the accumulated effects of dispersed practices. Rather, ideology takes hold of the subject at the point of the irrational excess outside the meaning or significance the ideological formation provides. This excess, nugget, or remainder marks the incompleteness of the formation and of the interpellated subject. It is that extra sticking point, a point of fixation and enjoyment (*objet petit a*). Fantasies organize and explain these sticking points. They cover over the gaps in the ideological formation as they promise enjoyment (the enjoyment that has been stolen, sacrificed, or barred to the subject) and in so doing, attach the subject to the group or community supposed by the ideology.

A Fixed Place in the Space of Flows

A number of compelling theories of the circulation and migration of people, information, capital, and opportunity characteristic of contemporary communicative capitalism emphasize notions of speed, flow, and mobility. For some, such as Michael Hardt and Antonio Negri and William Connolly, the key challenge of contemporary life arises from institutions or formations that endeavor to stop, contain, or territorialize these flows. Žižek's approach differs from these insofar as where they see movement, he finds fixity. As I explain in this section, he understands this fixity in terms of enjoyment. Enjoyment is what fixes the subject in its place.

According to the basic psychoanalytic story of the infant's primary attachment to the mother enjoyment is the remainder and promise of impossible fullness the desire for which animates the subject's fundamental fantasy and persists in the incommunicable excess of drive. The little remainder or reminder of enjoyment is the nugget, the object (*objet petit a*), that guarantees the consistency of the subject's being.[34] This nugget of enjoyment is thus strictly correlative to the subject.[35] In Žižek's words, enjoyment is the "place of the subject, his impossible Being-there."[31] It's why the symbolic order is not whole or complete, why the subject is split and not-self-identical. We might think of this place of the subject, then, as a limit point, a point of impossibility (insofar as it marks the lack in the other that the subject tries to make its own). We might also think of it as what sticks to the subject, as what the subject can never shake or escape. In both respects, enjoyment is a kind of fixity—something that holds the subject together and that provides it with a place. This place is not the same as a subject position or place in the symbolic order of language. Rather, it is the incommunicable nugget or excess that prevents the subject from ever fully occupying the place provided for it, which provides it, we might say, with another place.

We can approach this sense of the place or fixity enjoyment provides by considering the homology between surplus enjoyment and Marx's account of surplus value. As Žižek points out, Lacan models the notion of surplus enjoyment on Marx's surplus value.[36] The capitalist mode of production relies on excess; the capitalist gets back from the production process more than he puts into it. As the well-known passages from *Capital* explain, this excess seems somehow magical, an extra arising as an alchemical remainder of an exchange of equivalents. The worker produces an excess not his own, one that circulates in the other. Even as he loses the surplus of his labor insofar as it is enjoyed by the capitalist, the worker depends for his survival on continued production; he is trapped in, exists within the terms established by, the circulation of this leftover that embodies limit and excess, lack and surplus.[37] The circulation of the surplus provides him with his place.

In fact, as with enjoyment, so with capitalism is this surplus *constitutive*—just as enjoyment is always and necessarily an excess, so is the generation of an excess, the production of more than what was consumed, the emergence of something extra in the very process of circulation, what distinguishes capitalism from other modes of production. Emphasis is on growth, expansions, and increases, on the self-revolutionizing of the very material conditions of production, and on an ever-intensifying circulation that itself generates more.[38] Žižek concludes from this point that Marx was wrong to think that something like communism, some kind of order that would unleash and expand productivity, was possible. Rather, the very form of capitalism, its inner tension between the relations and forces of production, is what makes capitalist productivity possible. Žižek writes,

> In short, what Marx overlooked is that—to put it in classic Derridean terms—this inherent obstacle/antagonism, as the "condition of impossibility" of the full deployment of the productive forces, is simultaneously its "condition of possibility": if we abolish the obstacle, the inherent contradiction of capitalism, we do not get the fully unleashed drive to productivity finally delivered of its impediment, we lose precisely this productivity that seemed to be generated and simultaneously thwarted by capitalism—if we take away the obstacle, the very potential thwarted by this obstacle dissipates.[39]

The homology between surplus enjoyment and surplus value brings home the way that under capitalism, circulation and fixity are not opposed, but on the contrary, circulation itself introduces a certain fixity. To the extent that contemporary flows are flows of capital, immobility is necessary and unavoidable. The circulation of capital requires a leftover that fixes the subject. The homology between surplus value and surplus enjoyment is not complete, however. Whereas surplus value goes to the capitalist, surplus enjoyment returns to the subject. That is, the subject gets back some of the *jouissance* he sacrifices in order to enter the symbolic.[40] He may get this back in the form of little transgressions, for example, as well as in the form of obedience—submission. Thus, with respect to surplus enjoyment, the subject gets something for nothing; the impossible enjoyment he initially sacrificed returns to him as a little nugget of enjoyment. This something, then, attaches the subject to capitalism; it is the pay-off for playing the game, or, better, it is the promise of a pay-off, the promise of an excess, that capitalism holds out.

Thinking of enjoyment in terms of fixity enables us to distinguish Žižek's account of subjectivity from other versions prominent in political theory. First, his subject is clearly not the same as the liberal subject insofar as there is no notion of consciously free and rational will. Rather, the Žižekian subject is an emptiness held in place by enjoyment. Second, for Žižek the subject is not properly understood in terms of the concept of "subject-position" or the individual as it is constructed within the terms of a given hegemonic formation (as a woman/mother, black/minority, etc.). Third, the subject is not the illusory container of a potentially infinite plasticity or capacity for creative self-fashioning. Rather than a subject position or an opportunity for re-creation, the subject is a lack (in the structure, the other) marked by the limit point or nugget of an impossible enjoyment.

Although this idea of the subject of lack might at first glance appear rather bizarre and unhelpful, it nonetheless affiliates well with notions congenial to thinkers convinced by critiques of a specific reading of the enlightenment subject such as those offered by Marx, Nietzsche, and Freud and extended in Foucauldian, feminist, and post-Nietzschean thought. Žižek's account of the subject shares with these views the rejection of a primary will, rationality, wholeness, and transparency. Similarly, it acknowledges the role of the unconscious, the body, and language, bringing these three elements together in the account of enjoyment as limiting and rupturing language and providing the object that is the very condition of the subject. As it emphasizes the object conditioning the subject, moreover, Žižek's discussion of enjoyment as a political factor draws our attention to a certain fixity on the part of the subject. Far from the malleable self-creating subject championed by consumer capitalism, the Žižekian subject finds itself in a place not of its choosing, attached to fantasies of which it remains unaware that nevertheless structure its relation to enjoyment, thereby fastening it to the existing framework of domination.

Žižek often develops this last point via examples of the forced choice, such as "your money or your life!" In such a choice, each side precludes the other. If we choose money, we do not get to live. If we choose to live, we do not even get the security of living because we cannot trust the person who just forced us to choose. To the extent that we accept the terms of a forced choice, then, we remain trapped, confined, and fixed by a fundamental loss.[41] When American identity is construed in terms of supporting a war, say, one who is against the war may find herself trapped, unable to place herself as both American and antiwar. She will likely be told to "go home," as if there were some other place for her. (Shouts of "go home," I should add, were frequent during protests I participated in against the U.S. invasion of Iraq. At the time, they seemed quite strange. Now they seem to me to be markers of precisely this kind of forced choice.)

The difficult way out is refusing the forced choice. This refusal, I should add, is for Žižek a choice for the worst, a choice for unclarity, uncertainty, and the unknown, indeed a choice for subjective destitution in the sense that the subject has to give up the very symbolic coordinates that tell it who it is. So, does one accept the given order or jump into the abyss (which, in my example, may not actually be an abyss but more a morass of discussion, debate, and the challenge of imagining another America and another world)? For Žižek fixity ruptures the ideal of a self-aware, transparent subject even as it enables action. When we act, we never do so with full knowledge of the consequences, of our motives, or of how others understand the situation. Rather, we simply act. Žižek reads Kantian ethics, then, not as highlighting a tension between acting out of duty and acting out of some pathological motivation, but rather as asserting a more fundamental tension: "the free act in its abyss is unbearable, traumatic, so that when we accomplish an act out of freedom, in order to be able to bear it, we experience it as conditioned by some pathological motivation."[42] The challenge of freedom consists in accepting the absence of certainty, the lack of a security in some kind of imaginary cover or back up.[43]

Thus, Žižek holds that in a liberal political culture the very sense of an active free agent relies on a primary dependency: "utter passivity is the foreclosed fantasy that sustains our conscious experience as active, self-positing subjects."[44] It is the foreclosed fantasy in the sense that it is the excluded opposite conditioning the liberal ideal of freedom. This passivity is what has to be supposed and negated for the notion of liberal freedom to make sense. The fantasy prevents us from confronting the trap of the forced choice. For example, we might imagine a being completely determined by natural laws or laws of reason—as Kant does—and recognize, with Kant, that such a being would be incapable of agency. There would be nothing to decide, no capacity for decision insofar as all would be already determined. Alternatively, we might consider how arguments about nature and nurture threaten liberal ideas of autonomy insofar as each, in a different way, renders the person a kind of inert substance, an object of either natural or social systems. The idea of utter passivity, of being a plaything of alien forces, works as a foreclosed fantasy of liberal freedom in another sense as well, a sense that provides relief from the demands of freedom. Fantasies of victimization, of irresponsibility ("It's not my fault!"), and of instrumentality ("I had no choice!") protect the fragile agent from a confrontation with its accountability. They provide the imaginary cover for a more fundamental deadlock.

As a way of confronting ("traversing") this fundamental fantasy of passivity, Žižek introduces the figure of Bartleby, from Herman Melville's short story, "Bartleby the Scrivener." The attitude of Bartleby politics is that of "I would prefer not to."[45] This attitude might be thought of as one of subjective destitution—insofar as Bartleby declines the choices and activities generally associated with normal symbolic exchange, he becomes a kind of strange, unbearable object, one hard to recognize as human. Bartleby's formal gesture of refusal works as a stain or lump that cannot be readily assimilated or understood. The potential of this figure rests in the way that it reverses the standard notion of the subject as active and the object as passive. Having shown that the subject is fundamentally passive, one who submits, who is subjected, Žižek considers the way that the object *objects*, disturbing the established order of things.[46] Bartleby's inert refusal thus suggests the movement of an object, an objection to capitalist activity and circulation and to liberal fantasies of freedom.

I have read Žižek's notion of enjoyment as the impossible being-there of the subject in terms of fixity, that is, as that which holds the subject in place. I have emphasized how this fixity not only persists in capitalism but is necessary to the circulation of capital. Capitalism relies on the production of excesses, on intensifications and expansions that always exceed their initial conditions. Accordingly, the account of fixity differentiates Žižek's approach to the subject from other approaches in political theory.

For Žižek, the subject persists within the setting or structure in which it finds itself. We can understand this persistence through the idea of the "forced choice": no matter what the subject chooses, something is lost; yet, breaking out of the confines of this choice means changing the very conditions that make one a subject. We can also understand these confines in terms of the fantasy of passivity that accompanies the idea of liberal freedom. What provides the subject with a sense of agency is not a full knowledge of the circumstances (an impossibility) but a more fundamental fantasy that covers over the deadlock of the forced choice. Žižek draws from this account of the passive subject the possibility of the active object, one that "moves, annoys, disturbs and traumatizes us (subjects)."[47] He uses Bartleby to figure this possibility.

Displacement or Enjoying Through the Other

I have been discussing enjoyment as a kind of fixity insofar as it provides the place of the subject. I now approach this fixity from a different direction—that of substitution and displacement, of doing something through another (what Žižek terms "interpassivity").[38] I do so in order to consider specific attributes of the intersubjective dimension of enjoyment. Enjoyment is not a private ecstasy rupturing the subject. Nor is the intersubjectivity of enjoyment simply a matter of the overlap of the lacks in the subject and the other. Rather, Žižek emphasizes that one can enjoy through another, that another can enjoy for us, in our stead. We have already seen this displacement of enjoyment at work in ethnic nationalism in the idea that enjoyment can be stolen.

The case of ethnic nationalism points to an additional aspect of enjoyment, namely, that enjoyment pertains not to relations between subjects but to something stranger and more disturbing: others are objects for us. We might recall the way fantasies about the enjoyment of others provide us with a way to organize our own enjoyment. These others are objects for us, objects that are stuck in enjoyment while we go about our activities. Enjoyment, then, helps us account for the way relations with others may not be inter-subjective relations between subjects but relations between subjects and objects. Within our libidinal economies, others are not always other subjects for us; they also function as objects. Indeed, as objects, they enable us to act. Differently put, we are active to the extent that we can displace our enjoyment onto another. We have to get rid of our passive enjoyment and transfer or displace it somewhere else.

In this section, I emphasize the connection between our displacement of our enjoyment onto another and fixity: the external-ization of enjoyment also fixes the subject. Whereas the preceding section emphasized enjoyment as the place of the subject, this section construes enjoyment as the *displaced of the subject*. The fact of the displacement of enjoyment, in other words, introduces a second way to understand the subject's fixity. It attends to the libidinal economy, the arrangement of enjoyment, conditioning the subject's activity.

How does one enjoy through another? A first example might be Santa Claus. I go through elaborate efforts at Christmas to ensure that my children are thrilled and delighted. I enjoy Christmas through their delight—their enjoyment. At the same time, if I think about it, I can also recall a particular kind of agony I experienced as a child. I did not want to let my parents down. I did not want them to think that they had disappointed me, that I was not completely ecstatic every minute of Christmas day. I had to hide the little let down that occurs when the packages are all opened and it is time to clean up. Yet now as an adult, I find myself repeating the same pattern. Christmas seems to focus on the children, but this very focus involves my enjoying through them. I am now relieved of the burden of enjoyment; I do not have to enjoy for my parents anymore. Now, my children enjoy in my stead. "I defer *jouissance* to the Other who passively endures it (laughs, suffers, enjoys . . .) on my behalf."[49] They enjoy so that I do not have to.

This example can be extended to clarify Žižek's point that "the open display of the passive attitude of 'enjoying it' somehow deprives the subject of his dignity." I do not want to be caught again in the child's place of mindless, unself-conscious absorption in wanting to know what is hidden behind the wrapping paper, opening packages, and confronting the actuality of their contents. Ripping through the ribbons and bows seems somehow savage, excessive, and materialistic. What if my desire is exposed—my lack, the fact that no possible content will fill it, will be it? That vulnerability is more than I can bear. If the children enjoy Christmas for me, I am saved from this incapacitating enjoyment and can happily go about my business of wrapping, decorating, preparing food, and hosting friends and family, that is, the basic activities of the holidays.

For Žižek, the externalization of enjoyment in another is a necessary feature of subjectivity: "in order to be an active subject, I have to get rid of—to transpose on to the other—the inert passivity which contains the density of my substantial being."[50] Actually encountering the other enjoying for us, moreover, can be nearly unbearable insofar as it confronts us with our own passivity. The enjoying other is holding, is the location of, the enjoyment we have deferred to it. Our encounter with this other thus involves an encounter with the object in ourselves, with our absorption in enjoyment, with "the passive kernel" of our being. "I see *myself* in the guise of a suffering object: what reduces me to a fascinated passive observer is the scene of *myself* passively enduring it."[51] There is a kind of transfixed repulsion (the children ripping through the presents, their inevitable hope and let down) when we come upon the other to whom we have transferred our *jouissance* enjoying in our stead. We confront our own ultimate passivity, the enjoyment that fixes us in our place.

By highlighting the fact of this confrontation, this transfixed horror and fascination before the enjoyment of the other (which we also saw in the discussion of racism and ethnic nationalism), Žižek's approach clarifies the way our encounters with others are not necessarily encounters with other subjects, other people. The other who gives body to excessive enjoyment is not located within the field of intersubjectivity.[52] Hence, grappling with hatred involves confronting the fundamental fantasies organizing our enjoyment, a confrontation that inevitably and necessarily destroys who we are. Differently put, we cannot dislodge the contingent nugget around which our subjectivity is organized without destroying this very subjectivity, becoming some one or some we different from whom we were before. Of course, we can disavow it, displacing it onto the other, and carry on, our activity held in place by this ultimate passivity.

We can get a clearer sense of this link between our fundamental passivity and the displacement of enjoyment onto another by considering two examples: Alec Baldwin's performance in the film *Glengarry Glen Ross* and President George W. Bush's 2003 State of the Union address. Žižek holds that the most libidinally satisfying part of the movie is Baldwin's appearance. He writes, "It is the excessive enjoyment elicited by Baldwin's demeanour in this scene which accounts for the spectator's satisfaction in witnessing the humiliation of the poor agents. Such excessive enjoyment is the necessary support of social relationships of domination ..."[53] Initially, I was puzzled by Žižek's remarks. Was the enjoyment Baldwin's or the spectators'? Is Baldwin's character eliciting enjoyment in us or for himself? Figuring this out seems important if we are to understand Žižek's claim about domination. Is Žižek using the scene analogically—the relationship in which the poor agents are stuck is like ours?—or is he saying that insofar as we as spectators are enjoying, we are similarly involved in relationships of domination?

In the scene in question, Baldwin plays a sales executive who has come to push or inspire a group of real estate salesmen. It is a rainy night. The men are frustrated with their inability to sell property to the people whose names and information they have been provided: "the leads." The only man doing well, Ricky Roma (Al Pacino), does not show up for the meeting. The rest of the salesmen are then subject to the browbeating of this executive, sent from the bosses, "Mitch and Murray." Baldwin tells them that they are not salesmen; they are faggots, pieces of shit. He issues completely irrational orders: put that coffee down! He subjects the salesmen to a false choice: listen to what he has to say or get out, get fired. He gives them sales advice that makes no sense, writing on the chalkboard the words *attention, interest, decision*, and *action* and asking, "Have you made your decision for Christ?" When one of the salesmen asks him who he is, Baldwin answers "Fuck you! That's my name. Your name is you're wanting." After he leaves, there is rumbling thunder.

That Baldwin's character displays excessive enjoyment seems clear enough. But does he elicit enjoyment from us? Or, differently put, how is it that we enjoy through this scene? To the extent that we are transfixed and repulsed by the performance, we are captured, held in place by enjoyment.[54] Like the humiliated salesmen, we passively endure Baldwin's obscene tirade, flinching, overwhelmed by the excess. Insofar as this scene is a staging of our own passivity, it can be understood in terms of a fantasy that sustains activity. We imagine the denigrated salesmen as trapped, unfree, as unlike us; they are caught in a forced choice, in a particular economic horror. We are not—or at least we can fantasize that we are not, relieved by the fact that we are not pathetic and humiliated. In this case, then, we become like Baldwin, thinking of these men as, sure, nice guys, but when it comes right down to it, failures.

Conversely, we may see the salesmen's condition as our own; like them, we are trapped—but, it is not our fault. Like them, we could succeed if we only had that extra, the right stuff, or, in the film's specific version of the object-cause of desire, if we had the right leads. Thus, in one version, the salesmen are inert objects, instruments of Mitch and Murray's enrichment and Baldwin's enjoyment. In another, they are victims, not really responsible for the situation in which they are trapped. The enjoyment in the scene, then, arises out of this impossible, irresolvable situation. It stages the all or nothing oscillation of enjoyment, and this impossibility transfixes us.

We can compare this scene from *Glengarry Glen Ross* to President George W. Bush's 2003 State of the Union address. In reporting on progress in the so-called war on terror, Bush lists some of those "we have arrested or otherwise dealt with," specifying some "key commanders of Al Qaida." He continues, "All told, more than 3,000 suspected terrorists have been arrested in many countries. And many others have met a different fate. Let's put it this way: They are no longer a problem to the United States and our friends and allies." I shuddered when I saw this speech. It has stuck with me, particularly because of Bush's repulsive smirk. For me, it was not simply a matter of what I took to be Bush's clear allusion to torture. Rather, it was the fact that he enjoyed it. His clear enjoyment when mentioning torture and death made the speech compelling and unbearable—horrifying and unavoidable.

Does it make sense to consider Bush's speech in terms of displaced enjoyment? A perhaps obvious reading would emphasize some viewers' transference of a desire for revenge onto the President. He offers himself as an instrument of our will and we want him to carry it out, to act in our stead, to do those illegal and murderous deeds because we cannot—even though we want to. In this instance, displacing our enjoyment over to Bush enables us to avoid confronting it, to avoid acknowledging an illegality within law that we endorse. He acts, so that we can remain passive.

To be sure, not everyone who heard the speech agrees with Bush. Yet we are still transfixed—wherein lies our enjoyment? Perhaps we are captured by our own disavowed passivity. Bush's speech enables me to be self-righteously horrified, to write letters to the editor, talk with friends and colleagues, and send money to Move On, all while denying the way that I am nonetheless trapped, unable actually to change a thing. And, perhaps, here "Bartleby politics" involves a shift in perspective on precisely this trap, a turning of what appears to be an impossibility into the possibility that things might be otherwise, but a turn that cannot occur in the absence of a refusal to acknowledge our underlying passivity. I can imagine Republicans thrilled by the speech, but it is very difficult for me to imagine Democrats and progressives taking the difficult steps of organizing politically to impeach Bush, stop the war, and publicly recant previous support for the war by admitting they were wrong. I can criticize the speech, and the policies and the man behind it, even as my true, passive position is caught in enjoyment, trapped by "Oh, this is so horrible, but it's out of my hands, not my responsibility."[55]

In sum, as with the Baldwin example, the enjoyment in the Bush speech is double: viewers transfer their enjoyment to Bush, remaining passive while he acts for them; or we pursue all sorts of activity, talking and criticizing, disavowing the fact that these activities are ineffectual.[56] We are transfixed, then, by the impossibility of the situation, by the way we are compelled to confront and disavow in the same moment the horrific fact of the law violating the law *for us and in our stead*. Those of us who oppose Bush and his war are compelled to confront and disavow in the same moment our own failure to act, our own sense of helpless entrapment.

Enjoyment and Superego

The Baldwin and Bush examples shed light on a further aspect of enjoyment, namely, its superego support. Lacan has a somewhat counterintuitive concept of the superego. He holds that the fundamental superego injunction is "Enjoy!" Against the prohibitions of symbolic norms, superego solicits enjoyment.[57] Superego is an injunction, a law that is not included within the symbolic order; thus, it is a law of enjoyment that permeates and ruptures the symbolic.[58] We might think of visceral reactions to Presidents Bill Clinton and George W. Bush. Those who hated Clinton hated him primarily for his enjoyment, for his sexual appetites that seemed to them outside of permissible norms. Similarly, those who hate Bush hate him for his enjoyment, for his embrace of violence, torture, and excess wealth, again, for the way he exceeds and transgresses symbolic norms. In each instance, there is a certain enjoyment that cannot be accounted for within basic symbolic frames, something more than disagreement with policies and positions.

Baldwin's character in *Glengarry Glen Ross* clearly transgresses the boundaries of the conventional understanding of motivational speaking. Not only is he resolutely obscene—his name is "fuck you"; he ends his speech by displaying his brass balls—but he also highlights those elements of the symbolic order that his injunction compels the pathetic real estate agents to reject: being nice guys, good fathers, having names. His demands, in other words, cannot be met within or through symbolic norms. They are an obscene, unacknowledgeable supplement to normal practice—a supplement, incidentally, upon which the order relies: the real estate agents cannot continue within the symbolic, they cannot support themselves, if they fail to carry out Baldwin's demands. His injunction: take the money of the poor saps from the leads, if you are man enough. Be rich, like me. Treat the saps just like I'm treating you. "Go, and do likewise." Additionally, Baldwin's perversity is manifest in the way that he presents himself as an instrument of the other: Mitch and Murray sent him. Yet clearly, he is more than an instrument. As Žižek writes, "the 'truth' of the pervert's claim that he is accomplishing his act as the instrument of the big Other is its exact opposite: he is staging the fiction of the big Other in order to conceal the *jouissance* he derives from the destructive orgy of his acts."[59]

In his 2003 State of the Union address, Bush similarly highlights his externality to the symbolic, public law. He says many others have "met a different fate" and "let's put it this way," drawing our attention to what cannot be said, to what cannot be directly acknowledged.[60] His position is likewise similarly perverse. Bush presents himself as an instrument of the American people, of the civilized world, and of the cause of freedom. That his perversity is excessive, that he is not only doing his duty as an instrument but *enjoys* it, is apparent in his embrace of power and destruction: shock and awe. Finally, like Baldwin commanding the salesmen to break the rules and get rich, so does Bush position himself as a totalitarian master, a master who not only makes himself the object of another's enjoyment but who also enjoins us to enjoy.[61] As a totalitarian master, Bush gives us permission, indeed, encourages us, to enjoy. He gives us permission to enjoy torture, to enjoy the domain beyond the law, the domain of power, strength, and revenge. Ultimately, to the extent that the so-called war on terror involves a line in the sand, for us or against us, permitted enjoyment becomes commanded enjoyment. Enjoy! ... *if you are one of us.*

Three aspects of the superego injunction to enjoy are important to understanding enjoyment as a political factor: the connection between superego and enjoying through another, the division of the law between its public letter and its obscene superego supplement, and the relation between enjoyment and transgression.

First, the notion of a superego imperative accounts for the relief provided by enjoying through another. That one would displace enjoyment is, to a certain extent, paradoxical. If the lack of enjoyment sustains desire, why would we want to get rid of it? Wouldn't we want enjoyment? Isn't that what we are after? Žižek attributes the "satisfaction and liberating potential of being able to enjoy through the Other" to the fact that enjoyment is not "an immediate spontaneous state, but is sustained by a superego imperative."[62] The fact that enjoyment is commanded, in other words, is why we experience relief in displacing it onto another. When enjoyment is a duty, we want to escape from it, so the order to enjoy actually hinders our enjoyment. We might think here of the way the pressure to enjoy ourselves while on vacation can be exhausting. By the time we return home, we are relieved to be back at work so we are no longer compelled to keep having fun. Or we might imagine the way casual conversations can be more rewarding, more enjoyable, than those we force ourselves to have by setting up quality time or by arranging specific meetings or making lunch dates. Once we are in the situation where we are expected to have a good conversation, where we feel that it is our duty to be smart or interesting, we find ourselves at a loss for words. The point is that we are caught: the superego compels us to enjoy, yet that compulsion hinders our enjoyment. One way that we escape this compulsion is by displacing our *jouissance* onto another who enjoys for us.

Second, Žižek claims that "superego designates the intrusion of enjoyment into the field of ideology"; that is, it provides the enjoyment that supports meaning, that gives an ideological edifice its hold on the subject.[63] Insofar as enjoyment is not a natural state but a byproduct, it has to come from somewhere. It has to be provided. This is the job of superego or enjoyment as a remainder that compels, enjoins, and insists in a way beyond meaning, at a point where meaning fails.[64] When we view public law in terms of ideological meaning, we can see how superego functions as law's irrational underpinning. Public law is necessarily split between its explicit text, its ideological meaning, and its obscene (unacknowledgeable) superego support. The perhaps surprising result is the way law tolerates and incites what its explicit text prohibits.

As I set out more thoroughly in Chapter Four, this toleration and incitement works in two opposing ways: superego prohibits what the public law permits and superego permits what the public law prohibits. For example, according to the norms of liberal democracy, citizens are encouraged to voice their views, challenge authority, debate matters of shared concern. Yet there are myriad daily instances of the way that we, as citizens, discourage others from voicing their views, criticize those who challenge authority, and say that some things should just not be debated. Žižek sometimes refers to this dimension of superego as the "nightly law," the unwritten rules that keep people in their place.

Conversely, superego also enjoins people to do what is contrary to the law—as we have seen already in Bush's 2003 State of the Union address. Superego says go ahead, do your duty, break the law for the sake of the law. "As for the status of this obscene supplement," Žižek writes, one should

> neither glorify it as subversive nor dismiss it as a false trans-
> gression which stabilizes the power edifice . . . but insist on its
> *undecideable* character. Obscene unwritten rules sustain Power
> as long as they remain in the shadows; the moment they are pub-
> licly recognized, the edifice of Power is thrown into disarray.[65]

By attending to the superego supplement to the public law, we can account for the way that power is split. Public law is not simply opposed to transgression; it relies on its own internalized transgression, which it is forced to deny. The very operation of law depends on an obscene outlaw that it has to conceal.

In *The Ticklish Subject*, Žižek contrasts his account of law's split with the division between politics and the police as theorized by Jacques Ranciere. Žižek rightly points out that Ranciere opposes democratic energy to depoliticizing order, but this opposition is limited insofar as it fails to take into account an additional component of power: the way it has to transgress the very laws it establishes, the way its upholding of the law involves it in illegal activities. Žižek writes, "What Power refuses to see is not so much the (non) part of the 'people' excluded from the political space, but rather the invisible support of its own public police apparatus."[66] Law, the police, of course recognizes that there are criminals. It recognizes as well that there is a limit to its reach, to its purview, that some are excluded from its protections and denied participation in its construction. The American constitution, for example, includes provisions for its own revision and, indeed, one type of legal battle is over who law recognizes and how. We might think here of the way law has acknowledged, excluded, and included people of African and slave descent as Americans or how law has perceived, constrained, and recognized specific persons as women.

What law does not acknowledge is the criminality necessary for its own functioning. This is the aspect of itself that it has to hide—its own internal transgression. An obvious example, much loved by conspiracy theorists and oddly avoided by mainstream political scientists, is the existence of "black ops" and the black budget component of national security funding. The functioning of public authority requires that certain things be not said: a policy cannot be defended on the grounds that it lets the rich get richer; rather, it has to be said to stimulate the economy or to trickle down for the benefit of those at the bottom. In the words of former U.S. Attorney General, Ramsey Clark, "The United States is not nearly so concerned that its acts be kept secret from its intended victims as it is that the American people not know of them."[67] Thus, part of the scandal of Pat Robertson's August 2005 call for the assassination of Venezuelan President Hugo Chavez is the way he stated the obvious, the way he made explicit what the U.S. government must officially deny.

What follows from this distinction between Žižek and Ranciere is a matter of political strategy and leads to my third point regarding enjoyment and transgression. For Žižek, insofar as the superego supplement to the law solicits transgression, transgression on its own is not subversive. Because law is split, transgression may well violate the letter of the law in a way that affirms and reinforces law's superego supplement. That is, transgression may comply with the injunction to enjoy; it may be a vehicle for *jouissance* and thus fail to address the law at all. For example, transgression can provide the common link, the libidinal support that binds a collective together—our collective dirty secret.[68] Here superego tells members there is more to law than its official face, that they, the members, know what to do, that the official rules do not apply to them; they should go ahead, violate the laws, harass, assault, kill. We might think here of the solidarity of Southern white racists, as in the case of Emmett Till, a fourteen-year-old Chicago boy, murdered in Mississippi in 1955. His murderers, Roy Bryant and J. W. Milam, were quickly acquitted by an all-white jury. Soon after, they confessed to the crime, selling their story to *Look* magazine. People in their part of the rural Mississippi delta knew Bryant and Milam were guilty, but, far from this guilt being an outrage, it confirmed the whites in their collective racism. Southern law continued to rely on, indeed, to endorse, the racist superego supplement commanding whites to enjoy.

Among some critical theorists today, particularly those affiliated with some of the more extravagant moments in cultural studies, transgression has seemed worthwhile in and of itself. For these theorists, the dominance of established norms is necessarily constraining, creating unjustifiable limits on the freedom and creativity of selves coming into being. Žižek offers a more nuanced approach to transgression, one that allows for the potentially liberating work of laws and norms, their ability to relieve subjects from the superego compulsion to enjoy, on the one hand, and their dependence on a superego supplement, on the other.

Enjoying Pluralism

Thus far, I have presented Žižek's account of enjoyment in terms of the way it fixes the subject. Enjoyment provides the subject with its place; it also displaces the subject. In turn, even as this displacement enables the subject to act, it relies on an underlying fantasy (an organization of *jouissance*) in which the other is an object enjoying in our stead. At the level of fantasy, the other is not another subject, but the repository of enjoyment. I can imagine myself acting as a subject in a way that accords with the symbolic order, *I can be the person I see myself as*, precisely insofar as fantasy prevents me from confronting the lack in the symbolic (its inconsistency and rupture) and instead organizes this lack to promise and deliver enjoyment. As the vehicle for enjoyment, superego is thus a primary element of fantasy. It is the meaning-less command that supplements and subverts official ideology, the necessary and unavoidable irrationality that stains public law.

In my view, this theory of enjoyment provides a powerful way to understand and critique the contemporary political–economic formation of communicative capitalism. It helps us grasp why global flows of capital and information, the digital era's seemingly endless capacity for accessing, distributing, and producing ideas and opportunities, have not resulted in anything like a democratic "globalization from below" but instead result in new forms of inequality, exploitation, and enslavement. To make this point, I turn now to Žižek's account of the present in terms of the general-ized perversity of the society of enjoyment.

Žižek argues that the crucial feature of late capitalist societ-ies is the way that transgression has been normalized.[69] Rather than conforming to stereotypes of responsible men in the public sphere and caring women in the private, contemporary subjects are encouraged to challenge gender norms and boundaries. Men and women alike are enjoined to succeed in the work force and in their family lives, to find fulfilling careers and spend quality time with their children. Networked communication technologies (high-speed internet, cell phones) enable parents to work harder even as they attend to familial relationships. Similarly, emphases on the value of diverse cultural and ethnic traditions have replaced earlier injunctions to assimilate. These emphases find material support in consumer goods ranging from clothing and accessories targeted to specific demographic groups, to film, television, and print media, to, more recently, drugs and health plans designed for particular populations. What is now quite clear is a shift in the understanding of social membership away from the worker-citizen and toward the consumer.[70] Thus, what disciplinary society prohibited, contemporary consumerism encourages, indeed, demands.

Contemporary consumer culture relies on excess, on a general principle that more is better.[71] Excess drives the economy: super-sized meals at McDonald's and Burger King; gargantuan SUVs; fashion magazines urging shoppers to pick up "armloads" of the newest items; extreme sports; extreme makeovers; and, at the same time, bigger closets; the production of all sorts of organizing, filing, and containing systems; and a booming business in mini-storage units, all of which are supposed to help Americans deal with their excess stuff. These makeovers, these fashions and accessories, provide material support for injunctions to be oneself, to create and express one's free individuality, to become the unique and valuable person one already is, to break the bounds of conformity. Excess also appears in other aspects of life under communicative capitalism: 24/7 news, 800-channel television, blockbuster films, and television shows advertised as the "most unbelievable moment of the season" and the "unforgettable series finale." Self-help books tell us not just *how to achieve* sexual ecstasy, spiritual fulfillment, and a purpose-driven life—they tell us *to achieve* sexual ecstasy, spiritual fulfillment, and a purpose-driven life. As Žižek writes, "the superego aspect of today's 'non-repressive' hedonism (the constant provocations to which we are exposed, enjoining us to go right to the end, and explore all modes of *jouissance*) resides in the way permitted *jouissance* necessarily turns into obligatory *jouissance*."[72] We are daily enjoined to enjoy. Ours is a society of the superego.

One might object at this point that Žižek's emphasis on contemporary injunctions to enjoy is misplaced. Does not the rise of religious fundamentalism, for example, suggest just the opposite, that is, a return to old sexual prohibitions? What about persistent warnings concerning health: don't smoke, just say no to drugs, watch your weight, cut down on fat and carbohydrates. What are these if not new forms of discipline? Žižek's response is, first, that one should not confuse regulations with symbolic prohibitions and, second, that so-called fundamentalism also relies on an injunction to enjoy.[73]

In the first instance, the regulations we encounter every day, the instructions regarding moderation and balance, the careful regimes and guidance we come under as we navigate late capitalism, are not symbolic norms. They are regulations that lack a claim to normative authority but are instead installed by committees, by experts, and by pundits. Everyone knows they are ultimately contestable, carrying no symbolic weight. Experts argue all the time over proper diets, the necessary amount of exercise, the benefits of red wine. In Žižek's terms, these regulations are regulations of the very mode of transgression.[74] This makes sense when we recognize the way that these regulations fail to provide any real breathing space, any relief from the injunction to enjoy. They function perniciously, never failing to remind us that we are not enjoying properly, are not doing anything right. Pervasive regulations are ultimately worse—more repressive and more difficult to contest precisely insofar as they accept their own contestability—than symbolic norms. They reinforce the malevolent superego, empowering it to torment us all the more.

In the second instance, Žižek argues that contemporary fundamentalisms, as in the example of postmodern nationalism (and I'll add the religious right in the United States) also enjoin *jouissance*. Their seeming adherence to law is driven and sustained by a superego injunction to transgress contemporary regulations. I think of this in terms of a culture of cruelty. Opponents of gay marriage, in the name of family values, free their congregations to hate; indeed, they organize themselves via a fascination with the sexual enjoyment of same-sex couplings, thereby providing enjoyment. Opposition to gay marriage gives opponents permission, in fact it encourages them, to find and weed out homosexual attraction. Might a boy be too artistic, too gentle? Might a girl be too aggressive? Christian fundamentalists opposing gay marriage urge that ambiguous behavior be identified and corrected before it is too late. If necessary, of course, they can provide retraining, that is, they can install young people in camps and programs that will "turn them straight."

This fascination, this weeding out that exceeds and transgresses the law, lets us know we are dealing with enjoyment. We might also think of media figures like Ann Coulter. In her extreme conservatism, she inspires her readers and viewers to hate. Go ahead, you don't need to concern yourself with the poor, with "smelly homeless people," or the "savages" we are fighting in Baghdad.[75] Hate them! Don't be like those treasonist left-wing lunatics (among whom she includes Supreme Court Justice Ruth Bader Ginsburg). Again, the righteousness Coulter inspires provides a kind of extra excitement, a sense of struggle, of matters worth fighting for, of enjoyment. Like opponents of gay marriage, she gives people permission to break the rules of political correctness; they can stop worrying about strange holidays like Kwanzaa being forced upon their children and happily celebrate a truly American holiday like Christmas. Yet the preoccupation with excess is not confined to the right. Žižek emphasizes that this excessive attitude toward enjoyment also characterizes the multiculturalism and political correctness associated with leftist and liberal politics. Thus, he argues that liberal tolerance today is in fact a "zero tolerance" of the other in his excessive enjoyment.[76] If the other remains *too* tied to particular religious practices, say those that involve the subordination of women, the denial of medical treatment to children, the rejection of scientific findings regarding evolution and global warming, well, this other cannot be tolerated. This other is incompatible with liberal pluralism; differently put, liberalism wants an other deprived of its otherness.[77] White leftist multiculturalists, even as they encourage the flourishing of multiple modes of becoming, find themselves in a similar bind (one in which class difference is inscribed): their support of differentiated cultural traditions means that they oppose the racism, sexism, and religiosity that bind together some poor whites. Just as the superego imperative operates in conservatism to encourage hate, so can it be found in liberalism and leftist multiculturalism.

Correlative to the pervasive intrusion of superego enjoyment is a decline in the efficiency of symbolic norms, what Žižek refers to as the "collapse of the big Other."[78] The decline of symbolic efficiency refers to a fundamental uncertainty in our relation to the world, to the absence of a principle of charity that pertains across and through disagreement. We do not know on whom or what to rely, whom or what to trust. Arguments persuasive in one context carry little weight in another. In short, although the symbolic order is always and necessarily lacking—ruptured—today this lack is directly assumed. We no longer posit an overarching symbolic. We are so attuned to pretense and manipulation—"spin"—that we reject the very possibility of a truth beneath the lie or of a truth that cuts through the assortment of lies and injunctions to enjoy constitutive of the present ideological formation.

What we presume instead are a variety of partial fillers, partial substitutes. Thus, in place of symbolically anchored identities (structured in terms of conventions of gender, race, work, and national citizenship), we encounter imaginary injunctions to develop our creative potential and cultivate our individuality, injunctions supported by capital's provisions of the ever-new experiences and accessories we use to perform this self-fashioning (what Žižek refers to as the direct super-egoization of the imaginary ideal).[79] In place of norms grounded in claims to universal validity, we have rules and regulations that are clearly the result of compromises among competing parties or the contingent and fallible conclusions of committees of experts. In place of the norms that relieve us of the duty to enjoy, that provide the prohibitions that sustain desire, we find ourselves at the mercy of the superego's injunction. We are expected to have a good time, to have it all, to be happy, fit, and fulfilled.

This compulsion results in overwhelming guilt and anxiety. On one hand, we are guilty both when we fail to live up to the superego's injunction and when we follow it. On the other hand, we are anxious before the enjoyment of the other. Given our inabilities to enjoy, the enjoyment of the other seems all the more powerful and all the more threatening. The other all too easily threatens our imaginary balance. An ever-present reminder that someone else has more, is more fulfilled, more successful, more attractive, more spiritual, the other makes our own lack all the more present to us. That the fragility of contemporary subjects means others are experienced as threats helps make sense of the ready availability of the imaginary identity of the victim—one of the few positions from which one can speak. When others smoke, I am at risk. When others over-eat, make noise, flaunt their sexuality, then my *American way of life, my values*, are under attack. In the terms provided by the so-called war on terror, to be "civilized" today is to be a victim—a victim of fear of terrorism, a victim that has to be surveilled, searched, guarded, and protected from unpredictable violence. In all these cases, the imaginary identity of the victim authorizes the subject to speak even as it shields it from responsibility toward another.[80] The victim role, in other words, is one wherein the subject who speaks relies on and presupposes the other as an object enjoying in its stead, and, moreover, as threatening, even unbearable, in that enjoyment.

One might have thought that the disintegration of restrictive symbolic norms, especially in the context of the speed and flows of communicative capitalism, would have ushered in a time of remarkable freedom. People in pluralist and pluralizing societies would be free to make choices about who they want to be and how they want to live unhindered by racist and patriarchal conventions. Žižek's thesis, however, is that the decline of symbolic efficiency has introduced new opportunities for guilt and anxiety, new forms of submission, dependence, and domination. His account of the fixity of enjoyment explains why. Given that activity depends on passivity, that the very capacity to act relies on a nugget of enjoyment, the emergence of new opportunities for domination makes sense. In the face of injunctions to freedom, compulsions to individual self-creation, and demands to choose and decide even when there are no reliable grounds for a decision, subjects will cling all the more desperately to the objects that sustain them, whether these objects are the myriad available momentary enjoyments provided by capital or the others as objects enjoying in our stead. We depend on these contingent enjoyments to be at all.

Indeed, Žižek argues that contemporary imperatives to freedom produce even more radical attachments to domination and submission. This attachment repeats the simple dynamic of transgression. If authorities say do not do X, then doing X will provide enjoyment (because prohibition relies on the fantasy that were it not for the prohibited object, one would enjoy). Conversely, if authorities say do X, then not doing X provides enjoyment. Thus, Žižek insists that contemporary subjectivities confront an "obscene need for domination and submission" and he defends this point with reference to "the growth of sado-masochistic lesbian couples."[81] I think this example is absurd (and likely an instance of where Žižek's own enjoyment irrupts in the text). More powerful examples of contemporary attachments to domination can be found in the widespread enthusiasm for coercive law, strict sentencing, the death penalty, and zero tolerance toward law-breakers.[82] And, we can better account for impulses to submission, for the surprising willingness of many to accept even the most unconvincing pronouncements in a time of fear, uncertainty, and insecurity, by emphasizing, again, not sexual anecdotes but the need for relief from the injunction to decide for oneself when one has no grounds for choosing. Submission enables someone else to do what needs to be done for us, to be the object or instrument of our will. Displacing the need to know what to will and the very act of willing onto an other who wills for us, we escape from the pressures of guilt and responsibility.

When the concept of enjoyment is a category of political theory, our conception of the challenges of contemporary politics changes. The central political problem today is not the fundamentalism that opposes the unfolding of freedom in the world—despite the odd fact that radical, pluralist democrats and mainstream neoconservatives and neoliberals are united in the conviction that it is. Instead, insofar as this unfolding is tied to the expansions of global capitalism, it relies on nuggets of enjoyment; it reintroduces sites and objects of fixity. Thus, the central problem is how we are to relate to enjoyment, how we can escape (traverse) the fantasies that provide it, even as we acknowledge enjoyment as an irreducible component of what it is to be human. This is a mighty problem indeed, for confronting enjoyment requires that we disrupt our place, that is, that we refuse to accept imaginary and symbolic reassurance and undergo subjective destitution.

The difference between Žižek's view and that of radical pluralists appears clearly when we consider the work of William Connolly. In his valuable exploration of the interconnections between pluralization and fundamentalism, Connolly treats fundamentalism as an excess to be eliminated. Fundamentalism blocks more primary, generative, and destabilizing "movements of difference."[83] The challenge of contemporary political and ethical life, then, is cultivating a proper response to these movements, a response that is generous and ethical rather than narrow and restrictive. As Connolly emphasizes, cultivating such a response necessarily entails working on the self, that is, a critical attitude toward one's own fundaments or the contingent kernels to which one remains attached. What the notion of enjoyment makes clear is how fundamental, how radical, this work of generosity must be. Far from involving a kind of nudging of one's dispositions, the work of grappling with the fundamental fantasies that structure our enjoyment entails a thorough subjective destitution, the willingness to give up the very kernel of one's being. Connolly's account of generosity, while it need not avoid this leap into the abyss, too often understates the degree of work involved. That is, it leaves the subject intact.

We can approach the same point from a different direction: Connolly cannot tell us what to do with fundamentalists who enjoy their fundaments. His suggestions for techniques by which to cultivate gratitude and responsiveness to "new movements of cultural diversification" are helpful practices for those who want to be thankful and responsive, but, on the face of it, they simply do not apply to those who choose to be vindictive and small-minded.[84] I say "on the face of it" because despite Connolly's point that generosity and responsiveness cannot be commanded into being, there is nonetheless a presumed injunction in his ethics, one that bids those who might hear it to give up their attachments, to abandon their fundaments if they wish to be liberal democrats in a pluralistic society. The implication is that fundaments are intolerable, whether in others or in ourselves. We can think of this as a kind of neo-Stoic effort at producing the flexible subjects of late capitalism.

Two problems with Connolly's presentation of fundamentalism as the primary problem confronting contemporary societies thus present themselves. On the one hand, Connolly's suggestions for self-work end up replicating the regulations and manuals to which late capitalist subjects turn for relief. To this extent, they fail to address the investment in rules, in submission and attachment to domination, characteristic of contemporary subjects. His techniques, then, are techniques of accommodation that leave the primary organization of enjoyment intact. On the other hand, insofar as Connolly seeks to address elements of attachment, his techniques repeat the very processes of pluralization generating contemporary anxieties. Just as the enjoyment of the other is experienced as a threat to my fragile, narcissistic self, so is any passionate attachment potentially a sticking point for the flows of becoming. Whereas Žižek urges us to consider the ways fantasies arrange this investment, precisely because there is no way of eliminating enjoyment and our only alternative is to confront it and take responsibility for it, Connolly would have us try to eliminate it. Clearly, Connolly's approach is more hopeful. Yet Žižek's may well be more helpful in providing political theorists with concepts by which we can grapple with the challenges of freedom under communicative capitalism.

In the following chapters, I consider how the category of enjoyment helps us think better about political–ideological formations. Chapter Two discusses Žižek's rejection of *totalitarianism* as an analytical term in favor of a more precise set of distinctions between fascism and Stalinism. Chapter Three looks at liberal democracy, the formation Žižek prefers to understand as "totalitarian" today in the sense that it constitutes a barrier beyond which we cannot think. Chapter Four considers enjoyment in law in terms of law's superego supplement. These chapters set out systematically Žižek's theory of enjoyment as a political factor.

2
FASCISM AND STALINISM

Introduction

One of the key claims of Žižek's political theory is that every ideology relies on an unassimilable kernel of enjoyment.[1] As we saw in the previous chapter, this means subjects are attached to an ideological formation not simply because of a set of identifiable reasons or causes, but because of something extra. Ideological formations rely on an extra, nonrational nugget that goes beyond what we know to produce our sense of who we are and what the world is for us. This nugget of enjoyment can be what we desire but can never achieve, as in, say, national unity. It can also be what we want to eliminate, but never can, as in, for example, political corruption. Again, the idea of enjoyment as a political factor is that some contingent element of reality takes on a special, excessive role and so attaches us to a socio-political formation. In Žižek's words, this element "becomes elevated to the dignity of a Thing."[2] It becomes a fantastic stand-in for enjoyment.

Enjoyment, then, is a category that can help political theorists account for differences among ideological formations. A typical move for political theorists working in the liberal tradition is to emphasize the legitimacy of a political formation. For these theorists, what makes a formation legitimate is the presence of consent: can the power formation be understood as one on which people would agree? In contrast, Žižek differentiates among ideological formations in terms not of legitimacy but of enjoyment. A primary task for the political theorist, then, is to grasp how a given formation organizes enjoyment.

Accordingly, Žižek rejects "totalitarianism" as a category through which to analyze fascism and communism. The category is too broad, too embedded in a simple liberal framework of consent versus force, to account for how political subjects might be attached to and invested in fascist and communist arrangements of power. Breaking with liberal political and intellectual notions of "totalitarianism," Žižek argues for the difference between fascism and communism in terms of their organizations of enjoyment, in what steals it and what provides it.

Žižek's thesis is straightforward: the difference between fascism and Stalinism rests in their relationship to "class struggle," that is, to the fundamental antagonism rupturing society.[3] The Nazis attempted to neutralize class struggle by displacing it onto what they naturalized and racialized as an essential, foreign element to be eliminated. Stalinism, a perverse bureaucratic formation perceiving itself as having won and thus eliminated the class struggle, tried to retain and enhance economic productivity. It strove to direct exceptional economic production and growth without the constraints of the capitalist form.

In this chapter, I set out Žižek's analyses of the discursive structures of Nazism and Stalinism, showing how he reaches these conclusions. As I do so, I add to the concept of enjoyment an additional element of Žižek's political theory, namely, his use of Lacan's "four discourses." I begin by considering in more detail what is at stake in Žižek's refusal of the term *totalitarianism* as a way of thinking about fascism and communism.

The Totalitarian Threat

In his 2001 book, *Did Somebody Say Totalitarianism?*, Žižek argues that the term *totalitarian* prevents thought.[4] The elevation of Hannah Arendt "into an untouchable authority," he announces, "is perhaps the clearest sign of the theoretical defeat of the Left."[5] In subjecting the term *totalitarianism* to critique by differentiating among its objects, that is, by emphasizing *contra* Arendt that fascism and communism are not the same, that they mobilize enjoyment differently, have different projects and, indeed, have different degrees of greatness or authenticity, Žižek is trying to clear out a space for radical politics. As he clearly states in the conclusion of his 2004 book, *Organs without Bodies*, "Nazism was enacted by a group of people who wanted to do very bad things, and they did them; Stalinism, on the contrary, emerged as the result of a radical emancipatory attempt."[6] Three aspects of Žižek's effort to open up possibilities for radical thought by distinguishing between Nazism and Stalinism bear emphasizing.

First, when he rejects the idea that fascism and communism are "totalitarian" regimes, Žižek is resisting the forced choice that entraps radical thought. Challenges to the present combination of global capitalism and liberal democracy typically encounter the rejoinder that revolution always leads to totalitarianism, that the present is the best we can have because any attempt to change it will inevitably lead to something worse, as the experiments of the twentieth century made so bloodily clear.[7] Žižek argues that to accept this forced choice between acquiescence to the present and the risk of a totalitarian future, however, is to accept liberal democratic hegemony in advance, to close off the very possibility of thinking otherwise. If there is not one totalitarianism, one option, one alternative to liberal democracy, then the choice for liberal democracy is not so clear. One needs to think about it, to understand how other possibilities emerged and might emerge, what aspirations they held in the past and may hold in the future. One has to recognize the differences between Left and Right critiques of the present liberal democratic order.

Accordingly, Žižek, second, links the rise of fascism not to dogmatism but to liberalism's suspicion of every form of engagement.[8] Many leftist intellectuals today reject deep, constitutive attachments to practices or beliefs as primitive or dangerous. Liberal neutrality and so-called postmodern relativism overlap in a skepticism about convictions.[9] In Žižek's view, this rejection is indicative of a cynicism complicit with fascism. It produces the atmosphere of confusion and undecideability—*all ideas are equal, none is better than another*—into which the fascist decision for order intervenes. Precluding radical, dogmatic, defenses of equality or justice, suspicion toward engagement "defangs" leftist thought in advance by refusing the division or choice—*this, not that*—constitutive of politics.[10]

Third, Žižek seeks to recall the history of antifascism.[11] World War II involved an alliance between liberal democratic and socialist countries. The Cold War steadily eroded this alliance. In the wake of the demise of socialism, it seems all but forgotten. This forgetting supports intensifications of global capitalism and the present rise of neoconservativism and religious fundamentalism. The grip of neoliberal economic policy and its rhetorical alliance with classic liberal appeals to freedom has meant that, officially at least, socialism is a dead project—a false start. Lost in this ideological convergence is an ideal celebrated under Stalinism, namely, a view of material production and manual labor as a "privileged site of community and solidarity." What such a notion maintains, Žižek writes, is that "not only does engagement in the collective effort of production bring satisfaction in itself; [but also] private problems themselves (from divorce to illness) are put into their proper perspective by being discussed in one's working collective."[12]

Little effort has been made to learn from the socialist experiment—to consider its successes, possibilities, and the traumatic results of its failure. Accordingly, Žižek resolutely condemns Frankfurt School theorists for failing to consider in any serious or systematic way either the specificity of Stalinism or the "nightmare of real existing socialism."[13] One of the merits of Žižek's critique of totalitarianism is thus the way that it addresses directly the horrors of Stalinism in order to create a space for this work of recovery. As he says, a crucial political task "is to confront the radical ambiguity of Stalinist ideology which, even at its most 'totalitarian,' still exudes an emancipatory potential."[14] Stalinism was not totalizing in the sense that it closed the gap between real and ideal. It appealed to aspirations for justice and solidarity. Dissidents and critics could thus evoke *communist* ideals against the regime itself. In other words, they could draw on more than liberal democracy and more than market freedom. Real existing socialism was a tragedy *in socialism's own terms.*[15]

In the face of the prominent fury of religious and ethnic nationalism at the end of the twentieth and beginning of the twenty-first centuries, Žižek's account of fascism and Stalinism's differing organizations of enjoyment provides political theory with an important new way of understanding attachments to and excesses of political violence. His analysis of the difference between fascism and communism makes clear how not all opposition, not all revolution, is the same. In this respect, it can benefit emancipatory struggles against authoritarian and right-wing regimes as it learns from socialist experience and highlights the interconnections between capitalism and ethnic nationalism. Žižek's rejection of totalitarianism, then, is a crucial component of his effort to open up a space for the critique of liberal democracy and its capitalist suppositions.

As the following sections make clear, Žižek's engagement with fascism and communism changes in the course of his writing. For example, in *Did Somebody Say Totalitarianism?*, Žižek considers the Holocaust in Lacan's terms, as Nazism's "desperate attempt to restore ritual value to its proper place" through that "gigantic sacrifice to the obscure gods."[16] Yet, in "Lenin's Choice," the afterword to his edited collection of Lenin's writings, *Revolution at the Gates*, published in 2002, Žižek rejects Lacan's reading of the Holocaust, accepting instead Giorgio Agamben's notion of the Jews as *homo sacer*, ones who could be killed but not sacrificed.[17] He likewise changes his account of Stalinism, altering his early formulation of the "totalitarian" subject as he comes to emphasize what I argue is a kind of split Stalinism, a Stalinism split between its perverse operation and its official bureaucratic face.[18]

Additionally, Žižek is not always consistent in his terms. He may compare fascism and Stalinism, where fascism stands in for National Socialism. Conversely, he sometimes uses Nazism as an example of fascism. He may use Stalinism as a synonym for late socialism or he may distinguish between Lenin, the Stalinist fantasy of Leninism, the period of the New Economic Policy in the Soviet Union of the twenties, the purge of the *nomenklatura* in the thirties, and the late days of real existing socialism. My approach to these changes is, first, to emphasize the fundamental antagonism of class struggle as the kernel that remains the same throughout Žižek's discussion of fascism and communism and, second, to recognize that sometimes the changes signal that we are dealing with a "parallax gap," that is, the displacement of an object that comes about when it is viewed from different perspectives.[19]

To see parallax at work, stretch your arm out in front of you; point your index finger up; close one eye and then the other while looking at the tip of your finger. Your finger will seem to move back and forth. This movement, or shift, is parallax. The Mobius strip provides another example of parallax at work. The weird thing about the Mobius strip is that it seems to have two sides. But, when you try to follow or trace one side, you end up, not with two sides, but just one. At the very place where you would expect the two sides to meet, you encounter one side. So, really, the sides never meet. You can never have both sides together; it is either one or the other.[20] The notion of the parallax gap is a way of thinking of the two sides of the strip. The shift between desire and drive that I introduce in Chapter One is a further example of a parallax gap. These are two radically incommensurable organizations of enjoyment. Adopting one perspective on enjoyment displaces the other. The parallax gap thus expresses the way "the 'truth' is not the 'real' state of things, that is the 'direct' view of the object without perspectival distortion, but the very Real of the antagonism which causes perspectival distortion. The site of truth is … the very gap, passage, which separates one perspective from another."[21] Truth is neither one perspective nor multiple perspectives. Instead, it is found in the distortion or gap as such.

Important to Žižek is the way the concept of a parallax gap designates an insurmountable discord between different perspectives.[22] By means of this concept, Žižek accounts for perspectival shifts in his own work—the way that seemingly incommensurate claims are not simple contradictions but in fact indications of a more profound gap within the field or object under consideration. More importantly, though, he uses the notion of a parallax gap to revise Lacan's notion of the Real and to augment his reading of Hegel as a philosopher of negativity.

In brief, unlike Lacan's Real, Žižek's "parallax Real" is not something that remains the same beneath varying changes in symbolization. Instead, it has no substantial density; it is simply the gap in perspectives, the shift from one to another. The Real, Žižek writes, is

the disavowed X on account of which our vision of reality is anamorphically distorted; it is simultaneously the Thing to which direct access is not possible and the obstacle which prevents this direct access, the Thing which eludes our grasp and the distorting screen which makes us miss the Thing. More precisely, the Real is ultimately the very shift of perspective from the first standpoint to the second.[23]

We can understand this by considering the idea of multiple perspectives on the same event. Žižek's point is that we do not get to the truth of the event by considering one or even all of these perspectives. Nor do we get to it by trying to adopt a kind of impossible God's eye view that would take into account absolutely everything that led up to the event. Instead, the distortion among the differing views and the impossibility of the God's eye view each indicate the Real of the event. The Realness of the event is what generates the multiplicity, the impossibility of its being encompassed. So, what I've called in this example the "event," Žižek refers to as the impossible hard core of the Real, one that, in a first instance, we cannot confront directly but only through "a multitude of symbolic fictions," and, in a second instance, appears as "purely virtual, actually nonexistent, an X which can be reconstructed only retroactively, from the multitude of symbolic formations which are 'all that there actually is.'"[24]

My example of the event can also help elucidate how Žižek uses the notion of the parallax gap in his reading of Hegel. What was missing in my first use of this example is the fact that the very notion of an event installs a frame; to refer to something as an event is to take it out of the manifold of experiences and impressions, to enframe it. Indeed, any accounting of the event would necessarily rely on a prior framing through which we see the event. The frame tells us how the event appears to us. So, rather than the event we actually have an appearance of the event. The framing turns reality into an appearance. Žižek draws on this idea of framing to explain how Hegel's response to Kant's distinction between the phenomenal and noumenal realms (or between our experience of our actions as determined in the physical world of nature and as free in the domain of reason) does not involve reconciliation in a larger substantial unity. It simply repeats the gap between the two. As Žižek writes in *The Ticklish Subject*, "'Negation of the negation' presupposes no magic reversal; it simply signals the unavoidable displacement or thwartedness of the subject's teleological activity."[25] Designating this unavoidable displacement with the term "parallax gap," Žižek argues that Hegel's contribution was to assert, to make "for itself," the gap Kant identified, but failed to recognize as itself freedom. What Hegel demonstrates, in effect, is that Kant had already found what he was still looking for. Hegel renders what Kant understood as a failure (the split between the noumenal and the phenomenal realms) into a success. He reframes Kant, making the gap appear as what it is (rather than as some kind of illusion, the supposition which supports more conventional accounts of Hegel's overcoming of Kant through negation).[26]

Having addressed briefly Žižek's notion of the parallax gap, I turn in the following section to the concept of antagonism.

Antagonism

In Chapter One, I explain that enjoyment resembles a nugget or object that holds the subject in place. This excessive, unassimilable, nugget prevents the subject from achieving fullness or transparency. Žižek argues that coming to terms with this excess means acknowledging a fundamental deadlock or antagonism: fullness— complete self-knowledge, satisfied desire, total transparency—is a fantasy that, were it to be fulfilled, would result in the end or destruction of the subject, its complete absorption in the symbolic order of language, and the loss of its desire.

Žižek holds that a similar gap, or antagonism, ruptures and produces society. On this point, he agrees with Ernesto Laclau and

Chantal Mouffe.[27] It is their merit to have developed a theory of the social field, Žižek writes, founded on the notion of antagonism, "on the acknowledgement of an original 'trauma,' an impossible kernel which resists symbolization, totalization, symbolic integration."[28] The idea is that there is no "essence" of society or set of ordered relations constitutive of sociality as such. There is no society in which every element fully occupies a place.[29] Instead, society emerges around, through, and as a result of failures and solutions, struggles, combinations, and exclusions. One simple way to think about the impossibility of the social is with respect to the nonsocial. How might such a line be drawn? Would it refer to nature? The divine? Chaos? How would we be able to determine the contents or attributes of each side? Wouldn't we be compelled to draw the line within society, finding the natural, the divine, and the chaotic as gaps or ruptures in sociality? The very notion of the completeness of the social, moreover, presupposes a fixity of meaning incompatible with language. It erases anything like freedom, change, or contingency from human experience.

Typically, Marxists have understood the antagonism at the heart of society in terms of alienation and hence as resolvable. Social unity is possible. It will result when workers are no longer alienated from their labor, each other, and themselves, that is, when the revolution comes and capitalism is overthrown. Again, like Laclau and Mouffe, Žižek rejects the Marxist vision of an ultimately reconciled, unantagonistic society. Instead, he views antagonism or radical negativity as constitutive of the human condition. "There is no solution, no escape from it; the thing to do is not to 'overcome,' to 'abolish' it, but to come to terms with it, to learn to recognize it in its terrifying dimension and then, on the basis of this fundamental recognition, to try to articulate a *modus vivendi* with it."[30] We can't eliminate antagonism, but we can affect it. We can change the ways it is materialized—the structures that form around it.

Freud conceives the fundamental antagonism as the death drive. Hegelian dialectics treats this antagonism as a contradiction and a fundamental incompleteness.[31] Žižek, while endorsing and adopting both these views, adds to them the Marxist name for antagonism: "class struggle."

Žižek conceives class struggle as the struggle over the meaning of society: which class stands-in for society as a whole and which class is thereby constituted as a threat to it?[32] He thus does not view class struggle in positive terms, that is, as referring to an opposition between existing social groups. To treat class struggle positively would be to integrate it within the symbolic, to reduce it to already given terms, and thereby to eliminate the very dimension of antagonism. As Žižek points out, the fact that "class struggle" cannot be understood as positive in this sense is clear once we recognize how classes tend to be symbolically represented in *threes*, the upper, lower, and middle classes.[33] Representations of class, in other words, occlude social division, substituting distinct, naturalized categories for the reality of conflict. He writes, "The 'middle class' grounds its identity in the exclusion of both extremes which, when they are directly counterposed, give us 'class antagonism' at its purest ... the 'middle class' is, in its very 'real' existence, the *embodied* lie, the denial of antagonism."[34] Class struggle designates the impediment that gives rise to these different symbolizations, to the differing ways that the extremes are posited as well as to their fetishistic disavowal in the form of the middle class.

Second, class struggle for Žižek is not a species of identity politics. It is not one among a variety of struggles for hegemony in the social field. Class struggle operates according to a logic fundamentally different from that of identity politics. The basic goal of feminist, gay, and anti-racist activists is to find ways of getting along, to find new ways of accepting and valuing the diversity of ways of becoming, "to translate antagonism into difference."[35] In contrast, the aim of class struggle is to intensify antagonism, to transform the multiplicity of differences into a division between us and them and then to annihilate them (that is, the "socio-political role and function" of capitalists understood as a class). The goal is not mutual recognition or respect. It is transforming relations of production so as to eliminate capitalists altogether.

Additionally, class struggle determines the very horizon of political struggle today: "it structures in advance *the very terrain* on which the multitude of particular contents fight for hegemony."[36] Here again breaking with Laclau and Mouffe, Žižek separates class out of the proliferating political struggles around sex, sexuality, race, ethnicity, ability, religion, and the environment (new social movements, identity politics) to emphasize the way that this very proliferation is an aspect of postindustrial society. Global capitalism "created the conditions for the demise of 'essentialist' politics and the proliferation of new multiple political subjectivities."[35] Movements thus unfold in the spaces opened up (and closed off) in the course of the expansions and intensifications of capitalism—expansions and intensifications that are themselves manifestations of class struggle, both in terms of gains made by labor and in terms of capitalist successes.

To shift gears somewhat with a too simple example, in the late twentieth century, identity-based movements corresponded with changes in consumerism. Not only did marketers begin identifying niche markets such as youth, Blacks, gays, and senior citizens, but consumer choices themselves came to signify (and substitute for) a certain politics. One could signal one's radicality by a style of dress, by the music one purchased, and by the places one shopped. Accordingly, Žižek's point that class struggle is not reducible to identity politics draws our attention to the way class modifies and impacts particular and identity-based struggles, constituting a kind of extra barrier to their successes. Feminists have witnessed precisely this barrier as college-educated upper- and middle-class women rely on lower-class women to work in our homes and care for our children. Opportunities for some women have not meant opportunities for all but have reinforced already existing inequalities. In acknowledging the appropriateness of Žižek's prioritizing of class struggle, we might also think of the challenges of political organizing in the intensely mediated terrains of communicative capitalism: it requires lots of time and money.[38] Here again we have an indication of the way that the very terrain of politics is configured so as to privilege financial and corporate interests.

In sum, for Žižek, class struggle is the antagonism inherent to and constitutive of the social field. It is the formal gap that accounts for the fact that other struggles can link together in different ways, for the fact that not all feminist and antiracist struggles, for example, are necessarily progressive. Class struggle suggests a division that traverses or splits all existing, positive divisions.

As I see it, Žižek's rendering of the fundamental antagonism constitutive of the social as "class struggle" is strictly correlative to his emphasis on the way that Capital overdetermines every aspect of contemporary life.[39] That it seems impossible today to imagine a world without capitalism, that the constraints and demands of productivity, trade, investment, accumulation, and employment seem natural, inevitable, and unavoidable is both the result of class struggle, the horizon in which it occurs, and the very form that it takes. Class struggle, then, marks the division in capitalist society, the specificity of the rupture in the social field of communicative capitalism. In referring to the fundamental antagonism as class struggle, Žižek highlights Capital as the determining fact of the current historical epoch even as he allows for movement, change, and struggle. Differently put, class struggle is another name for Capital, or it is Capital viewed from a different perspective: the parallax gap involved in thinking social relations under Capital. We could even say that class struggle is the excess that even as it drives capitalist development, designates its limit. If that obstacle is removed—that ultimate inequality, ownership, and exploitation—there is no capitalist production.

I read Žižek's version of class struggle, then, as involving both antagonism as the fundamental gap constituting society and a shift in our perspective on Capital.[40] Class struggle is Real in the Lacanian sense that it is inaccessible through the symbolic (where it appears instead as three classes or is present only in the distortion it effects on any representation) and unavoidable, or determining. In this way, class struggle encapsulates Žižek's claim that "there is no relationship between economy and politics" such that we can grasp both levels at the same point.[41] Thinking about economy and politics together produces a pronounced parallax; it involves a set of shifts back and forth from one to the other and the inevitable displacement that results. Class struggle is for Žižek what "sexual difference" is for Lacan.[42] Just as Lacan explains sexual difference by saying "there is no sexual relationship," no place or perspective where feminine and masculine are equal or commensurate, so should we read Žižek's term *class struggle* as a way of designating the lack of a relationship between economy and politics, the gap and distortion in our thinking from one to the other.

As I mention at the beginning of this chapter, Žižek's rejection of the notion of totalitarianism as a category through which to analyze fascism and communism hinges on his claim that fascism and communism deal with class struggle in different ways. Fascism tries to resolve class struggle by displacing the antagonism onto race, placing all the blame for the upheavals of capitalism onto the Jew.[43] The Jew is figured as a foreign body, corrupting the organic unity of the nation. The fascist solution is thus to purify the social body by eliminating the Jew. Racial difference takes the place of class struggle. In contrast, communism confronts antagonism directly. It attempts to hold onto unbridled productivity, striving to realize the capitalist fantasy of ever-accelerating development unconstrained by the capitalist form.[44]

Fascism: The Discourse of the Master

Žižek's discussions of fascism focus on Nazi Germany and the way the Nazis attempted to force order onto the excesses of capitalism by displacing class struggle onto the naturalized and racialized figure of the Jew. He emphasizes the role of the fascist, "totalitarian" Master in delineating the political body to be ordered and protected. He attends as well to the workings of the Nazi bureaucracy and to aesthetic dimensions of Nazi rule. Each perspective involves a shift from the other, alerting us to the underlying, traumatic gap of the Real even as each can be understood in terms of the more conventional Lacanian account of the registers of the Real, the symbolic, and the imaginary. The imaginary refers to fantastic images and figurations. The symbolic denotes the order of language and norms (as well as their violations). The Real exceeds, ruptures, and conditions these norms and images; we can understand it here via the notion of antagonism. My claim, then, is that Žižek's three accounts of Nazi rule exemplify the parallax Real. In so doing, the Real appears as an aspect or dimension of itself.[45]

National socialism, Žižek explains, was an attempt to change something so that nothing would change.[46] It confronted capitalism's revolutionizing, destabilizing tendencies, yet it did so in a way that sought to ensure the continuity of capitalist production. Nazism tried to eliminate the antagonism fundamental to capitalism (and to society) by locating it in a specific cause that could then be eliminated.[47] Instead of acknowledging social division, it conceived society as a unified body. Nevertheless, it could not avoid the very real disruptions fracturing Germany in the wake of its defeat in World War I. Nazism treated this unity as an empirical social fact, one that could be identified and restored. Differently put, Nazism attempted to retain capitalist productivity by subjecting it to political control, that is, by displacing the economic crisis onto a set of political coordinates where the problem was identified and embodied as the Jews.

Žižek's account of Nazism as an effort to have capitalism without capitalism relies on the notion of class struggle in two key senses. The first is historical and involves class struggle in its positive dimension: National Socialism emerged as a specific response to capitalism's excesses and disruptions (to economic and financial crises), labor unrest, and the work of organized communist and socialist parties. The Nazis rose to power through the suppression and elimination of communists. The second sense is conceptual and involves class struggle as abstract, as antagonism or a kind of negation. Nazism attempts to control and contain the self-revolutionizing excesses of capitalism by displacing them onto the figure of the Jew as the cause of all disruption. It responds to antagonism by treating what is constitutive as accidental, natural, and remediable.

Žižek draws on Lacan's formula of the discourse of the Master to explain the functioning of the social bond provided by National Socialism. The discourse of the Master is the first of Lacan's four discourses—those of Master, hysteric, university, and analyst. Lacan developed these four discourses in part to account for differences in the ways that discourses function, differences in the kinds of social links they provide and the kinds of suppositions and requirements that structure them. Claims uttered in the name of scientific knowledge, for example, rely on a discursive formation different from that upon which moral injunctions rely. A full account of Lacan's four discourses is beyond the scope of this book.[48] Nevertheless, it is important to attend to them since Žižek draws upon them frequently as he theorizes the ways that ideological formations organize enjoyment. The four discourses constitute one of the primary systematic elements of his thought and they provide a useful heuristic for thinking through the ways that discursive structures differentially rely on and produce authority, truth, and enjoyment.

In brief, the four discourses are sets of formulae that distinguish between speaking and the place from which something is spoken. For example, my question, "What are you doing?" can be understood in a variety of ways, depending on to whom I am addressing the question and what underlies or supports my asking of the question. If I ask my young daughter, "What are you doing?" I am likely speaking from a position of parental authority. If I ask an associate in my laboratory, "What are you doing?" I may be speaking as a fellow scientist. If I ask a political leader, "What are you doing?" I may be challenging her authority, calling upon her to justify her policies and decisions. Lacan formulates the differences among these questions as different discourses, different ways that communication establishes a social link. These three situations are examples of the discourse of the Master, the discourse of the university, and the discourse of the hysteric. I discuss the fourth discourse, the discourse of the analyst, later in this chapter.

The formulae for the four discourses are based on Lacan's formula of the signifier: the signifier represents the subject for another signifier. If we return to my example of asking my daughter, "What are you doing?" we can say that the signifier Mommy represents me in relation to another signifier, daughter. That she does not call me by first name is a sign of our relation to one another. We might also think of email addresses. My email address represents me for another email address. It can travel all over the place, often becoming integrated into enormous mailing lists and serving me spam. My name represents me to other names. I cannot control the dissemination and circulation of my name; people can attribute words and views to my name that I would never recognize as my own. Understood more generally, then, Lacan's formula of the signifier tells us that a signifier is that which has a meaning effect, that this effect occurs in relation to other signifiers, and that this effect will exceed these relations.[49]

The discourse of the Master is the first of Lacan's four discourses or four accounts of the social link provided in communication. Its structure is rooted in the absolute authority of the Master's word. The Master's word is law—even if it seems unfair or crazy. So the Master can say, "do this" or "do that," "pick that cotton," "kneel!" or "go fight that battle!" Any of these injunctions is acceptable within the discourse of the Master simply because the Master said it.

Lacan's "matheme" or symbol for the Master is S1. In the discourse of the Master, this symbol occupies the first (upper left) position in the formula. Lacan calls this position the position of the "agent," that is, the one who is speaking. The formula is written:

$$\frac{S1}{\$} \quad \frac{S2}{a}$$

The formula tells us that the Master (S1) is speaking, that he is the agent. Moving one step clockwise to the right, we have the position of the other, or addressee. One might expect that the addressee of the Master would be the slave and that S2 would then be the matheme for slave. Unfortunately, matters are more complicated. S2 stands for "knowledge" or the "chain of signifiers." The idea is that in working for the Master, the slave acquires knowledge that the Master both lacks and does not care anything about. We can see, then, the top half of the formula as expressing the idea of an arbitrary signifier (S1) holding together or directing a chain of signifiers or knowledge (S2). Another example might be that of the capitalist addressing the worker. The capitalist likely has no idea how to fix the machine or produce the goods that the worker is producing, and he does not really care how things are done; he just wants them done. The important thing here is that S2 stands for knowledge.

What about the bottom half of the formula, $-a$? First, $ is the matheme for the Lacanian split subject, the subject who is always decentered with respect to the symbolic order of language, as we saw in Chapter One. As we also saw in Chapter One, a stands for an excessive kernel or nugget of enjoyment, that which disrupts the subject. Second, the positions that $ and a occupy in the discourse of the Master are those of "truth" and "production," respectively. The bottom left position in the formula stands for the truth that underpins the speaker or agent, a truth that must be hidden or suppressed. The bottom right position in the formula is the excess produced in the relation expressed between the two sides of the top half of the formula. Third, the formula $-a$ is also the Lacanian formula for fantasy.

The formula for the discourse of the Master thus expresses in a kind of weird algebra some basic attributes of this specific kind of social bond. It tells us that the Master's words provide knowledge with a support in fundamental truth. Why? Because truth underpins the Master's injunction to the slave. Yet the fact that $ is in the position of truth tells us that there is something fishy in the Master's claim to speak from the position of truth. It tells us that the Master is hiding the fact that he, too, is a split subject. The Master is covering his own weakness or lack, the way that, like everybody else, he also fails to occupy language fully. He, too, had to give up the fantasy of full enjoyment when he entered the symbolic, even as his words require fantastic supplement. Thus, there is an excess to his words, an enjoyment that exceeds speaking, truth, and knowledge. Hence, *objet petit a* is in the position of production. Finally, because the lower half of the formula for the discourse of the Master is itself the formula for fantasy, we see that the Master's authority depends on fantasy as its necessary support.

What does this have to do with fascism? Žižek reads Nazism as introducing a Master into a chaotic social field. National Socialism operates as a discourse of the Master. Describing German anti-Semitism in the 1920s, Žižek writes, "People felt disoriented, succumbing to an undeserved military defeat, an economic crisis which ate away at their life savings, political inefficiency, moral degeneration ... and the Nazis provided a single agent which accounted for it all: the Jew, the Jewish plot. That is the magic of a Master ..."[50] Crucial to the Nazi appeal to order is the production of meaning, the provision of an explanation that could tell Germans who they were. The Master's speech orders the social field, telling Germans that they are a great, unified, people, a people tied by their blood to their land. In providing Germans with their place, moreover, the Nazi Master necessarily produces a remainder, something that exceeds the social field or unified body of the people.

Nazism identifies and naturalizes this remainder in the fantastic figure of the Jew. Differently put, the order that the Nazi Master establishes is based on a fantasy (recall that the bottom half of the discourse of the Master is the formula for fantasy, $\$-a$). More specifically, this fantasy is that the subject is an object for the other's enjoyment (an idea we encountered in the preceding chapter).[51] The German subject is fantasized as the object of the Jews' enjoyment. Instead of the Germans themselves enjoying, the Jews were enjoying in their place. Instead of the Germans themselves profiting, living well, happy, and secure, all this profit, happiness, and security is fantasized as possible, reachable, were it not for the activities of the Jews who have stolen it. The very activity, strength, and agency that the fascist Master promises and seemingly installs in his people is thus premised on his subjects' ultimate passivity, that they have been and are the victims of an other who steals their enjoyment. The Master guarantees their enjoyment, indeed, their very possibility of understanding themselves as a nation characterized by a national Thing, by presenting that enjoyment as threatened or stolen.

I have explained thus far Žižek's theorization of the social bond provided by fascism in terms of the discourse of the Master.

National Socialism confronts the upheavals of class struggle by attempting to retain capitalism and displace its disruptions onto a naturalized and racialized fantasy of the Jew. In this ideological formation, the Real of antagonism overlaps with the fantasy of stolen enjoyment. I turn now to the structure of National Socialism as a symbolic order. To understand fascism symbolically, as a set of norms and laws, involves a shift in perspective. For Žižek, this is a shift to the Nazi bureaucracy.

Taking up the vast bureaucratic infrastructure of the Third Reich, Žižek rejects Hannah Arendt's notion of the banality of evil.[52] In her account of the trial of Nazi war criminal Adolf Eichmann, Arendt emphasizes Eichmann's meticulous investment in rules, order, bureaucracy, and paperwork. In Arendt's work, the horror of mass extermination appears not as some terrifying monstrous evil but as the accumulation of details, the mindlessness of displacing responsibility by just following orders. The Nazi regime is the rules and laws that make it up and allow it to function. Žižek argues that the Holocaust can in no way be reduced to a machinic byproduct of bureaucratic administration. Rather, it needs to be understood in terms of its relation to enjoyment.

Under the Third Reich, the systematic extermination of Jews, Poles, Roma, and homosexuals was, even when known, not openly avowed (unlike, for example, the imprisonment of communists and sterilization of the "mentally defective"). As Žižek points out, "the execution of the Holocaust was treated *by the Nazi apparatus itself* as a kind of obscene dirty secret, not publicly acknowledged, resisting simple and direct translation into the anonymous bureaucratic machine."[53] The fact that the administration of the death camps had hidden components, that exactly what was being administered had to remain concealed, is what makes Arendt's account ultimately unsatisfying. There was clearly more to the Holocaust than the administration of rules by civil servants, namely, the relation of the rules to enjoyment.

Žižek suggests three ways in which the symbolic logic of the bureaucracy operated with respect to enjoyment. The rules enabled subjects to maintain a gap between their duties and the horrors they were perpetrating. In this sense, the rules were a kind of shield, a big Other on whose behalf subjects were acting. They provided subjects with a symbolic screen against the Real of enjoyment. Additionally, the rules enabled subjects to participate in shared transgression. Precisely because the horrors of the extermination camps could not be officially acknowledged, precisely because the crimes remained crimes, remained obscene violations of German ethical codes, those carrying them out participated in a shared transgression. Collective violation thus provided a libidinal support for or sense of Nazi commonality.[54] They were all in this together. Finally, the rules delivered their own libidinal kick, that excess that provides enjoyment to those who are carrying out orders. Describing the way bureaucratization itself was a source of enjoyment, Žižek writes,

> Does it not provide an additional kick if one performs the killing as a complicated administrative-criminal operation? Is it not more satisfying to torture prisoners as part of some orderly procedure—say, the meaningless "morning exercises" which served only to torment them—didn't it give another "kick" to the guards' satisfaction when they were inflicting pain on their victims not by directly beating them up but in the guise of an activity officially destined to maintain their health?[55]

(If this seems far-fetched, one might consider villains in Hollywood movies. They set up elaborate mechanisms to torture and confront the heroes, whereas the extras are simply shot. This point was made directly by Doctor Evil's son in Michael Myers' film, *Austin Powers*. Incredulous before his father's comically elaborate plan, involving sharks with laser beams attached to their heads, Scott, the son, asks, "Why don't you just shoot him?")

In addition to analyzing Nazism from the perspective of the Real of antagonism and from that of the symbolic order of its bureaucratic rules, Žižek also considers the imaginary dimension of Nazi ideology. We can understand this ideology as what the Master provides and what the symbolic rules are established to secure. Yet, insofar as there is an irreducible gap between these three domains, they will not be strictly commensurate.

To summarize the analysis thus far, we first saw how the Master's discourse responded to the antagonism of class struggle and displaced it onto race. Here Nazism both tries to control capitalism's disorder and relies on this disorder for its own power; it can identify what corrupts society and purify society of this corruption. The racialization of antagonism through the Master effects a closure, a full incorporation of the system's excess. Even the level of fantasy supports rather than disrupts the discourse of the fascist Master insofar as it confirms the theft of enjoyment. Recall, the fantasy promises enjoyment by positing it as missing and by explaining why: *it was stolen by the Jews.* Second, we approached Nazism from the perspective of the symbolic. This shifted our attention to the split between the official face of the rules and the obscene enjoyment that supports it. This perspective helps account for the attachment of German subjects to the regime, to the way the rules themselves delivered enjoyment. The account of enjoyment from the perspective of the symbolic, then, is not the same as the fantasy of stolen enjoyment we encountered when we began from the Real of antagonism. There is a gap between the analyses, yet singularly each misses important dimensions of fascist rule.

I now move to the third perspective on fascist rule: the imaginary or the fantastic images and scenes that inspired National Socialism. The shift to this third domain draws out yet another relation to enjoyment crucial to Nazism, namely, an attachment to an aestheticized ideal of community.

Contra Martin Heidegger and with Alain Badiou, Žižek asserts that Nazism did not contain any "inner greatness."[56] Nonetheless, this does not mean it lacked an "authentic" vision.[57] This vision, "a notion of the deep solidarity which keeps the community of people together" was a kernel of nonideology, an ideal or aspiration that cannot be reduced to an instrument of power.[58] Žižek argues, "Of course Fascist ideology 'manipulates' authentic popular longing for a true community and social solidarity against fierce competition and exploitation; of course it 'distorts' the expression of this longing in order to legitimize the continuation of the relations of social domination and exploitation. In order to be able to achieve this effect, however, it none the less had to incorporate authentic popular longing."[59] People are not simply coerced. Nor do they directly accept open plays of power. Rather, their tie to an ideological formation is secured by utopian longings for something more, something better. *Every* ideology, *including fascism*, relies on such a nonideological kernel.

In Nazism, this kernel was rendered as "an ecstatic aestheticized experience of Community."[60] Far from an element of the total politicization of society, Nazi spectacles relied on the suspension of the political through elaborately staged rituals. They were theatrical enactments that produced an illusion of community, a mirroring of community, by covering over the way modernization and technological mobilization necessarily disrupted the imagined organic social body.[61]

Not only was the experience of community aestheticized, but so was its horrific other, the concentration camp. Žižek emphasizes that the Nazi camps involved an "aesthetics of evil."[62] "The humiliation and torture of inmates," he writes, "was an end in itself." It served no rational purpose and in fact was counter to efficient use of the inmates in forced labor.[63] Instead, it produced broken, barely human beings, beings who having lost any will to live, simply persisted. They seemed to feel no pain and showed little reaction to stimuli. Their attitude was one of complete and fundamental indifference. Žižek's discussion of the aesthetics of evil in the camps thus draws on Giorgio Agamben's account of the *Muselmann* (Muslim). He joins Agamben in viewing the *Muselmann* as the "zero-level of humanity" or unsymbolizable point of the Real.[64] The *Muselmann* can be considered neither animal nor human. Nor can his experience be formulated in terms of authenticity or inauthenticity. Instead, the *Muselmann* is the point at which all such oppositions break down. He emerges as an excess of the Real over the imaginary, spectacularized, and aestheticized production of a German community.

In taking up Žižek's account of fascism, I have emphasized his analysis of Nazism as a displacement of the Real of class struggle onto the racialized figure of the Jew, as the symbolic operation of bureaucratic rules and the relation of this operation to enjoyment, and as an imaginary longing for community aestheticized and theatrically enacted. Yet these differing analyses do not fit into a single explanation. They arise instead out of the parallax gap between economy and politics, our inability to think both together. In these analyses, it is clear that "there is no relation between economy and politics," that economy and politics do not meet but that their relation involves an inevitable gap. This parallax, moreover, overlaps with the Real of antagonism, with the displacements and distortions that result from the effort to avoid class struggle—to have capitalism without capitalism. The Nazis attempt to have capitalist modernization without its disruptions and upheavals, to replace class struggle with a "naturalized" power struggle between organic society and its corrupting excess. Thus, for Žižek their revolution was not a revolution at all but just a fake, a spectacular enactment covering over and sustaining its failure to confront this antagonism directly.

Stalinism

Unlike Nazism, Stalinism, Žižek argues, involved a Real Event. It grew out of real revolutionary change, a real attempt to confront antagonism directly. Even the horrifying excesses of Stalinist terror testify to its inner greatness.[65] For Žižek, the contrast between Stalinism and Nazism appears most clearly at precisely that point where supporters of the notion of totalitarianism find an identity between the two regimes—the camps and the purges. Yet, as I explain, this contrast in itself cannot sufficiently explain the different structures of communism and fascism, the way they provide enjoyment. Žižek's account of these different structures, moreover, shifts as he grapples with the legacy of real existing socialism and comes to emphasize the difference between Stalinism and Nazism and the similarity between Stalinism and liberal democracy. Accordingly, after I set out Žižek's comparison of the *Muselmann* (Muslim) and the victim of the Stalinist show trials, I return to Lacan's four discourses, using their formulation of changes in the social link as a basis for thinking through Žižek's analysis of a Stalinism split between perversity and bureaucracy.[66]

The Discourse of the Pervert

To understand Stalinism in terms of the discourse of the pervert, I begin by comparing the Nazi extermination camps with the Soviet gulag, moving then to consider the difference between the *Muselmann* and the victim of the Soviet show trial. This comparison yields two key results. First, we see how, for Žižek, even the worst excesses of Stalinism retained an emancipatory dimension, an ideal that cannot be reduced to the horrors of Stalinist terror. Second, and consequently, this glimmer of hope corresponds to the difference in the place of law in Nazism and Stalinism. Whereas Nazi rule relied on a state of exception and a suspension of law in the camps, Stalinist law consolidates at the point when the revolutionary state of emergency ended and the communists declared victory in the class struggle. The show trials, in other words, operated within and as the law of the new regime. To this extent, they enact a simultaneous realization and perversion of law. The structure of law under Stalinism thus does not follow the structure theorized by Agamben (following Carl Schmitt) in terms of the norm and the exception. Instead, nothing, even the gulag, was external to the system; everything was part of it. Nevertheless, "at the same time, the system is non-all, it is never able to totalize itself, fully to contain the excesses it generates."[67] The same moves or agents that facilitated the revolution could destroy or derail it; what was a middle course at one point could be a rightist deviation at another; over-fulfilling the Party's expectations could become counter-revolutionary sabotage. Indeed, the same law that codified collective ideals could become a perverse vehicle for enjoyment, an excuse for doing one's duty.

As I mention in the previous section, Žižek draws from Agamben in treating the *Muselmann* (Muslim) as the key figure in the Nazi concentration camps. In the Stalinist camps, Žižek points out, one rarely finds an equivalent figure. He cites Primo Levy: "It is possible, even easy, to picture a Socialism without prison camps. A Nazism without concentration camps is, instead, unimaginable."[68] The Stalinist camps were not essential components of socialist rule. Rather than relying on an "aesthetics of evil" that inverted the idealized, ecstatic vision of community as offered by the Nazis, the gulag extended basic socialist notions, treating its prisoners as an expendable work force. It would get as much work from the imprisoned as possible and then dispose of the remainders. For Žižek, this difference between the camps tells us that under Stalin "ethical miracles of mass defiance and demonstrative public solidarity were still possible."[69]

To exemplify his point, Žižek describes a series of strikes that broke out throughout Siberian labor camps in 1953. Most of the strikes collapsed in the face of threats and promises from Moscow. One, Mine 29 at Vorkuta, held out. Žižek writes,

When the troops finally entered the main gate, they saw the prisoners standing behind it in a solid phalanx, their arms linked, singing. After a brief hesitation, the heavy machine-guns opened up—the miners remained massed and erect, defiantly continuing to sing, the dead held up by the living. After about a minute, reality prevailed, and the corpses began to litter the ground. However, this brief minute in which the strikers' defiance seemed to suspend the very laws of nature, transubstantiating their exhausted bodies into the appearance of an immortal singing collective Body, was the occurrence of the Sublime at its purest, the prolonged moment in which, in a way, time stood still. It is difficult to imagine something like this taking place in a Nazi extermination camp.[70]

That such an act of solidarity and collective resistance was possible suggests to Žižek the fundamental difference between the Nazi and Soviet camps. The defiant unity of the miners confronted the Soviet regime with its own perverted revolutionary ideal. It is as if, at least in this instance, those imprisoned by the regime believed more in the regime than the regime believed in itself.

The incommensurable "logics" of the Nazi and Soviet camps marks a fundamental difference between fascism and communism. The Nazis were determined to purify the nation of a foreign intruder. The camps were the space of this exclusion. As theorized by Agamben, the camps were a state of exception where law was "in force in the form of a suspension," where what was outside and external to the law was indistinguishable from what was internal to the law, where there was no difference between following and transgressing a norm.[71] In the Soviet case, the camps involved not purification and exclusion but continuation of a radical revolutionary project. As the example of the strikes makes clear, socialist ideals were not excluded from the gulag; the Soviet work camps were not spaces exempt from these ideals; on the contrary, the presence of the camps marks the incompleteness of the socialist project, its failed realization despite the boasts of the official rhetoric to victory in class war. Nothing was external to the system; nevertheless, the system could not totalize itself. Instead, it drew from its own internalized negativity, to revolutionary upheavals now instantiated as rule by the Party.

Žižek highlights this fundamental distinction between Nazi and Soviet terror by comparing the *Muselmann* to the victim of the Stalinist show trials: "The Nazi treatment produces the Muslim; the Stalinist treatment produces the accused who confesses."[72] These two figures occupy "the Void." Deprived of all life, they are past caring about either their existence or their historical place, yet they differ insofar as the victim of the show trial must participate in his degradation. Although a staging and a perversion, the show trial remains within and part of the law; the victim is expected to act his part, to play the role the Party assigns to him. The victim is thus not simply tortured and rendered lifeless and abject; rather, he is forced actively to relinquish his human dignity. He must be made willingly to sacrifice every remnant of ethical integrity for the sake of the Party.[73] Only by confessing to betraying the Party can he uphold it.

Žižek reads the 1937 trial of Nikolai Bukharin in terms of this tragic dilemma (more precisely, in terms of a "horror beyond tragedy").[74] Bukharin could not face the sacrifice of his ultimate commitments, of that beyond to life that makes his life as a revolutionary worth living. In one of his last speeches before the Central Committee, Bukharin explained that, for the sake of the Party, he would not commit suicide but would simply continue his hunger strike. On the one hand, he accepted the Party line that suicide signifies an insidious counter-revolutionary plot. Far from a heroic, authentic act, suicide was understood completely instrumentally, as a way to deceive the Party and disgrace the Central Committee. Bukharin even accepted that there "is something *great and bold about the political idea of a general purge.*"[75] On the other hand, while he recognized that he had committed some "political sins," he denied the guilt thrust upon him and would "deny it forever."[76] He continued to insist upon his subjective position, his innocence, and his complete sincerity. In a desperate, emotional letter to Stalin earlier that same year, he agonized over the possibility that Stalin might actually think he was guilty: "But believe me, my heart boils over when I think that you might *believe* that I am guilty of these crimes and that in your heart of hearts you *yourself* think that I am really guilty of all these horrors. *In that case*, what would it mean?"[77]

Žižek points out that, in his letter, Bukharin inverts the standard ethical relationship between guilt and responsibility. We typically think it unjust to punish someone who is innocent of the crimes of which he is accused. What really worried Bukharin, however, is not that Stalin would punish him unjustly, but that Stalin actually believed the punishment was warranted. Preferable would have been Stalin's acknowledgment that Bukharin was innocent but nonetheless had to be sacrificed for the good of the Revolution. This acknowledgment, this attachment beyond mere life, is precisely what Bukharin was denied.

For Žižek, Bukharin's insistence on his innocence confirms his guilt. He writes,

> Thus Bukharin still clings to the logic of *confession* deployed by Foucault—as if the Stalinist demand for a confession was actually aimed at the accused's deep self-examination, which would unearth the most intimate secret in his heart of hearts. More precisely, Bukharin's fatal mistake was to think that he could, in a way, have his cake and eat it: to the very end, while professing

his utter devotion to the Party and to Stalin personally, he was not ready to renounce the minimum of subjective autonomy.[78]

What Bukharin would not give up, what he would not sacrifice, is what we might call his own personhood. His insistence on his subjective innocence means he did not fully accept that the Party determined the truth. Rather, for Bukharin, there were objective facts that needed to be taken into account beyond the Party. He proceeded as if the trial were a ritual for determining the truth, as if somehow the Party were subject to another law, a law beyond its own making. From the standpoint of the Party, however, the trial was a procedure for demonstrating the truth that it knew. To the extent that Bukharin denied this demonstration, he *was* guilty. He failed to give everything to the Party, to allow it to be everything.[79]

Žižek also argues that the Stalinist communists themselves were similarly "impure." They, too, were impure insofar as they enjoyed (got off on) demanding that Party members fully sacrifice everything. Their very excessive preoccupation with duty above all else, with a duty violently and terroristically enforced, points to an obscene enjoyment. Žižek thus views Stalinism proper as perverse (as a making of oneself into the instrument of another's enjoyment): the Stalinist communist exculpates himself (for enjoying) with reference to the big Other of the Revolution or of the Progress of Humanity. Stalinism thus differs from Nazism in that it structures enjoyment perversely, as an enjoyment that comes from doing one's duty. One can inflict all sorts of pain on another guilt free, fully exonerated from any sense of responsibility.

The discourse of the pervert is not one of Lacan's four discourses (Master, hysteric, university, and analyst). Nevertheless, its formal structure is identical to that of the discourse of the analyst.[80] Here is the formula for the discourse of the analyst/perverse discourse:

$$\frac{a}{S2} \quad \frac{\$}{S1}$$

In this formula, *objet petit a* is in the position of agent; the split subject is in the position of Other or addressee; knowledge (S2) is in the position of truth; the Master (S1) is in the position of production. The formula tells us that this is a discursive structure where the object, remainder, or excessive kernel of enjoyment speaks. This object may be imaginary; it may be covering a void. Either way, it is a kind of nonassimilable kernel that addresses the subject. The formula also tells us that this speaking excess is supported by knowledge. The subject who is addressed by it, then, supposes that the object's words are based in knowledge (or that the object covers some kind of fundamental, hidden, truth). The outcome of this discourse is authority: (S1) the Master. Because it is produced as a kind of surplus, however, it is not fully operable. It does not anchor knowledge or guarantee truth. We can think of it, then, as a kind of nonfunctioning authority.

Applied to Stalinism, the formula of the discourse of the pervert tells us not to expect rational utterances. Insofar as an unassimilable object speaks, Stalinist injunctions can be irrational and nonsensical. Their content does not matter; some kind of excess or extra is doing the talking. Accordingly, Žižek points out that not only did the investigations part of the Stalinist purges rely on clearly fabricated accusations, but these very accusations fluctuated arbitrarily, latching onto different groups purely in an effort to meet district liquidation quotas.[81] The orders issued from the Party leadership were vague and contradictory, at times supporting the *nomenklatura* against the rank and file, at times supporting the rank and file against the *nomenklatura*, and all the while demanding harsh measures even as it warned against excess. For this reason, Žižek argues that by 1937, Stalinism ceased to function as a discourse. Its perverse structure used language not as a social link but as a pure, meaningless instrument.[82]

S2 beneath *objet petit a* reminds us that the irrational, pointless orders were supported by the "objective knowledge of the laws of history" or by the Soviet bureaucracy. We note as well that the discourse is not anchored in a Master (S1) and thus can "run amok."[83] The discourse is thus less one of authority than of irrational power. During the self-destructive frenzy of the purges, there was no governance or authority to speak of. Rather, there were panicky actions and reactions, an acting out that attempted to cover a more fundamental impotence. Authority proper is foreign, excessive to, Stalinist rule. For Žižek, a clear indication of Stalin's inability to rule appears in the personality cult that grew up around Stalin in the thirties. Stalin was depicted as the supreme genius, providing advice and wisdom on everyday matters of gardening and tractor repair. Žižek writes, "What the Leader's intervention in everyday life means is that things do not function on the most everyday level—what kind of country is this, when the supreme Leader himself has to dispense advice about how to repair tractors?"[84]

In Žižek's view, the irrationality of the Stalinist purges testifies to the authenticity of the Russian Revolution. They were the form in which the "betrayed revolutionary project" haunted the regime."[85] To support this contention, Žižek rejects accounts of the revolution that locate its defeat in the mid-1920s (as in Trotsky's argument that the revolution failed when the Party accepted the doctrine of "socialism in one country") or in the very move to take state power and function as a state (the position of Alain Badiou and Sylvain Lazarus).[86] He advocates instead a view defended by historian Sheila Fitzpatrick: the revolution ended in 1937 when the great purges started coming to an end.[87] The most profoundly revolutionary period occurred during the years 1928 through 1934, when Russian society was radically transformed. Žižek explains:

It was only the thrust of 1928 that directly and brutally aimed at transforming the very composure of the social body, liquidating peasants as a class of individual owners, replacing the old intelligentsia (teachers, doctors, scientists, engineers, and technicians) with a new one ... The difficult thing to grasp about the terrible years after 1929, the years of the great push forward, was that, in all the horrors beyond recognition, one can discern a ruthless, but sincere and enthusiastic, will to a total revolutionary upheaval of the social body, to create a new state, intelligentsia, legal system, and so forth.[88]

In Žižek's view, Stalinism was a perversion of the revolution, but perversion does not mean the misdirection of the revolution or its betrayal in the form of rule by the Party. Rather, perversion refers to the way it was instrumentalized, to the furthering of violence for the sake of the big Other of history or progress. What we see in Stalinism is a regime confronting the conflict between governance and revolution. Stalinism extended the basic negativity of revolution, the truth of its confrontation with antagonism, back into the regime itself. This prevented any kind of stabilization or completion of the revolutionary moment, acknowledging, in a way, the very conflict between revolutionary energy and the law the revolution attempts to install. Stalinism functioned as a kind of violent transition and point of overlap between revolutionary violence and bureaucratic rule, a "vanishing mediator" (a concept I take up more thoroughly in the following chapter) between the authentic Leninist revolution and the stagnant period of bureaucratic rule that followed.

That the purges continued the violent upheaval and transformation of the revolution is manifest not only in their brutality and irrationality but also in their very notion: "the struggle of the Stalinist Party against the enemy becomes the struggle of humanity itself against its non-human excrement."[89] More specifically, the Stalinist terror was at its fiercest after the new constitution was accepted in 1935. That is, its most extreme and irrational moments took place after the regime claimed victory in the class struggle and took upon itself the role of ensuring ever-increasing productivity. Žižek emphasizes that ratification of the Soviet constitution, as it ended the state of emergency, universalized the right to vote, and reinstated the civil rights of groups previously treated as enemies, was supposed to signal the end of class war and the formation of a new, classless, socialist order. The state, then, was not a vehicle for class rule but for rule by the people. Anyone opposed to the regime was thus not an enemy of the working class, but an enemy of the people, "worthless scum which must be excluded from humanity itself."[90] The Stalinist state treated any difference from or rupture in the social as a threat to humanity precisely because it declared itself victorious in class war.

Thus far I have discussed Žižek's treatment of Stalinism as a perverse discourse. For Žižek, the brutal violence of Stalinism testifies to the authenticity of the Russian Revolution. Its pervasive irrationality, its inward turn against the Party, and even the demands for sacrifice made during the show trials are evidence of the extraordinary confrontation with class struggle and the effort to transform society in its entirety. Additionally, I have highlighted Žižek's comparisons of the *Muselmann* and the victim of the show trial and of the Nazi and Soviet camps. Each comparison suggests a difference between the legal logics of fascism and communism. Whereas the Nazi model relies on the idea of a state of exception that blurs the distinction between law and its constitutive outside, the Stalinist case finds law to be pervasive, all-encompassing, but necessarily incomplete. Law can be found even in the most horrifying reaches of the gulag. This suggests both the possibility of glimmers of hope, of ideals that might still be operative, and the perverse instrumentalization of law. I turn now to Stalinism's other, bureaucratic face.

Bureaucracy: Stalinism and the Discourse of the University

Žižek points out that one of the key differences between Stalin's and Lenin's time, and hence one of the indications of the perversion of the revolution, is the status of political terror. Under Lenin, terror was openly admitted. Under Stalin, terror was hidden, "the obscene, shadowy supplement of public official discourses."[91] As discussed above, the perversity of the Stalinist purges marks in part the continuation of revolutionary negativity against precisely that Party attempting to consolidate state power; it is the Party's own conflict over its betrayal of revolution, its compulsion to "(re)inscribe its betrayal of the Revolution within itself, to 'reflect' or 'remark' it in the guise of arbitrary arrests and killings."[92] The purges thus bear witness to the way the revolution involved a real confrontation with class struggle. They are "the very form in which the betrayed revolutionary heritage survives and haunts the regime."[93]

Nonetheless, the purges are not the only way Stalinism confronts class struggle. Its official face, its public, bureaucratic, existence testifies as well to Stalinism's alleged victory over capitalism, its attempt to have capitalist productivity without capitalism. What, then, is the structure of Stalinist bureaucracy?

To answer this question, I return to Lacan's four discourses, turning now to the discourse of the university. Žižek argues that Stalinist bureaucracy is one of two forms of the university discourse that dominates modernity: capitalism and bureaucratic "totalitarianism."[94] This tells us that, for Žižek, capitalism and Stalinism have a similar structure, a fundamental formal similarity. Stalinism, he argues, was a symptom of capitalism.[95] To see how this works, we need to look at the discourse of the university:

$$\frac{S2}{S1} \quad \frac{a}{\$}$$

A first glance tells us that S2, or knowledge, is in the position of the speaking agent. S2 addresses *objet petit a*, the little nugget or remainder of enjoyment. S1 (the Master) is in the position of truth, and the subject ($) is in the position of production.

We can understand the discourse of the university as a discourse in which knowledge speaks. We can think of it, then, as the rule of experts. These experts provide facts. To be sure, they do not tell us what the facts mean, what we should do with them, or how we should evaluate them. The formula makes this lack of an explicit evaluation visible by putting the subject ($) in the position of production or surplus. The poor subject is left out, split and uncertain, provided no real, solid position by the knowledge that speaks. The knowledge that speaks addresses the object (*a* in the position of addressee), as if the subject were, for example, the object of the medicalized gaze theorized so well by Foucault. We might also say that the facts address subjects only in terms of their object-like qualities, that is, only as what Agamben conceives as "bare life," only as bodily beings and not as beings oriented toward a higher purpose or cause.[96]

What is hidden under the facts, however, what the facts want to deny, is the way they are supported by power and authority (S1 below the bar, in the lower left-hand corner; the Master in the position of truth). As Žižek argues, the "constitutive lie" of university discourse is its disavowal of its own performative dimension. University discourse proceeds as if it were not supported by power, as if it were neutral, as if it were not, after all, dependent upon and invested in specific political decisions.[97]

Capitalism and bureaucratic socialism, as a generation of critiques of technocracy and instrumental reason made clear, emphasize expertise.[98] Capitalists ground their expertise in efficiency as understood by economic theory. Stalinism, or the bureaucracy of late socialism, grounds its expertise in its ability fully to plan social life so as to maximize productivity. Each disavows the nonscientific component of political power underlying its administration.[99] Likewise, each addresses the subject as a kind of object, providing no real ideological or symbolic locus of subjective meaning. We see this in the way capitalism undermines symbolic identities, how it undermines such forms of attachment through the revolutionary force of ever-expanding and intensifying markets. Instead of a symbolic identity of the kind provided by a Master, capitalism offers its subjects enjoyment (*objet petit a*).[100] Late socialism also failed to provide a symbolic identity. Those who identified with socialism, those who really believed, were dangerous to a system that relied on its subjects' cynical dis-identification, at best, and actual moral bankrupty (lying about basic facts of life, cheating the system, trading on the black market), at worst.[101] Žižek thus describes Stalinism's obsessive effort to keep up appearances:

> We all know that behind the scenes there are wild factional struggles going on; nevertheless, we must keep at any price the appearance of Party unity; nobody really believes in the ruling ideology, every individual preserves a cynical distance from it and everybody knows that nobody believes in it but still, the appearance has to be maintained at any price that people are enthusiastically building socialism, supporting the Party, and so on.[102]

We can imagine the result of actual identification with socialist ideals—a dissident calling out of corrupt Party hacks with their cars, dachas, foreign currency stores, and well-furnished apartments while regular working people wait in line for bread and live in squalid, over-crowded, poorly built housing complexes out on the edges of the cities.

For Žižek, the most interesting aspect of modern power captured by the formula of the discourse of the university stems from the distinction between the upper and lower levels of the diagram.

The upper level (S2-*a*), he explains, expresses the fact of contemporary biopolitics (knowledge addressing objects, treating subjects as objects) while the lower (S1–$) marks the "crisis of investiture," or the collapse of the big Other that I introduced in the first chapter (there is authority, but the subject is a remainder; differently put, authority is not subjectivized). In contemporary capitalist society biopolitics appears in two forms: the life that has to be respected and the excess of the living other that one finds harassing, unbearable, and intolerable. Thus, in one respect, the other is fragile and vulnerable. It must be fully respected. In another, the fragility of the other is so great, the need for respect so strong, that anything can harm it; everything is dangerous. Žižek argues that the discourse of the university enables us to understand how these two attitudes are two sides of the same coin. They are both brought about by a crisis in meaning, by "the underlying refusal of any higher Causes, the notion that the ultimate goal of our lives is life itself."[103] That is to say, the structure of university discourse reminds us that authority is presupposed yet denied by expert rule; the Master does not speak and does not occupy the position of agent; rather, he occupies the position of Truth.

What about socialist society? Although Žižek's discussions of cynicism address the lower level of university discourse, the cynical expression of empty verbiage characteristic of real existing socialism, he neglects the biopolitical aspects of Stalinism. A plausible reconstruction, which would require strong empirical evidence, might consider the specificities of Soviet medical science and public health policies as well as the racial aspects of Russian dominance in a country of multiple languages and ethnicities. Perhaps more to Žižek's point, such a reconstruction would necessarily focus on the way that, particularly under Stalin, medicine, science, health, and population were linked into a larger focus on production and productivity per se.

As does capitalism, so did socialism rely on "integrating its excess," that is, on a constant revolutionizing. Yet whereas capitalism is a self-revolutionizing economic form, one whose very crises, inequities, and excesses drive its productivity, Stalinism was a self-revolutionizing political form. Stalinism tried to attain (and surpass!) capitalist productivity without the capitalist form, without, in other words, class struggle. Once class struggle officially ended with the 1935 constitution, the revolutionizing impulse of capitalism came under the control of the political domain in the form of terror. As a consequence, the inequities of capitalism shifted into social life as more direct forms of hierarchy and domination. Žižek writes, "In the Soviet Union from the late 1920s onwards, the key social division was defined not by property, but by direct access to power mechanisms and to the privileged material and cultural conditions of life (food, accommodation, healthcare, freedom of travel, education)."[104] For this reason, Žižek can say that Stalinism was the "symptom" of capitalism. It was a symptom insofar as it revealed the truth about the social relations of domination that capitalist ideology presents as free and equal.[105]

As I read it, Žižek's account of Stalinism points to a Stalinism split between its bureaucratic operation as a kind of technocratic attempt at productivity unstained by class struggle, on the one side, and as a perverse effort to realize the truth of a vision of human progress toward communism, on the other. Žižek thus confronts the combination of horror and utopian aspiration particular to this socialist attempt to bring the economy fully under political control.

Žižek's analysis of Stalinism as structurally similar to capitalism is particularly important today—Stalinism was perhaps one of the first "postproperty" societies. Citing battles over intellectual property, licensing, and copyright brought about by digitalization, Žižek concludes that a similar dissolution of property now faces capitalist societies.[106] Clearly, under the conditions of contemporary communicative capitalism, rights of use and access take on a greater importance than those associated exclusively with ownership. And, even more relevant in my view is the increased dominance of global finance and the concentration of financial control in the hands of a capitalist elite. Under the neoliberal form of capitalism that has become hegemonic since the end of the 1970s, economic power has shifted from "production to the world of finance."[107] In any case, Žižek's point is that capitalist societies confront ever more directly raw power relations—the immediate forms of hierarchy and domination characteristic of real existing socialism. The danger accompanying the gradual disappearance of the role of property is the emergence of "some new (racist or expert-rule) form of hierarchy, directly founded in individual qualities, and thus canceling even the 'formal' bourgeois equality and freedom. In short, insofar as the determining factor of social power be in/exclusion from the privileged set (of access to knowledge, control, etc.), we can expect an increase in various forms of exclusion, up to downright racism."[108] What shape will a postproperty society take? Will it be egalitarian or hierarchical? Struggling over this shape will be the most fundamental political problem in coming years. In Žižek's view, neither the old Marxist utopia of hyperproductive communism nor the liberal–democratic emphasis on neutral procedures and human rights is adequate to this challenge, a point I develop in the following chapter. Thus, it is necessary to undertake the slow, difficult work of building something new.

So What About Lenin?

I have presented Žižek's critique of the notion of totalitarianism and his discussion of Nazism and Stalinism in terms of the primacy of class struggle. The Nazis attempted to create an organic social whole unrent by antagonism. To do so, they racialized antagonism and worked violently to purify the social body of foreign, staining elements, elements they located primarily in the figure of the Jew. Hence, National Socialism followed the discourse of the Master: anti-Semitism posits enjoyment as attainable yet stolen by the Jews. Stalinism perverts an authentic revolutionary moment. It thus confronted class struggle directly, yet in so doing, in subjecting the economy to complete political control, in trying to have capitalist productivity without the capitalist form of private property, it relied on direct forms of hierarchy and domination. Stalinist terror functioned (or disfunctioned) perversely. The pointless, irrational injunctions of the terror were supported by the "truth" of the laws of history, of the absolute knowledge of the Party. Fascism and Stalinism, then, are not the same. Understanding how they are different sheds light on current problems of globalized racism and ethnic nationalism, on the one hand, and the challenges posed by neoliberalism, on the other.

Is the only lesson we can take from the socialist experience a negative one? Is Žižek's message ultimately a conservative warning against radical change? As I read him, the answer is no. I thus conclude this chapter by introducing Žižek's use of Lenin and explore his discussion of Lenin more thoroughly in the last chapter. What we need to keep in mind here is that Stalinism is, for Žižek, a *perversion* of an authentic revolution. What, then, does an authentic revolution look like? What can we learn from Lenin? For this discussion to be clear, I return again to Lacan's four discourses, more specifically, to the discourse of the analyst.

As Žižek points out, the discourse of the analyst has the same structure as the perverse discourse (Lacan did not consider the perverse discourse as one of the four discourses, emphasizing instead the discourse of the analyst).[109] Again, the formula is

$$\frac{a}{S2} \quad \frac{\$}{S1}$$

The difference between the discourse of the analyst and the perverse discourse rests in the ambiguity of *objet petit a* (occupying here the position of agent). In the perverse discourse, *objet petit a* designates the subject's ($ in the position of addressee) enjoyment. That is, the pervert is the one who knows what the subject desires and makes himself into an instrument of that desire. Accordingly, we see how the formula places knowledge (S2) in the position of truth, supporting the object that speaks.

In the discourse of the analyst, this knowledge (S2) is the "supposed knowledge of the analyst." This means that in the analytic setting, the subject presumes that the analyst knows the secret of its desire. But, this presumption is false. The enigmatic analyst simply adopts this position, reducing himself to a void (*objet petit a*) in order that the subject will confront the truth of her desire.[110] The analyst is not supported by objective or historical knowledge. Rather, the position is supported only by the knowledge supposed by the subject through transference. Analysis is over when the subject comes to recognize the contingency and emptiness of this place. Žižek follows Lacan in understanding this process as "traversing the fantasy," of giving up the fundamental fantasy that sustains desire.[111] Thus, whereas the pervert knows the truth of desire, the analyst knows that there is no truth of desire to know.

The process of traversing the fantasy, of confronting *objet petit a* as a void, involves "subjective destitution." As the addressee of the speaking object, the subject gives up any sense of a deep special uniqueness, of certain qualities that make him who he is, and comes to see himself as an excremental remainder, to recognize himself as an object. Neither the symbolic order nor the imaginary realm of fantasy provides any ultimate guarantees. They cannot establish for the subject a clear, certain, and uncontested identity. They cannot provide him with fundamental, incontrovertible moral guidelines. What is left out, then, is the authority of the Master (S1, now in the position of production).

Žižek views the discourse of the analyst as homologous to revolutionary emancipatory politics. What speaks in revolutionary politics is thus like *objet petit a*, a part that is no part, a part that cannot be recuperated into a larger symbolic or imaginary unity. Such a part, in other words, is in excess of the whole. In emphasizing the structural identity between revolutionary politics and the discourse of the analyst, moreover, Žižek is arguing that the revolutionary act proper has no intrinsic meaning. It is a risk, a venture that may succeed or fail. Precisely what makes revolution revolutionary is that it leaves out (produces as remainder) the authority of a Master: there are no guarantees.

For Žižek, what was remarkable about Lenin was his willingness to adopt this position. Žižek emphasizes two specific moments: 1914 and 1917. In 1914, Lenin was shocked and alone as all the European Social Democratic parties (excluding the Russian Bolsheviks and the Serb Social Democrats) turned to patriotism, approving war credits and generally falling in with the prevailing nationalist fervor. Yet this very catastrophic shattering of a sense of international workers' solidarity, Žižek argues, "cleared the ground for the Leninist event, for breaking the evolutionary historicism of the Second International—and Lenin was the only one who realized this, the only one who articulated the Truth of the catastrophe."[112] Likewise, in April 1917, most of Lenin's colleagues scorned his call for revolution. Even his wife, Nadezhda Krupskaya, worried that Lenin had gone mad, but Lenin knew that there is no proper time for revolution, that there are no guarantees that it will succeed.[113] More importantly, he knew that waiting for such an imagined proper time was precisely the way to prevent revolution from occurring. For Žižek, then, Lenin is remarkable in his willingness to take the risk and engage in an act for which there are no guarantees. We should recall that the odds were fully against Lenin—in peasant Russia he did not even have a working class that could take power.

Against communist dogma regarding the laws of historical development and the proper maturity of the working class, Lenin urged pushing through with the revolution. He did not rely on objective laws of history. He also did not wait for permission or democratic support. He acted without grounds, inventing new solutions in a moment when it was completely unclear what would happen. He refused to wait for authorization or do what others thought he "ought" to do, doing instead what he had to do. Lenin, then, takes the position of *objet petit a*. The truth of his view does not rest in laws of history but in its own formal position in an uncertain situation, a position marked by the Leninist Party.

Recall Žižek's account of Stalinist perversion: its official face was one of bureaucratic, expert rule while its obscene underside was perverse, a violence cloaking itself in duty to the Party. Žižek argues that the problem was that the Stalinist Party was not "pure" enough; it got caught up in enjoying doing its duty.[114] The difference between the Stalinist and the Leninist Party, then, can be found precisely here. For Lenin, the Party was a form for class struggle. It provided an external, organizing form, a way to cut into, or intervene in, a situation. Its knowledge (S2) was strictly identical to its formal position as "true."[115] There was nothing objective or neutral about it: it was a partisan, political truth, the truth of class struggle, of the hard work of organizing, transforming, and even producing a revolutionary alliance of peasants and workers. Lenin accepted the notion that the state is an instrument of oppression, the dictatorship of one class over another, and thus was open to the use of terror.[116] In contrast, the Stalinist party claimed neutrality and objectivity, both in terms of the laws of history and in terms of the end of class struggle in the triumph of the socialist state. The ultimate tragedy, says Žižek, is that the strength of the Leninist revolutionary Party made Stalinism possible.

There is one last, potentially puzzling, link between Stalinism and Leninism that I want to address, that between the revolutionary willing to go to the limit and the victim of the show trial. Žižek uses the same words, "subjective destitution," to describe them both. Their position is homologous: internal and external to the situation at the same time, markers of the truth of a formation. How should we understand these two figures?

One possibility is that the revolutionary is somehow ethically superior to the victim. The victim pathetically holds onto his individuality, refusing to relinquish it for the sake of the Party. Another possibility is that whereas the revolutionary willingly forsakes all symbolic guarantees, the victim is forced to sacrifice them, forced to undergo a second death. Neither of these is satisfying. The first option presumes a kind of ethical stability that the revolutionary moment disrupts. The second presumes a kind of agency that Žižek finds absent from the revolutionary moment: true revolutionary struggle means one is not free not to act; one is forced into it.

The difference between the discourse of the pervert and the discourse of the analyst suggests a better way to understand these two figures. The victim of the show trial, the victim of the demands made by the Party, alerts us to the tragedy of the perversion of Lenin's revolutionary step. It marks the shift from the urgency of what Žižek understands as "enacted utopia" to the desire to evade responsibility for one's acts by grounding them in duty to a big Other. As I argue in Chapter Four, this difference also embodies a different relation to law, one crucial to Žižek's overall political theory. Unlike some radical thinkers writing today (such as Agamben), Žižek does not abandon law and sovereignty. Lenin's greatness is not simply that of a risk-taker but of a founder, one who takes responsibility for introducing a new order. As we shall see, addressing the fundamental political problems of the day—antagonism in an era post-property and the exclusions and violence of neoliberal capitalism—is a matter not of escaping or abandoning the law but of traversing the fantasies that support the law, confronting the perversity and enjoyment in our relations to law. For these problems to be clear, I move in the following chapter to Žižek's critique of contemporary democracy. I then return to law, emphasizing both the split in law and the possibility of moving from law to love.

3
Democratic Fundamentalism

Introduction

Our discussion of Žižek's critique of the concept of totalitarianism drew out the different ways in which fascism and Stalinism responded to class struggle and organized enjoyment. Žižek argues that fascism condensed and displaced class struggle onto a naturalized and racialized figure of the Jew. The Nazis attempted to secure capitalism and society from capitalism, to have productivity without upheaval. Shifting our perspective, we saw how National Socialism functioned as the discourse of the Master, grounding knowledge in the Master's word on one level, while relying on a fundamental fantasy on another. As Žižek makes clear, this fantasy structure accounts for the fascist organization of enjoyment. Fascism provided enjoyment by positing it as stolen by another.

Likewise, we saw the radical difference in the organization of enjoyment under Stalinism. Žižek presents a "split-Stalinism," a Stalinism split into two discursive structures: the discourse of the pervert and the discourse of the university. Stalinism perverted the authentic revolutionary impulse of Lenin. As a state formation based in a claim to victory in class war, it provided enjoyment in the form of doing one's duty; excessive violence was justified, or excused, in the name of the success of the Party's work. This perversion, however, has to be denied. Accordingly, the official face of the regime relied on expertise, that is, on the successful managing of the economy, on pushing and stimulating productivity. Because the socialist state ran the economy, failures, imbalances, or excesses of productivity could not be attributed to class struggle but pointed instead to problems with the state. And, to come full circle, pointing out problems with the state clearly indicated that one did not accept the Party as the source of knowledge. Duty to the Party demanded silence, compliance, or elimination.

How, then, is enjoyment organized in contemporary liberal democracies? In considering this question, we need to keep in mind that liberal democracy is the political form of capitalism. We will thus need to shift back and forth between political and economic perspectives on the present, aware that this shift will involve a parallax gap: the object—contemporary society (or what I term *communicative capitalism*)—will appear different from each perspective even as one perspective seems to blend into the other (like the two sides of the Mobius strip that become one). In taking up Žižek's account of democracy, I begin with a brief discussion of capitalism as the version of university discourse characteristic of liberal democracies. I then shift to Žižek's critique of democracy, emphasizing his engagement with Claude Lefort's notion of democracy as an empty place and comparing his position with others prominent in contemporary political theory.

University Discourse in and as Capitalism

As I mention in the previous chapter, Žižek asserts the structural resemblance between socialism and liberal democracy. The discourse of the university provides the formula for each. Whereas under socialism this discourse takes the external form of the bureaucracy, in liberal democracies it takes the form of capitalism. For political theorists, an important aspect of Žižek's claim for the discourse of the university as the primary structure of the social link is its challenge to basic suppositions of democratic debate. Democratic theorists, media pundits, and everyday citizens appeal to an ideal of debate among equals, the free exchange of opinions, and the marketplace of ideals. Public officials are presumed, at least ideally, to be accountable to the people, to have to defend their positions before the public, and, when they cannot, to face being booted out of office. One might say, then, that democratic debate prioritizes questioning: exchanges among citizens and between citizens and officials are not simply exchanges of opinions but responses to questions and criticisms.[1] The best ideas are supposed to be those that can answer the strongest questions. In asserting the primacy of the discourse of the university, Žižek breaks with this singular model of democratic discourse. He offers instead a view of liberal democracies as integrated not simply through the market but through the market organization of knowledge and debate. Accordingly, before turning to the focus of this chapter, Žižek's challenge to the view that democracy is that political arrangement that all of those seeking freedom, equality, and social justice should support and his contesting of the claim that democracy is the ultimate horizon of left political aspiration, I need to set out in more detail how capitalism works in terms of the discourse of the university.

Let's recall the formula for the discourse of the university:

$$\frac{S2}{S1} \quad \frac{a}{\$}$$

S2 (knowledge, the string of signifiers) is in the first position, that of the agent or speaker. This tells us that under capitalism, the facts speak. They are not grounded in a Master (S1), although they rely on a hidden or underlying supposition of power, of the authority that they command (S1 is in the position of truth). Because this authority is hidden, the facts claim that they speak for themselves. What do they mean? Well, that is a matter of opinion—*and each is entitled to his own opinion*. The facts, or the knowledge that speaks in the discourse of the university, are not integrated into a comprehensive symbolic arrangement; instead, they are the ever-conflicting guidelines and opinions of myriad experts. Thus, they can advise people to eat certain foods, use certain teeth-whiteners, wear certain clothes, and drive certain cars. The experts may evaluate and judge all these commodities, finding some safer or more reliable and others better values for the money. Experts may make economic and financial suggestions, using data to back up their predictions.

S2 addresses *a*, and, hidden underneath *a* is the subject, $. This tells us that knowledge, or the experts, address the subject as an object, an excess, or a kernel of enjoyment. The object addressed by the experts, then, might be the person as a body or set of needs, the person as a collection of quantifiable attributes, or the person as a member of a particular demographic, but the person is not addressed as what we might typically understand as the reasonable subject of liberal democratic politics. The person is addressed as an object and thus is less a rational chooser than an impulse buyer, a bundle of needs and insecurities, desires and drives, an object that can be propelled and compelled by multiple forces. As a version of the university discourse, capitalism does not provide the subject with a symbolic identity. The formula shows that $ does not identify with S1. The subject is merely the remainder of a process in which knowledge addresses enjoyment.[2]

This reading of the discourse of the university expresses as a formula a number of ideas that we encountered in our initial discussion of enjoyment in the first chapter. Recall that Žižek argues that late capitalist societies are marked by (1) an injunction to enjoy and (2) the decline of symbolic efficiency. Late capitalist subjects are encouraged to find, develop, and express themselves. They are enjoined to have fulfilling sex lives and rewarding careers, to look their very best—no matter what the cost—and to cultivate their spirituality. That these injunctions conflict, that one cannot do them all at once, and that they are accompanied by ever-present warnings against potential side effects, reminds us that we are dealing with the superego (as Žižek writes, "the S1 of the S2 itself, the dimension of an unconditional injunction that is inherent to knowledge").[3] We see here a key difference between late capitalist and socialist versions of the discourse of the university. Whereas the Stalinist provision of enjoyment is primarily in the form of the perverse discourse that accompanies the discourse of the university and that renders enjoyment as the benefit of doing one's duty, late capitalism directly commands the subject to enjoy, so enjoyment does not simply accompany one's duty. Enjoying is one's duty. (Perhaps the most telling example of this injunction came from President George W. Bush after the attacks of September 11, 2001. He urged Americans to hug their children, return to normal life, and go shopping.) The socialist and capitalist arrangements of the university discourse, then, are two sides of the same coin: one provides enjoyment by urging sacrifice, the other by urging pleasurable indulgence.

The decline of symbolic efficiency (or collapse of the big Other) refers to the ultimate uncertainty in which late capitalist subjects find themselves. The formula for the discourse of the university expresses this idea in its lower half: S1–$. Late capitalism does not offer subjects a symbolic identity; it offers them imaginary identities—ways to imagine themselves enjoying. These identities shift and change, taking on different meanings and attributes in different contexts. Indeed, part of the confusion in contemporary life stems from our inability to read many of the images it offers.

What is radical and transgressive at one moment becomes conformist kitsch at another. One might respond that Žižek's account of the decline of symbolic efficiency is overstated. Is not law rooted in symbolic norms and expectations, does it not codify these very expectations? And, do we not find appeals to law, to rights, now exceeding state forms and thereby suggesting a larger, potentially universal dimension of human rights? Thus, even if one accepts that capitalism of course conditions contemporary democracies, and in highly negative ways, does democracy not continue to provide, particularly in the form of rights, possibilities for symbolic identification and social integration?

This chapter and the next discuss Žižek's critique of democracy and theory of law with these questions in mind. In his most scathing attacks on human rights, Žižek views them as rights to break the Ten Commandments (what is a right to privacy but a right to commit adultery? the right to property but a right to theft? the right to religious freedom but a right to worship false gods?) and rights to solicit or control enjoyment.[4] Yet this in no way means that Žižek abandons rights altogether.[5] Rights are a vital political form, ways of designating and practicing the capacity of an identity or a claim to stand for something beyond itself. The problem is their depoliticization within the liberal democracies of contemporary capitalism. Put differently, for Žižek the problem with rights today is the way they are not universal enough, the way they are stained by excesses of enjoyment and violence. For example, in contemporary political discourse, human rights are depoliticized in the sense that they are attached to suffering victims such that the victims themselves cannot be understood as political subjects. Action on their behalf effectively results not in their rights but in "the right of Western powers themselves to intervene politically, economically, culturally and militarily in the Third World countries of their choice, in the name of defending human rights."[6] To be sure, this depoliticization does not mean we can do without rights. It means we have to find new ways to think about and practice them, and, in Žižek's view, a key component of this task is to challenge the hegemony of liberal democracy.

Horizon or Barrier?

Is democracy the ultimate horizon of political aspirations to equality, freedom, and a hope for justice? In the face of the demise of socialism in Eastern Europe, the welfare state in Western Europe and Great Britain, and confidence in state or public approaches to social and economic problems in the United States, is democracy our primary signifier of the potential of emancipatory political struggle? If so, does this not indicate a diminishment in political dreams—the loss of hopes for equity and social justice?

Liberal and pragmatic approaches to politics accept the diminishment of political aspirations as a realistic accommodation to the complexities of late capitalist societies. They also assert themselves as the only alternative to what they present as the inevitable danger of totalitarianism accompanying Marxist and revolutionary theories. In contrast, Žižek confronts directly the trap involved in acquiescence to a diminished political field: within the ideological matrix of liberal democracy, any move against nationalism, fundamentalism, or ethnic violence ends up reinforcing Capital and guaranteeing democracy's failure. Arguing that formal democracy is irrevocably and necessarily "stained" by a particular content that conditions and limits its universalizability, Žižek challenges us to relinquish our attachment to democracy. If we know that the procedures and institutions of constitutional democracies privilege the wealthy and exclude the poor, if we know that efforts toward inclusion remain tied to national boundaries, thereby disenfranchising yet again those impacted by certain national decisions and policies, and if we know that the expansion and intensification of networked communications that was supposed to enhance democratic participation serves primarily to integrate and consolidate communicative capitalism, why do we present our political hopes as aspirations to democracy rather than something else? Why, in the face of democracy's obvious inability to represent justice in the social field that has emerged in the incompatibility between the globalized economy and welfare states to displace the political, do critical left political and cultural theorists continue to emphasize a set of arrangements that can be filled in, or substantialized, by fundamentalisms, nationalisms, populisms, and conservatisms diametrically opposed to progressive visions of social and economic equality?

Žižek's answer is that democracy is the form our attachment to Capital takes; it is the way we organize our enjoyment. He writes, "what prevents the radical question of 'capitalism' itself is precisely *belief in the democratic form of the struggle against capitalism*."[7] Faithful to democracy, we eschew the demanding task of politicizing the economy and envisioning a different political order.

Some theorists think Žižek's position here is mere posturing. They thus construe him as an intellectual bad boy trying to out-radicalize those he dismisses as deconstructionists, multiculturalists, Spinozans, and leftist scoundrels and dwarves. Ernesto Laclau, in a dialogue with Žižek and Judith Butler, refers scornfully to the "naïve self-complacence" of one of Žižek's "r-r-revolutionary" passages: "Žižek had told us that he wanted to overthrow capitalism; now we are served notice that he also wants to do away with liberal democratic regimes."[8] Laclau implies that Žižek's antidemocratic stance is something new.

Attention to Žižek's writing shows, to the contrary, that a skepticism toward democracy has long been a crucial component of his project. It is not, therefore, simply a radical gesture. In a number of his early books published in English, Žižek voices a sense of betrayal at the bait and switch occurring in Eastern Europe when they "went for" democracy and got capitalism and nationalism instead. For example, in *For They Know Not What They Do*, his first book written after the collapse of "actually existing socialism," Žižek wonders if the Left is "condemned to pledge all its forces to the victory of democracy?"[9] He notes that in the initial days of communism's disintegration in Eastern Europe, the democratic project breathed with new life. Democracy held out promises of hope and freedom, of arrangements that would enable people to determine collectively the rules and practices through which they would live their lives, but instead of collective governance in the common interest, people in the new democracies got rule by Capital. Their political choices became constrained within and determined by the neoliberal market logics of globalized capitalism already dominating Western Europe, Great Britain, and the United States. What emerged after the communists were gone was the combination of neoliberal capitalism and nationalist fundamentalism, what Žižek calls a "scoundrel time" when capitalism appears as democracy and democracy as and through capitalism. Is this what the Left is doomed to defend?

That skepticism toward democracy is not a recent radical gesture but a central element in Žižek's thinking is also clear in the fact that one of his most fundamental theoretical insights concerns the constitutive nonuniversalizability of liberal democracy. Thus, in *The Sublime Object of Ideology*, written before the collapse of communism, Žižek refers to the universal notion of democracy as a "necessary fiction." Adopting Hegel's insight that the Universal "can realize itself only in impure, deformed, corrupted forms," he emphasizes the impossibility of grasping the Universal as an intact purity.[10] In all his work thereafter, Žižek struggles with the relation between democracy and universality, concerned with the way contemporary adherence to democracy prevents the universalizing move proper to politics.

In subsequent work, Žižek names the limit to current thinking "democratic fundamentalism."[11] I read the term in two ways. First, democratic fundamentalism refers to the connection between liberal democracy and ethnic and religious fundamentalism. Rather than two opposing forces in an ideological battle (as presented in mainstream U.S. media and politics), liberal democracy and fundamentalism are two components of the current ideological formation.[12] Fundamentalism is not the preservation of authentic traditions against forces of modernization. Rather, it is the postmodern appropriation of cultural forms in the context of global capitalism. Likewise, liberal democracy is not an alternative to fundamentalism; indeed, it is laced through with fundamentalisms. The choice liberal democracy sets up—fundamentalism or democracy—is thus false; not only is it premised on the hegemony of democracy but it disavows its own relationship to fundamentalism.[13] This false choice is one of the ways liberal democracy attempts to ensure that "nothing will really happen in politics," that everything (global capitalism) will go as before.

The second way I read *democratic fundamentalism* is in terms of this hegemony, this basic framework so apparently immune to contestation and renegotiation. Democracy today is not the living, breathing activity of politics. The apparent suspension of social hierarchy in elections is the form of its opposite: it is a disavowal of the antagonisms rupturing the social.[14] Differently put, why should anyone be content with a democracy reduced to elections—precisely what has occurred in liberal democratic regimes? Where is the democracy in finance-driven, spectacularized contests between rich elites who agree on nearly everything? By reducing democracy to elections, democratic fundamentalism attempts to ensure that nothing will happen. It precludes politics, if by politics we have in mind actions that can produce major change. This second sense of democratic fundamentalism thus refers to the way democracy binds our thinking—anything that is not democratic is necessarily horrible, totalitarian, and unacceptable to any rational person.

Democratic universality thus appears in Žižek's early thinking as a necessary fiction, as an impossible universality that opens up because of an excess, obstacle, or stain that impedes it (an idea I detail below). In the wake of the demise of socialism and the expansion and intensification of neoliberal capitalism and racist fundamentalisms, Žižek finds that the democratic opening no longer exists, that it has been closed off. As I demonstrate, the empty place of democracy now appears politically hopeless as Capital, that other system that relies on disruption, crisis, and excess, displaces the excess necessary for democracy. Continued service to democracy today functions as our disavowal of the foreclosure of the political under global capitalism. Instead of a political practice structured around change—what one might expect from elections—we have a democratic fundamentalism that renders change unthinkable.

Contra Laclau, then, I read Žižek's questioning of democracy as genuine. When he says the "only question which confronts political philosophy today" is whether liberal democracy is "the ultimate horizon of our political practice," he means it.[15] I now look more closely at Žižek's questioning, setting out first his formal account of democracy and clarifying the link he posits between democracy, violence, enjoyment, and capitalism. With this account in place, I consider his more recent arguments regarding democratic fundamentalism's preclusion of politics. To this end, I contrast Žižek's concern with the loss of a space for the political with alternative positions prominent in Left critical cultural and political theory.

The Form of Democracy

Žižek's theorization of democracy relies on a conceptual insight into the impossibility of a pure form (this argument is thus correlative to the account of enjoyment I provide in Chapter One). A pure form will always be "stained" or in some way impure. The symbolic order, for example, or a given ideological field, will have within it nonrational kernels of intensity, objects of attachment, and excesses of enjoyment. Formal arrangements like the moral law and the "democratic invention" (Žižek follows Claude Lefort here) cannot escape this excess; indeed, they produce and rely on it. Thus, the democratic invention is extraordinary, yet it is also rooted in a fundamental impossibility: a pure form. When theorizing about democracy, then, one is confronted by the question of the proper relation to this impossibility of a pure form. Should one view it as the strength of democracy and thereby assume this impossibility, this inevitable failure and barrier?[16] Should one specify and contextualize it, seeking thereby to understand how it might function in a given historic period or what its relationship is to a given mode of production? Or should one strive for something more than democracy, to recover past hopes and undertake the hard work of bringing something new into being? I read Žižek as taking the third position. Understanding why this answer is compelling requires further attention to his analysis of the democratic stain.

Žižek develops his account of the formal stain through an exploration of the structural homology between Kant's categorical imperative, the Jacobin's democratic terror, and the psychoanalytic account of castration. All begin with "an act of radical emptying."[17] To establish the categorical imperative, Kant eliminates all possible contents. The moral law appears in and occupies this place emptied of empirical contingencies. Terroristically relying on an abstract principle of equality, the Jacobins attempted to protect democracy. Democracy requires that the place of power remain empty; the Jacobins sought to ensure this emptiness, recognizing that any attempt to occupy the empty place is by definition a usurpation. Finally, Freud explains the "strange economy of our psychic apparatus" by positing an initial pure loss.[18] "This loss has an ontological function," Žižek writes. "The renunciation of the incestuous object changes the status, the mode of being, of all objects which appear in its place—they are all present *against the background of a radical absence* opened up by the 'wiping out' of the incestuous Supreme Good."[19] As we saw in Chapter One, moreover, this fantasized loss is one of an originary enjoyment. Kant, the democratic Terror, and psychoanalysis all employ a logic that relies on a void, an empty place, the absence of enjoyment.

Important for Žižek is the production of this void, or the "act of radical emptying." Who is doing it? Who is the instrument who carries out the necessary cleansing or purification? The Jacobins tried to see themselves as such an instrument; their revolutionary Terror was premised on the aspiration that they were equal to the charge of democracy and that their responsibility to democracy demanded that they eliminate those who were not. Kant does not separate out the moral law from the enunciator of the moral law; the demands of the law simply confront the will with neutral, incontrovertible, reason. Kant's failure to distinguish between the "subject of the enunciated" (the subject of the content) and the "subject of the enunciation" (the one doing the enunciating) is the entry point of psychoanalysis. Lacan, Žižek explains, makes clear how the Kantian subject of the enunciation is actually the Freudian superego—that malevolent, malicious agent, torturing the subject in an obscene organization of enjoyment (a point we return to in Chapter Four). Pertaining to the very form of the moral law is an obscene enjoyment—a sadistic injunction to do one's duty, to obey, and to enjoy. "What does the subject discover in himself after he renounces his 'pathological' interests for the sake of the autonomous moral law?" Žižek asks. "An unconditional injunction which exerts ferocious pressure upon him, disregarding his well-being."[20] The structural homology between Kant and the democratic terror of the Jacobins thus involves more than absence; it also involves unavoidable violence and enjoyment.

At this point, one might object that Žižek's move to violence and enjoyment is too quick. Why could not the Jacobins' adherence to abstract equality be installed in rational procedures? Differently put, what is at work in the homology between the obscene superego underpinning the categorical imperative and the revolutionary Terror serving the democratic invention? The short answer is *objet petit a*. That is to say, Žižek explores the homology between Kant and the Jacobins in order to get at the limit point of abstraction or universalization, that is, to locate the stain or impossible object produced in the very process of formalization.

The problem of this limit is not new: political theorists are familiar with it as the paradox of founding, of the undemocratic violence prior to democracy. Hegel's critique of Kant in this regard is also well known: Kant cannot give an account of a choice for autonomy. What Žižek does, then, is draw from Lacanian psychoanalysis to explain our attachment to these persisting, unavoidable limits, antagonisms, or kernels of the Real.

With respect to the moral law, the stain of enjoyment does not involve any pathological content or empirical object. Rather, the wiping out of all pathological objects produces a new kind of nonpathological object—*objet petit a*, the object-cause of desire. Žižek explains, "We could thus define *objet petit a*, the object-cause of desire embodying surplus enjoyment, precisely as the surplus that escapes the network of universal exchange."[21] As I discuss in Chapter One, we should also understand this stain of surplus enjoyment as an object within the subject of the enunciation, as the gap exceeding it and its place as the subject of the enunciated. Superego occupies this place, issuing its injunctions to enjoy with no regard to the circumstances of the subject, that is, impersonally, neutrally, and senselessly. This is why Lacan says that Sade is the truth of Kant: "this object whose experience is avoided by Kant emerges in Sade's work, in the guise of the *executioner*, the agent who practices his 'sadistic' activity on the victim."[22] The executioner acts from duty alone. He makes himself an instrument of the Other's will.

Žižek explains (again, drawing from Lefort) that the Jacobins were never fully able to make themselves into pure instruments; they could not escape their own personal wills and decisions and directly embody, for example, the force of reason or the will of history. Nevertheless, as protectors of democracy as an empty place of power, the Jacobins remained caught in the Kantian trap: they could defend democracy only at the level of the enunciated content. Once they took on the role of subject of the enunciation, they were necessarily brutally and unconditionally occupying the empty place of power.[23] Thus, the crucial link between Kant and the Jacobins, between the categorical imperative and democratic invention, involves *objet petit a*: just as superego stains the moral law, so does it appear as a stain on the empty place of democracy.

This stain on the empty place of democracy takes the form of the sublime, pure, body of the People, that is, of the Nation. Žižek writes, "Before its proper birth, the Nation is present as a superego voice charging the Convention with the task of giving birth to it."[24] Revolutionaries understand themselves as charged to create a new people out of the old society, but who gives them this charge? The not-yet-existent people.[25] In this way, formal democracy is tied to a contingent, material content, to some sort of nation or ethnicity, to a fantasy point that resists universalization.[26] The nation is the condition for democracy: who else calls it into being?[27]

So, formal democracy is stained by a contingent, material content. The empty place of formal democracy, the extraordinary achievement of the democratic invention, is impossible. Is this democracy what the Left is condemned to defend? Are we destined to fetishize democracy, that is, to adopt the attitude, *I know democracy is a form stained by a pathological imbalance, but nevertheless I act as if democracy were possible*?[28] Is it necessary to remain faithful to castration and, if so, why?

Mediators Vanishing or Displaced

My discussion of Kant, the Jacobins, and psychoanalysis has focused on *objet petit a* as the limit of universalization. One result of this has been the claim that democracy is ultimately inseparable from nationalist violence. It is linked to the fantasy point of a people that calls it into being. I now shift back to capitalism, that other element in Žižek's disparaging of the present scoundrel time. I emphasize first Žižek's application of a concept he takes from Fredric Jameson: the "vanishing mediator." I turn second to his account of the violent interconnections between capitalism and ethnic nationalism in Eastern Europe.

An element of Jameson's explanation as to how Max Weber's theory of the Protestant ethic is compatible with Marxism, the vanishing mediator refers to a concrete and necessary condition for historical change, or a "dialectical necessity" that accounts for the shift from "in itself" to "for itself."[29] The closed society of medieval feudalism does not automatically or immediately transition into bourgeois capitalism. How do we get there? How is it possible to get from medieval corporatism to capitalist individualism? Protestantism. Protestantism extends the religious attitude beyond specific observances and into an ascetics of the everyday. Once the Protestant work ethic is universalized as central to economic life, it drops away or vanishes; religious activity can be relegated to the bourgeois private sphere.

In the face of the political and economic impact of Protestantism in the United States today—in the combination of neoconservatism and neoliberalism that extols privatization, regressive taxation, and the elimination of social services even as it emphasizes Christian family values and a divine endorsement of American military aggression—the term *vanishing mediator* rings hollow. The Calvinist need for assurance in the face of predestination and the moralized, spiritualized work ethic described by Weber (as an ideal type) may not be as pervasive now as they were then. Nevertheless, Protestantism continues to play a role in producing the subjects and practices necessary for the current hegemonic formation. A better term might thus be *displaced mediator*—a mediator whose functioning is displaced from what might have been understood (retroactively) as its original role. As I explain below, the term *displaced mediator* better accounts for an additional mediator that Žižek designates as vanishing, namely, new social movements.

At any rate, Žižek reads the Jacobins as vanishing mediators: they were not some kind of aberration but were necessary for the transition from the *ancien regime* to the bourgeois political structure. Jacobinism takes the bourgeois political ideals of equality, freedom, and brotherhood literally. Yet just as the religious ideals of Protestantism become superfluous after the work ethic is universalized, so does the Jacobins' egalitarianism pave the way for the egotistic, acquisitive bourgeoisie. As Žižek writes, "Vulgar, egotistic bourgeois everyday life is the actuality of freedom, equality and brotherhood: freedom of free trade, formal equality in the eyes of the law, and so on."[30] Thus, in Žižek's discussion of the Jacobin terror we find not only the formal analysis of a stain on the empty place of democracy. We also have a concrete account of the historical link between democracy and capitalism.

One might think that once democracy is established it would shed its previous link to violence and capitalism, yet this has not been the case. Attachment to a national or ethnic cause continues violently to subvert democratic pluralism, an attachment that seems only to have intensified as formerly communist states have become subjected to the neoliberal logics of contemporary global capitalism. Accordingly, Žižek considers the way the onset of capitalism in Eastern Europe ushered in hideous nationalism rather than a robust democracy. He extends his analysis to identify the same process in Western countries: fundamentalism necessarily flourishes in the space opened up by formal democracy and in response to the deterritorializing logic of Capital.

Žižek's account of East-European nationalism relies on the idea of a national Thing, of that inexpressible collection of practices and attributes that make us who we are and that constitute our way of life. The Thing is not the set per se, nor is it that characteristic shared by members of the set. Rather, it "shines through" the set as a kind of underlying belief in the set's meaningfulness. The Thing cannot be understood simply as a performative effect of people's belief in it. Rather, the Thing achieves its consistency because of a certain kernel of enjoyment. The national Thing "is ultimately nothing but the way subjects in a given ethnic community organize their enjoyment through national myths."[31]

As we saw in the first chapter, ethnic tensions and hatreds involve the national Thing. Others are always trying to take our Thing, or, that is what we think because this is the only way we have a Thing in the first place. Žižek writes, "What we conceal by imputing to the Other the theft of enjoyment is the traumatic fact that *we never had what was stolen from us*: the lack ('castration') is originary, enjoyment constitutes itself as 'stolen.'"[32] National myths organize a community with reference to external threats. These threats threaten our national Thing. To this extent, we need others: they provide the mechanism through which, via fantasy, we organize our enjoyment. If others do not steal our enjoyment, we will not have it. In this way, the others are actually part of us. As Žižek puts its, "The fascinating image of the Other gives a body to our own innermost split, to what is 'in us more than ourselves' and thus prevents us from achieving full identity with ourselves. *The hatred of the Other is the hatred of our own excess of enjoyment.*"[33] In short, with the notion of the Thing and the idea of the theft of enjoyment, Žižek gives an account of the nonuniversalizable kernel of fantasy in the organization of community.[34]

What interests Žižek with regard to the national Thing in postcommunist Eastern Europe is how its interaction with capitalism thwarts pluralist democracy. Nationalism is a kind of shock-absorber against the structural imbalance of capitalism, against its inevitable excess, expansion, and openness. Eliminating the ethnic other works as the fantasy organization of the desire for a stable, well-defined, social body, for a community unrent by capitalist upheaval. "And since this social body is experienced as that of a nation," Žižek argues, "the cause of any imbalance 'spontaneously' assumes the form of a 'national enemy.'"[35]

Of course, liberal intellectuals in Eastern and Western Europe were and are critical of nationalism and ethnic violence. The problem with their position, Žižek points out, is that it remains caught in the same fantasy framework and thereby ultimately supports capitalism. How? Because what bothers leftist liberals is enjoyment, that is any excessive identification with or attachment to a specific way of life or tradition. If the way of life is sufficiently distant, then Western intellectuals affirm it as a practice of the Other. If it is too close, however, like the practices and beliefs of American poor whites living in the rural south, then this enjoyment must be eliminated—sacrificed. Not only does the fear of over-identification rely on the same fantasy framework as the national Thing, but insofar as it urges the sacrifice of the Thing, it eliminates a barrier to capitalist intensification, to capitalism's reformatting of ever more domains of life as objects and experiences of consumption.

Before I move to Žižek's more recent arguments against democracy, I want to mention again the vanishing mediator, now with regard to the shift from socialism to capitalism in Eastern Europe. Here, too, as with the shift from feudalism to capitalism, the mediators who "triggered the process" do not exactly vanish; rather, they are displaced from their earlier position by the rush of privatization and the demands of neoliberal capitalism.

In East Germany and Yugoslavia these displaced mediators were the New Left, punk, and new social movements, who believed passionately in democracy and their opportunity to create something new.[36] Their moment passed quickly as they ushered in the scoundrel time.

To summarize, Žižek argues that the democratic form runs up against a nonuniversalizable remainder or nugget. He understands this nugget as a stain of enjoyment, as an irreducible attachment to an intense pleasure-pain. The empty place of democracy is never fully empty. It comes up against points of nonuniversalizability: founding violence, ethnic particularity, the national Thing. Indeed, insofar as democracy has been a project of the Nation, its very starting point, its position of enunciation, requires this nonuniversalizable nugget. To the extent that liberal democracy tries to eliminate this stain—tries to exclude ethic fundamentalism and nationalist attachment—it necessarily fails. Under conditions of late capitalism, the problem is even worse. Like liberal democracy, Capital wants to eliminate particular attachments. Liberal-democratic attacks on ethnic fundamentalism, then, serve capitalist ends as they attack some of the few remaining sites of opposition to capitalism. Nationalist, ethnic, racist violence thus persists today at the intersection of two modes of failed universalization: democracy and capitalism. The question is whether a new political universality is possible.

Becoming Postpolitical

Žižek's later salvos against democracy today rely on and repeat this earlier account of the nationalist stain on the empty place of democracy and the way that our fetishizing of democracy—our sense that, *yes, democracy is impossible, nevertheless it's better than the fundamentalist alternative*—supports Capital and remains tied to ethnic violence. With increasing intensity and in varying contexts he returns to this account, reiterating his point that "the real dilemma is what to do with—how the Left is to relate to—the predominant *liberal democratic* imaginary."[37] His primary concern is with the way Left approaches remain trapped in the matrix of democratic fundamentalism insofar as they accept key precepts of global capitalism. I explore this concern as it appears in three themes: multiculturalism, universalization, and the act. I contrast Žižek's position with alternative views prominent in Left critical cultural and political theory.

I am particularly interested in the differences between Žižek's account and those of Gilles Deleuze and Felix Guattari, William Connolly, and Michael Hardt and Antonio Negri.[38] In place of an emphasis on a multitude of singularities or the plurality of modes of becoming, Žižek emphasizes Capital as a totality. In place of a positive field of pure immanence to which there is no outside, Žižek urges a universality premised on division and hence exclusion. Finally, in place of the micropolitics of dispersed practices, resistances, and affects, Žižek emphasizes the act. The axis of disagreement stretching throughout these three themes involves politicization and the space of politics. At stake is the foreclosure of the possibility of politics and the tacit embrace of global capitalism.

Multiculturalism

Unlike most critical thinkers identified with the Left, Žižek rejects the current emphasis on multicultural tolerance. He has three primary reasons for rejecting multiculturalism as it is currently understood in cultural studies and democratic theory. First, agreeing with Wendy Brown, he argues that multiculturalism today rests on an acceptance of global capitalism.[39] Insofar as Capital's deterritorializations create the conditions for the proliferation of multiple, fluid, political subjectivities, new social movements and identity politics rely on a political terrain established by global capitalism. As I explained with regard to the notion of class struggle in

Chapter Two, multiculturalism ultimately accepts and depends on the depoliticization of the economy: "the way the economy functions (the need to cut social welfare, etc.) is accepted as a simple insight into the objective state of things."[40] We might think here of feminist struggles over the right to an abortion, political work toward marriage benefits for same-sex couples, and energies spent on behalf of movies and television networks that target black audiences. In efforts such as these, political energy focuses on culture and leaves the economy as a kind of unquestioned, taken-for-granted basis of the way things are. This is not to say that identity politics are trivial. On the contrary, Žižek fully acknowledges the way these new forms of political subjectivization "thoroughly reshaped our entire political and cultural landscape."[41] The problem is that capitalism has adapted to these new political forms, incorporating previously transgressive urges and turning culture itself into its central component.[42]

To be sure, Žižek's argument would be stronger were he to think of new social movements as vanishing or displaced mediators. Identity politics opened up new spaces and opportunities for capitalist intensification. As new social movements transformed the lifeworld into something to be questioned and changed, they disrupted fixed identities and created opportunities for experimentation. The market entered to provide these opportunities.

Consider gay media. Joshua Gamson observes that while gay portal sites initially promised to offer safe and friendly spaces for gay community building, they now function primarily "to deliver a market share to corporations." In this gay media, "community needs are conflated with consumption desires, and community equated with market."[43] Social victories paved the way for market incursions into and the commodification of ever more aspects of experience. Once cultural politics morphed into capitalist culture, identity politics lost its radical edge. With predictable frequency, the Republican Right in the United States regularly accuses the

Left of playing the race card whenever there is opposition to a non-Anglo political appointee.

A second argument Žižek employs against multiculturalism concerns the way multicultural tolerance is part of the same matrix as racist violence. On the one hand, multicultural respect for the other is a way of asserting the superiority of the multiculturalist.[44] The multiculturalist adopts an emptied-out, disembodied perspective toward an embodied, ethnic other. The ethnic other makes the universal position of the multiculturalist possible. Not only does this attitude disavow the particularity of the multiculturalist's own position, but it also repeats the key gesture of global corporate capitalism: the big corporations will eat up, colonize, exploit, and commodify anything. They are not biased. They are empty machines following the logic of Capital.

On the other hand, tolerance toward the other "passes imperceptibly into a destructive hatred of all ('fundamentalist') Others who do not fit into our idea of tolerance—in short, against all *actual* Others."[45] The idea is that the liberal democrat, or multiculturalist, is against hatred and harassment. Tolerance is tolerance for another who also does not hate or harass, that is, tolerance for an other who is not really so other at all.[46] It thus works in tandem with a right not to be harassed, not to be victimized, inconvenienced by, or exposed to the particular enjoyment of another.[47] To this extent, the multicultural position blurs into a kind of racism such that respect is premised on agreement and identity. The Other with deep fundamental beliefs, who is invested in a set of unquestionable convictions, whose enjoyment is utterly incomprehensible to me, is not the other of multiculturalism. For Žižek, then, today's tolerant liberal multiculturalism is "an experience of the Other deprived of its Otherness (the idealized Other who dances fascinating dances and has an ecologically sound holistic approach to reality, while practices like wife-beating remain out of sight ...)."[48] Just as in Eastern Europe after the fall of communism, so today's reflexive multicultural tolerance has as its opposite, and thus remains caught in the matrix of, a hard kernel of fundamentalism, of irrational, excessive, enjoyment. The concrete realization of rational inclusion and tolerance coincides with contingent, irrational, violence.

Finally, Žižek's third argument against multiculturalism is that it precludes politicization. Žižek uses the example of the animated film series about dinosaurs, *The Land Before Time*, produced by Steven Spielberg.[49] The "clearest articulation of the hegemonic liberal multiculturalist ideology," *The Land Before Time* iterates the basic message that everyone is different and all should learn to live with these differences—big and small, strong and weak, carnivore and herbivore. In the films, the dinosaurs sing songs about how one should not worry about being eaten because underneath those big teeth are real fears and anxieties that everyone shares. Of course, this image of cooperative dinosaurs is profoundly false. As Žižek asks, what does it really mean to say that it takes all kinds? "Does that mean nice and brutal, poor and rich, victims and torturers?"[50] The vision of a plurality of horizontal differences precludes the notion of a vertical antagonism that cuts through the social body. Some are more powerful. Some do want to kill—and denying this in an acceptance of differences prevents the politicization of this inequality. To say that in our difference we are really all alike, underneath it all, disavows the underlying social antagonism. It prevents us from acknowledging and confronting the way that class struggle cuts through and conditions the multiplicity of differences.

We can approach the same point from another direction. Identity politics today emphasizes the specificity of each identity and experience. Particular differences are supposed to be acknowledged and respected. As Žižek points out, the notion of social justice that corresponds to this view depends on asserting the rights of and redressing the wrongs inflicted upon victims. Institutionally, then, identity politics "requires an intricate police apparatus (for identifying the group in question, for punishing offenders against its rights ... for providing the preferential treatment which should compensate for the wrong this group has suffered."[51] Rather than opening up a terrain of political struggle, functioning as human rights that designate the very space of politicization, identity politics works through a whole series of depoliticizing moves to locate, separate, and redress wrongs.[52] Systemic problems are reformulated as personal issues. No particular wrong or harm can then stand in for the "universal wrong."[53] Multiculturalism is thus a dimension of postpolitics insofar as it prevents the universalization of particular demands.

Žižek's three arguments against multiculturalism—its failure to challenge global capitalism, its speculative identity with irrational violence, and its preclusion of politicization—can be read in terms of divergences from Connolly, Hardt and Negri, and Deleuze and Guattari. Not only do Connolly's emphasis on the pluralization of modes of becoming and Hardt's and Negri's account of a multitude of singularities seek to open the political terrain beyond an orthodox focus on class antagonism, for example, but Deleuze's and Guattari's concepts of becoming machine, the communication of affective intensities, and the rhizomatic structures of being and thinking are effectively the ideology of the "netocracy," or digital elite.[54] For Žižek, the fundamental homology between these concepts and networked information and communication technologies decreases their radicality. Furthermore, Žižek's emphasis on the speculative identity of toleration and irrational violence contrasts with efforts on behalf of an ethos of generosity or critical responsiveness in Connolly's work. Insofar as such an ethos aims to combat and eliminate dogmatic certainty, it rests on precisely that fundament of irrational, contingent attachment it seeks to erase.[55] Finally, Žižek's rejection of a multitude of singularities should be read as an alternative to Hardt and Negri. Singular positions are not political. They can become political when they are split between their particularity and a capacity to stand for something else, that is, when they are politicized in terms of class struggle. Echoing Alain Badiou, Žižek argues that emphasis on multitude and diversity masks "the underlying monotony of today's global life."[56] He writes, "Is there anything more monotonous than the Deleuzian poetry of contemporary life as the decentred proliferation of multitudes, of non-totalizable differences? What occludes (and thereby sustains) this monotony is the multiplicity of resignifications and displacements to which the basic ideological texture is submitted."[57] The more things change, the more they remain the same, or, lots of little micro-struggles do not automatically produce macro-level change. Accordingly, one could say that even though Žižek is an avowed theorist of totality, Deleuze is the totalizing theorist, the theorist whose all-inclusive account of the social cannot account for the division necessary for political struggle.[58] Deleuze, and with him Connolly and Hardt and Negri, embraces an ethics of affirmation that eliminates negativity from the political. Politics becomes immanent, part of the nature of things, arising as a force both destructive and productive, deterritorializing and territorializing.[59] All this teaming activity is ultimately inseparable from the flows and intensities circulating through the networks of communicative capitalism.

Universalization

I have argued thus far that Žižek rejects the celebration of diversity insofar as he finds it ultimately embedded in global capitalism. I have mentioned as well his specific criticism of multiculturalism on the grounds that it prevents the universalization necessary for politicization. I now look more carefully at Žižek's account of universalization and how it links with politics. In a nutshell, for Žižek, universalization is the key to politicization: without the claim to universality, there simply is no politics.[60] This rendering of the political is a second primary difference between his position and alternative approaches prominent in Left critical cultural and political theory: for Žižek, division and exclusion are crucial aspects of politics.

One way to approach Žižek's account of universalization is by way of a common critique of universality, namely, that it is always necessarily exclusive and hence not only not universal but ideologically or malignly so—the claim of universality depends on the exclusion and denigration of particular contents, indeed, of particular others. For some thinkers, the way around this problem is through the assertion of contingency and singularity. Because universality never escapes from the horizon of a particular, an ethical relation to difference calls for an appreciation of the multiplicity of modes of becoming instead of the inevitably divisive move to the universal. Indeed, not only is the move to the universal dangerous and divisive; it is unnecessary. As Hardt and Negri write, "Politics is given immediately; it is a field of pure immanence."[61] This, to say the least, is not the view Žižek advocates. Rather, he accepts the point that universality is inevitably exclusive and argues that this exclusion creates the space of politicization.

What does universality exclude? Žižek argues that it is not "primarily the underprivileged Other whose status is reduced, constrained, and so on, but *its own* permanent founding gesture—a set of unwritten, unacknowledged rules and practices which, while publicly disavowed, are none the less the ultimate support of the existing power edifice."[62] As I have discussed, this exclusion is at work in superego's underpinning of the moral law as well as in the democratic terror of the Jacobins. The violence of both is a condition for the emergence of the formal, empty place of universality. Within the democratic form, for example, one can include all sorts of different people—workers, women, sexual and ethnic minorities—but what one cannot include is the moment of transition to democracy or those who oppose democracy. As a political form, democracy is necessarily partial, and this partiality is a condition for its universality. Some operation of exclusion, some founding violence, is necessary for the emergence of a universal frame. Moreover, given that this violence and exclusion underlies the liberal-democratic order, this order can be disrupted from the standpoint of its exclusion. From such an abject standpoint, in other words, it is possible to challenge the existing order in the name of the universal. This is what Žižek has in mind when he talks about the social symptom: "the part which, although inherent to the existing universal order, has no 'proper place' within it (say illegal immigrants or the homeless in our societies)."[63]

We can approach the exclusion at work in universality from a different direction. Žižek agrees with Laclau that the "the universal is operative only through the split in the particular."[64] The universal appears when the particular splits into itself and something it represents or as the gap that prevents the particular from achieving self-identity. It is a split of the community from itself. As Žižek explains with regard to human rights, they amount to a "right to universality as such—the right of a political agent to assert its radical non-coincidence with itself."[65] Politicization (and rights as vehicles of politicization) involves struggles to open up something beyond itself, struggles to represent this element as displaced, as rupturing the social Whole. For Žižek, politicization *is* universalization. Politics proper, he explains, is "the moment in which a particular demand is not simply part of the negotiation of interests but aims at something more, and starts to function as the metaphoric condensation of the global restructuring of the entire space."[66] Thus, nothing is naturally or automatically political. Transgressions and resistances may be politicized, but there is nothing about them that makes them inevitably political. This makes sense when we recall that transgression is context dependent and that resistances are immanent to and inseparable from power. An act or practice of resistance, then, has to become political; it has to be reiterated in another register, a register beyond itself (even as there is no "itself" absent this "beyond").

Žižek illustrates this point with an example from his political experience in Slovenia: a specific slogan came to stand for more than itself, for the demand that the regime be overthrown. An example from the United States might be Rosa Parks: at issue was not simply her particular seat on a bus or even the racist practices of buses in Montgomery, Alabama. Rather, the laws of segregation, and the racism of U.S. law most broadly, of U.S. willingness to enforce a system of apartheid, were at stake. One can imagine what could have occurred should the therapeutic and particularized practices of institutionalized identity politics have been in place: Rosa Parks would have discussed her feelings about being discriminated against; the bus driver would have dealt with his racism, explaining that he had been brought up that way; and perhaps there would have been a settlement enabling Parks to ride at a discounted fare on weekends and holidays. Maybe the two would have appeared together on a television talk show, the host urging each to understand and respect the opinion of the other. Ultimately, the entire situation would have been seen as about Park's specific experience rather than about legalized segregation more generally. It would not have been political; it would have been policed (to use terminology from Jacques Ranciere).

The political problem today, then, is that global capitalism works as the frame or condition of our current, depoliticized, post-political situation. In a way, it appears as itself, rather than as something else; rather than, or perversely, *even as*, a horrific machine of brutalization, global capitalism is just the way things are. Put differently, an aspect of the current political impasse is the extraordinary difficulty of representing (metaphorically condensing) particular events or positions (Hurricane Katrina, the collapse of Enron, the war against Iraq, immigrants, the Afghani people) in such a way as to unsettle or challenge the existing order.

I can now specify what is at stake politically in Žižek's version of universality by contrasting it with the approach taken by Hardt and Negri. Hardt's and Negri's political ontology accepts the reduction of politics to policing. For example, their characterization of the relation between empire and multitude turns on the notion of crisis; the struggles of the multitude induce the crises into which authority is called to intervene, put down, or police.[67] All these singular events, resistances that strike at the heart of empire, are what Hardt and Negri understand as politics. To be sure, their description of empire and Žižek's account of the postpolitical totality of global capitalism are not far apart: both views take the position that the political space is threatened or dissipated, diffused because of globalization. Whereas Hardt and Negri treat this loss of the autonomy of the political as an opportunity insofar as now conflict can be anywhere, anytime, Žižek looks at this loss as a depoliticization that forecloses any real, political challenge to globalization. He writes, "Globalization is precisely the name of the emerging postpolitical logic which progressively precludes the dimension of universality that appears in politicization proper."[68]

From the perspective provided by Žižek's account of universality, we can locate a fundamental problem with Hardt and Negri's political ontology: the impossibility of discerning whether an action or event supports the empire or empowers the multitude. This is impossible because in their order things simply are—given or immanent. However, politics requires—demands—representation.[69] Politically, it is not enough to say that something could be both or that something is simply undecideable. Rather, one needs to say from what perspective or what standpoint an action or event has a certain meaning. To say this is to accept the political necessity of the division that orients and anchors struggle.[70]

A couple of years ago, I saw a large advertisement painted on a wall in Budapest. The wall was on one of the streets in the heavily trafficked tourist area near the city's center. The advertisement, for a restaurant, was written in English; its promise: risk free dining! Unlike Hardt and Negri, Žižek assumes that politics involves risk, indeed, violence and exclusion. This does not necessarily mean armed conflict, though it could. Rather, what the understanding of universality's exclusion of and dependence on violence and division does is try to break out of the suffocating foreclosure of the political in the postpolitical totality of global Capital.

The Act

Thus far I have focused on multiculturalism and universality. In so doing, I have tried to bring to the fore Žižek's ongoing critique of democracy. Rather than components of a more democratic society, inclusion and tolerance remain tied to a disavowed fundamentalism. At the same time, they foreclose the possibility of politicization and thus operate as postpolitics. Likewise, universality, rather than a neutral position transcending politics, opens up as a split within the particular, as that which is displaced, or out of joint.[71] I now turn to the third theme, the idea of the "act" in contrast to micropolitics. For Žižek, the possibility of acts that disrupt the socio-symbolic order, ruptures of the Real, can break through the stultifying deadlock of postpolitics. In the act, in other words, we can find hope for something more.

I approach this theme by way of what might appear as a detour: the political right in the United States. Given Žižek's emphasis on exclusion and violence, not to mention his critique of multiculturalism and general skepticism toward democracy, one might think American conservatism demonstrates precisely that political will Žižek admires. Žižek observes that "it is only right-wing populism which today displays the authentic *political* passion of accepting the *struggle*, of openly admitting that, precisely insofar as one claims to speak from a universal standpoint, one does not aim to please everybody, but is ready to introduce a *division* of 'Us' versus 'Them.'"[72] Given Žižek's reading of Christianity in terms of the traumatic event that transforms and commands the believer from the standpoint of a universal Truth (a reading I explore more fully in the following chapter), George W. Bush and his supporters on the religious right could seem perfect Žižekians. Not surprisingly, this superficial description is too quick and too, well, superficial. Žižek's point is not that any political position that comes from conviction is objectively correct or true. Such an idea would deny the truth of perspectival distortion, the way that the Real is characterized by a parallax gap. Or, it would presume the possibility of an idealized consensus, disavowing thereby the underlying antagonism rupturing (and producing) society. Accordingly, Žižek argues that Truth is *radically subjective*.[73] More precisely, "Truth itself is not a property of statements, but *that which makes them true*."[74] Žižek explains that a paradoxical dimension of Truth lies in the fact that Truth is the position from which a statement is made (a point we encountered already in the explication of the structure of Lacan's four discourses). To speak from this position, to be an agent of Truth, is thus to speak in way that will be inevitably distorted by a parallax gap, by a fundamental social antagonism (or that will produce an unavoidable excess or remainder). The wrongness of Bush (or racism or capitalism) is not an ontological given; it is a political claim. Adhering to a notion of "universal partisan truth," Žižek asserts unequivocally the need to exclude right-wing populists and extremists, the need to reject them out of hand rather than to tolerate them, debate with them, hear them out, or look for opportunities to compromise.[75] From the position of this partisan truth, it is clearly the case that Bush's politics are profoundly inauthentic, postpolitical, and antiuniversal.

Bush's politics (like Nazism) are inauthentic because they rely on the fantasy of a social Whole.[76] Rather than beginning from a universality posited from the point of exclusion, from antagonism or class struggle, as does Žižek, right-wing politics attempts to restore a ruptured society to its original unity. In direct opposition to Žižek's emphasis on those outcast from the social order, Bush's politics (like, unfortunately, nearly all mainstream party politics in the United States) are rooted in the most privileged members of society. This is why Bush's politics are postpolitical: they are designed to make sure nothing changes, that corporations remain powerful, for example, or that nothing threatens the interests of oil and energy companies. Indeed, the endeavor to make sure that nothing changes explains what might otherwise appear to be an inconsistency in right-wing politics: the combination of support for neoliberal economics and conservative social regulations.[77] Moralizing conservatives fight against precisely that consumerism, "lifestyle decadence, " and "erosion of values" generated and accelerated by intensifications in capitalism. One half of the right-wing coalition endeavors to protect "society" from what the other half is doing; it tries to have capitalism without capitalism.

Although motivated by the Truth of his conversion, Bush's politics do not politicize; they do the opposite. Not only did the early months of his presidency emphasize bipartisanship and consensus (an emphasis that became an assumption as politics was foreclosed after September 11), but the primary institutions of his rule are the Army and the Church—"examples of the *disavowal* of the proper political dimension."[78] The American religious right is powerful today because of the way it links together irreconcilable opposites: a rejection of government *and* an increase in state power, an endorsement of the market *and* the imaginary resolution of its antagonisms in religion, an emphasis on the global, on a worldwide war against terror *and* a rejection of global governing bodies. The Left has accepted this matrix when what it should do is explode it. It follows, then, that Bush's politics, for all their faith-based rhetoric, are global rather than universal. This contrast is crucial to Žižek, who emphasizes that the universal is opposed to globalism: "the universal 'shines through' the symptomatic displaced element which belongs to the Whole without being properly its part."[79] Bush wants to destroy the displaced element. This right-wing detour, then, emphasizes Žižek's notion of universal partisan Truth, a political Truth. According to Žižek, what democrats, multiculturalists, and "reborn pseudo-Nietzscheans" foreclose is a "politics of truth."[80] None of these positions is willing to take a side, to assert and claim that there is a truth of a situation. Instead, they embrace a multiplicity of narratives and forms of political engagement, as if these different perspectives could be combined without distortion. At the same time, these left positions limit political engagement to resistance, as if this resistance were not itself already allowed for in the hegemonic framework.[81] For Žižek, the failure of such an approach is that

> radical political practice itself is conceived of as an unending process which can destabilize, displace, and so on, the power structure, without ever being able to undermine it effectively— the ultimate goal of radical politics is ultimately to displace the limit of social exclusions, empowering the excluded agents (sexual and ethnic minorities) by creating marginal spaces in which they can articulate and question their identity ... there are no final victories and ultimate demarcations.[82]

Not only do such approaches to radical politics leave the overarching political-economic frame intact, but the very political tactics chosen are those conducive to the deterritorializing flows of global capitalism.[83]

For Žižek, the radical political act is a way to break out of this stultifying deadlock.[84] As I explain more thoroughly in Chapter Five, Žižek conceives the act as a radical, uncertain gesture that breaks through the symbolic order. From the standpoint of this order and like the foundation of the order itself, the act is shattering and unethical—and this is the point, to break through the boundaries of the situation, to change its basic contours. In this way, the act is nondemocratic; it is not democratically legitimized in advance. Rather, it is a risk.[85] There are no guarantees of success. Only retroactively, in light of what follows, can there be any sense of the act. Žižek writes, "An act is always a specific intervention within a socio-symbolic context; the *same* gesture can be an act or a ridiculous empty posture, depending on this context."[86] Rather than a radical step toward freedom, the Boston Tea Party could well have been a pathetic act of vandalism by men in unfortunate costumes. Likewise, the Los Angeles riots could have been the moment when the structures of class and race were radically transformed rather than merely the moment when rage combusted into violence and looting.

Žižek emphasizes two features of the political act. First, it is external to the subject. The act is not something that the subject figures out and decides to do having rationally considered a number of different options. On the contrary, insofar as the act is an intrusion of the Real, "the act is precisely something which unexpectedly 'just occurs.'"[87] An act is not intentional; it is something that the subject had to do, that it could not do otherwise, that just happened. Second, the genuinely political act intervenes from the position of the social symptom; it is not merely a transformation of the subject. Žižek explains, "An authentic act is not simply external with regard to the hegemonic field disturbed by it: an act is an act only *with regard to* some symbolic field, as an intervention into it."[88] To transform this field, rather than remain trapped within it, an act has to intervene from the standpoint of its hidden structuring principle, of its inherent exception. For example, the political strategy of the Democratic Leadership Council in the United States has for all intents and purposes been to race the Republicans to the right. Clinton Democrats emphasized "welfare reform" (turning it into workfare and capping lifetime receipt of benefits at five years) as they tried to appeal to what they perceived to be average or middle-class Americans. Lost in this strategy are the poor: the exclusion of the poor was necessary for the restructuring of the Democratic party. The poor, then, would constitute the symptom of the Democratic party, and an act would intervene from this position. Before I conclude, let me note a reservation regarding Žižek's notion of the act. Žižek writes most often about the violence necessarily connected to the political act, viewing this violence as what the Left refuses to accept responsibility for. Given the brutal violence of neoliberal capitalism and the nationalist, ethnic, racist fundamentalism infusing the contemporary postpolitical matrix, that violence may accompany disruptive acts seems obvious and necessary. The courage of Palestinian suicide bombers is but one example of such a willingness to accept responsibility for violence.

A perhaps more likely repercussion of Žižek's emphasis on an act that happens to a subject is extreme passivity. If the act is supposed to intervene from outside the symbolic order, how can one organize for it or try to produce conditions conducive to it? Žižek responsibly rejects the temptation to "provoke a catastrophe" in hope that then "the act will somehow occur."[89] Thus, in *The Parallax View*, he uses Melville's Bartleby as a figure for passivity as itself a kind of violence that could disrupt the manic, fruitless, resistances more typical of leftist politics and potentially underlie work toward constructing something new. Bartleby refuses, saying "I would prefer not to." Advocating Bartleby politics, Žižek writes, "today 'I would prefer not to' is not primarily 'I would prefer not to participate in the market economy, in capitalist competition and profiteering,' but—much more problematically for some—'I would prefer not to give to charity to support a Black orphan in Africa, engage in the struggle to prevent oil-drilling in a wildlife swamp, send books to educate our liberal-feminist-spirited women in Afghanistan ...'"[90] I confess that it is difficult for me to see how such a "preference" is not, in fact, the provocation of a catastrophe in the hope that an act will somehow occur—a catastrophe particularly for those who might be left alone and unsupported. At the same time, the very audaciousness of such a position, the way it confronts those of us with leftist sensibilities with our own complicity in and enjoyment of the present deadlock, cannot be denied. In a way, Bartleby is less an alternative than he is a realization, an acknowledgment of the contemporary political-economic impasse.

In work prior to *The Parallax View*, Žižek suggests other alternatives to waiting for an act. One such idea involves "shooting oneself in the foot."[91] By getting rid of what is most dear, most central to oneself, one liberates oneself from the constraints of a situation. With respect to political struggle, this might mean embracing the possibility of loss and failure in order to change the political environment. (To this extent, Bartleby politics can be thought of as a leftist version of shooting oneself in the self: activists are to give up what they hold most dear, their very activity, the very work and engagement that gives them a sense of meaning and purpose, that lets them believe that they are making a difference.) It could mean refusing to accept an outcome and continuing the struggle. The Republican party in the United States pursued just this sort of strategy in impeaching Bill Clinton and organizing a vote to recall California governor Gray Davis. Under George W. Bush, moreover, it steadfastly demands the impossible—war without taxes—and transforms the political debate in the process. Another alternative to waiting for the act might be found in Žižek's emphasis on identifying with the letter of the law against its own obscene underpinning.[92] One could imagine Democrats agreeing that lowering taxes and fighting wars are equally important, but, nevertheless, one must stick to the law and not incur huge deficits. Neither of these examples, however, does justice to Žižek's emphasis on the act insofar as both remain within the confines of liberal-democratic politics. This, today, is what Žižek wants us to reject.

No Reassurance, No Forgiveness

I conclude with a reference to an essay by Harvard political scientist Stanley Hoffman.[93] In a rather odd sentence near the middle of his essay, Hoffman writes, "The U.S. remains a liberal democracy, but ..." First, why does he say the U.S. remains a liberal democracy? Given that, as Žižek points out, anxiety is a response to a lack in the Other, it seems to me like Hoffman wants to reassure his readers that the United States remains a liberal democracy because his previous three paragraphs suggest the opposite.[94] Hoffman details the curbing of civil liberties, the "Republicans' relentless war against the state's welfare functions," the change in U.S. strategic doctrine such that preeminence is official policy, and the ceding of effective political control over all the branches of government to the president through congressional and judicial acceptance of the "notion that the President's war powers override all other concerns." In the face of these excesses, Hoffman wants to reassure readers that the United States is still a liberal democracy, "but ... ." But what? "But," Hoffman continues,

> those who have hoped for progressive policies at home and enlightened policies abroad may be forgiven if they have become deeply discouraged by a not-so-benign soft imperialism, by a fiscal and social policy that takes good care of the rich but shuns the poor on grounds of a far from 'compassionate conservatism,' and by the conformism, both dictated by the administration and often spontaneous among the public, that Tocqueville observed 130 years ago.

The United States is still a liberal democracy, but nevertheless Hoffman wants to acknowledge—and forgive—the justifiable discouragement of those who hoped that liberal democracy might be more or better than it is.

If the United States remains a liberal democracy, then liberal democracy is the problem. Insofar as Hoffman's sentences include within this remaining liberal democracy imperialism, detention without counsel, support for the rich, and shunning of the poor, then those of us who hoped for better and are now discouraged should not be forgiven. In the name of *this* liberal democracy, we have endorsed a political form fully accepting of deep and global inequality and inimical to projects toward commonality and justice. What Žižek's political theory tells us is that against *this* liberal democracy we should no longer emphasize compromise, acceptance, inclusivity, and generosity; we should adopt instead the divisive attitude of universal Truth.

4
LAW
FROM SUPEREGO TO LOVE

Introduction

Žižek's account of law is built upon the reiteration of the idea that law is split or that there is a parallax gap between the public letter and its obscene superego supplement.[1] This chapter focuses on the split in law, drawing out its repercussions for thinking about law more generally. As Paul A. Passavant observes, among postmodernists there is a recurring emphasis on moving beyond law because of law's perceived rigidity and determinacy, as if law were a domain safe from the shifts, remainders, and instabilities necessarily part of any text.[2] Some contemporary thinkers, such as Giorgio Agamben, suggest the possibility of a form of life beyond law. Others, inspired politically by anarchism and philosophically by Deleuze and Guattari, want to sever the relation between radical politics and law, to escape sovereignty's capture. For these contemporary thinkers, law's failures prevent law from serving social justice.

For Žižek, however, law is necessary and potentially liberatory. Appearing in multiple arrangements—the symbolic law of language and norms, the public law of states and regimes, the transgressive "nightly" law of superego, as well as the religious law of Judaism and the Pauline law of faith—law persists as a constituent element of human practical experience. Yet law as such is incomplete. As part of our empirical condition, law cannot be understood as a finite totality; rather, it is non-all. Law changes, adapts, unfolds, and expands in ways that cannot be fully systematized. Any such systematization will produce a remainder, accounting for which opens up our thinking about law anew. Žižek argues that this incompleteness, the fact that law is non-all, allows spaces for something more, something better. As we shall see, Žižek describes this something better as love.

An initial way to grasp Žižek's insight is to think of it as explaining the impossibility of a pure law or an authority that is perfectly just or completely justifiable. What Žižek's approach makes clear is the way law relies on a traumatic stain—an excess or violence. We might think, for example, of the voice of God issuing the Ten Commandments, the revolutionary overthrow of one regime to begin another, and the shock and awe of foreign violence claiming to bring freedom to an enslaved people. In all these instances, law is internally, constitutively divided between irrational command *and* enunciated, potentially reasonable content.

Žižek develops these ideas by working through Lacan's discussion, "Kant *avec* Sade." In this essay, Lacan reads the Kantian moral law in conjunction with the extreme perversity of the Marquis de Sade in order to isolate the superego command to enjoy (a combination we encountered already in the preceding chapter). Žižek finds this reading to be important for its exposure of the way law is split between the external social law and the obscene superego supplement. Hence, he rejects notions of law as a power edifice marked by an excluded other or as a set of norms and institutions that necessarily generate their own transgression. Superego, Žižek argues, is the underside of the social laws that hold together the community.

With this account of superego, Žižek can move beyond contemporary poststructuralist rejections of law to recognize how law provides insight into the excesses and lawlessness, the crime and violence, that inhere in law in the form of superego. The external, public law makes them visible and, potentially, remediable. Even more powerfully, the split in law points to an incompleteness in law that, with work, can be supplemented by love rather than delivered over to the superego injunction to enjoy.

Accordingly, I present Žižek's account of law in three moments: law's founding, law's split, and the love beyond yet within law.

Law's Founding

Where does law come from? Does it come from God, written by divine fire upon tablets of stone? Is it simply the force of custom? Does it arrive when primitive people somehow acquire language and find themselves in a fantastic moment of mutual consent and constitution making? Is it imposed upon people through the shock and awe of a conquering power? Žižek argues that any story of how law came to be is really a story about how law is. More specifically, his account of law's installation is synchronic: founding is always retroactively posited from the standpoint of that which was founded. I focus here on two versions of founding: founding crime and founding law. Here is a brief summary of the argument that follows.

If one understands law as fundamentally split in its very structure or as characterized by a parallax gap, as Žižek does, then accounts of law's founding are attempts to name, narrate, and conceal this gap. To be law, a given legal order must cover over the crime that founds it, but the crime is itself a fantasy construction that functions to conceal the antagonism fissuring the legal order. Žižek explains, "The loop is therefore perfect: the Structure can function only through the occultation of the violence of its founding Event, yet the very narrative of this Event is ultimately nothing but a fantasy destined to resolve the debilitating antagonism/inconsistency of the structuring/synchronous Order."[3] Stories of the violent installation of the law, then, are really stories about a violence that continues to stain and sustain the legal order. Indeed, we should extend Žižek's point here: the primordial gesture of concealment is the move that turns violence into law. The move to conceal produces an indeterminate, chaotic violence as a particular crime that grounds the law rather than a debilitating, ineliminable antagonism that renders law impossible.

Founding violence is not all there is to law. In fact, Žižek attends to the disalienating, the liberating, role of law. A kernel of irrational violence may inhere in law, but this violence does not undermine law's authority. Nor is it opposed to the liberating potential of law. Rather, in this violence, or excess, Žižek locates a condition for the belief that attaches subjects to law. We can neither escape law's traumatic kernel, nor do without it. What ultimately matters is the character of this traumatic excess and our relation to it. Is it an excess that we conceal? Is it one that pushes us to enjoy? Might it be an excess that we can assume directly as we acknowledge that law is both necessary and incomplete?

Founding Crime

In *For They Know Not What They Do*, Žižek writes,

> 'At the beginning' of the law, there is a certain 'outlaw,' a certain Real of violence which coincides with the act itself of the establishment of the reign of law: the ultimate truth about the reign of law is that of a usurpation, and all classical politico-philosophical thought rests on the disavowal of this violent act

of foundation ... this illegitimate violence by which law sustains itself must be concealed at any price because this concealment is the positive condition of the functioning of law: it functions insofar as its subjects are deceived, insofar as they experience the authority of law as authentic and eternal.[4]

Law begins in trauma.[5] From the standpoint of the old law, the violent establishing of something new is crime. The old law is disobeyed, overthrown, transgressed, and usurped. From the standpoint of the new law, this crime is self-negating. It vanishes (or is concealed) as a crime once the new order is constituted. Put differently, the establishment of law overthrows law, for example, the law of custom, the law of nature, or even law as an ideal that only existed at the very moment of its loss. Because establishing is overthrowing, there is a risk: the negation of law. Establishing manifests a disregard for law as it perversely (or criminally) turns crime into law. This paradox, this traumatic identity of law and crime, is the repressed origin of law.

The transition from the Articles of Confederation to the Constitution of the United States well illustrates such a traumatic identity of law and crime.[6] Delegates from the thirteen states had been commissioned to revise the Articles, but when they met in Philadelphia in 1787, they ran away with the convention. Instead of simply altering the Articles, they rewrote them from the bottom up, shifting sovereignty from the states to the people. From the standpoint of their critics, this was a usurpation, an unauthorized transmutation of the government. At least one delegate to the convention worried that it would lead to a civil war.[7]

Supporters of the Constitution acknowledged that in instituting a new government the delegates had exceeded their charge. Indeed, this excess was marked by a fundamental gap in legality, by an illegality or a criminality. The Articles had included a provision for amendment: any change had to be ratified by all thirteen states.

The Constitution, however, held that it only needed to be ratified by nine states. Elbridge Gerry, delegate from Massachusetts, "urged the indecency and pernicious tendency of dissolving, in so slight a manner, the solemn obligations of the articles of confederation. If nine out of thirteen can dissolve the compact, Six out of nine will be just as able to dissolve the new one hereafter."[8] From the standpoint of the Articles, the Constitution was illegal—an installation of illegality endangering the very possibility of law.

In *Federalist* number 40, James Madison fully accepts this gap wherein legality and criminality coincide: "In one particular it is admitted that the convention have departed from the tenor of their commission. Instead of reporting a plan requiring the confirmation *of all the States*, they have reported a plan which is to be confirmed and may be carried into effect by *nine States only*."[9] Madison reads this traumatic moment in which the delegates exceeded their powers as fully warranted by the circumstances— the delegates dared to act, to bring something new into being. He suggests as well a retroactive justification for their actions, a justification that works back from the very Constitution it is supposed to justify, namely "the views and happiness of the people of America," precisely that *people* thereby being constituted.[10]

The paradox of this retroactive justification, this short circuit in which constitution precedes authorization, was recognized—and fought over—at the time. Writing in the *Massachusetts Gazette* in 1788, MASSACHUSETTENSIS observed,

> that should the new constitution be received as it stands, it can never be proved that it originated from any proper state authority; because there is no such authority recognized either in the form of it, or in the mode fixed upon for its ratification. It says, "We the people of the United States," etc., make this constitution; but does this phrase, "We the people of the United States," prove that the people are acting in state character ...?[11]

Asking, does the phrase "we the people" itself ground the claim that the people are actually the originating force of the constitution, MASSACHUSETTENSIS clearly thinks the answer to his question is, "No—the very phrase 'We the people of the United States' proves that the founding was a crime, that the Constitution fundamentally violated the Articles of Confederation." There was neither authority nor people. Both are constituted retroactively as the founding crime is occluded.

Žižek's psychoanalytic account of the traumatic moment of identity between law and crime extends out of Freud's discussion in *Totem and Taboo*. In his well-known myth of the birth of law, Freud draws from Darwin to describe presocietal humans as a primal horde ruled by a violent, jealous father who kept all the females for himself. Hating the father because he "stood so powerfully in the way of their sexual demands and their desire for power," the brothers join together and kill him.[12] This violent killing of the father is more than murder, more than a crime from the impossible but real temporality of *before*.[13] Prior to the overthrow of the father, the sons' access to power and enjoyment is itself criminal and excluded. With the father's death, however, such access becomes the very notion of the rule of law.[14] It is the source of the rights law is invoked to protect, the measure of law, the ideal up to which laws are held. Law is to guarantee this access by limiting it: no one brother will be able to have it all, as the father did; rather, to keep order they will all equally renounce some of their access (the incest prohibition).

We can contrast the primal killing with the liberal social contract. For Žižek, the contract is a fantasy that covers over the brutal advent of the law. The outcome of the social contract—free and equal persons—is posited as one of its prerequisites. How is it, really, that the war of all against all in the Hobbesian state of nature can lead to a decision to give up one's rights and obey a sovereign? The fantasy of rational agreement founds law by concealing the violent move from nature to culture, the traumatic transmutation of the law of nature into sovereign authority. (The violence reappears in contract theory with respect to those who do not consent, who remain "outside" as enemies who can be killed. A similar fear manifested itself in the debate over the U.S. Constitution in the worry that the gap between ratification by thirteen and ratification by nine could lead to civil war: would the dissenting states be forced into Union?)

Žižek emphasizes the Real of founding violence. As with Freud's myth of origins, this Real cannot be reduced to historical facticity; rather, it is Real in the sense that it has to be posited in order to account for the existing notion of law, for the basic form of the legal, social, cultural order. It is an event that has to be presupposed if one is to explain the emergence of the space of the structure of law—an event not unlike the timeless time of Hobbes' state of nature.

For law to function as law, the Real of violence must be concealed. As Žižek explains (with reference to Kant), law's validity requires that we remain within law, that we do not go outside law and emphasize its historical founding.[15] If we do go outside the law, we cannot even see the order as law; its claim to authority becomes just another contingency or act of violence. Žižek is not making a facile point regarding stupid subjects duped by a malevolent legal order. Rather, he is emphasizing the fact that law involves more than arbitrary control. People need a kind of faith in law; they have to believe it (to believe that others believe it) for it to function at all. The fantasy of an original contract, for example, provides something in which people can believe; this fantasy attaches them to law as it conceals the Real of violence. Belief in law is that something extra that distinguishes law from violence, that separates the founding moment of violence from what comes after it.

How is it that people come to believe in law, especially if they are not simply forced or tricked into belief? How does authority come to be invested in law? As I have mentioned, contract theory offers a particular staging of this moment of investiture. By concealing the violence of law in the story of an original authorization, it offers a justification for the violence of which law avails itself. In Locke's *Second Treatise*, for example, persons come together in an original compact to authorize the making of civil laws. They also appeal to the law as that which can protect them, constituting law through this naturalization: it is already there. Both consent and appellation, then, invest law with authority, installing in it that element of faith or attachment that makes it more than violent force. The contingent moment of law's installation is displaced by the necessary advent of the authority of the eternal or the natural—reason, freedom, justice, and so on.

Žižek offers alternative explanations for how the Real of violence that haunts the law can be repressed—for how contingent law can be transformed into something perceived as necessary, eternal, authorized, and transcendent. His most basic explanation for the investment of meaning in law arises out of his reading of Kafka's *Trial* in conjunction with Pascal. In both Kafka and Pascal the idea appears that people cannot accept the fact that law has no authority outside itself, that people have to repress the fact that law is necessary without being true. Žižek argues that the illusion that drives people to believe that truth resides in law can be described by the mechanism of transference: "transference is this supposition of a Truth, of a meaning behind the stupid, traumatic, inconsistent fact of the Law. In other words, 'transference' names the vicious circle of belief: the reasons why we should believe are persuasive only to those who already believe."[16] People repress the violent origins of law by positing a Truth behind law to which they transfer their faith or confidence. Law is law because of this Truth, but people only accept the "because" insofar as they already believe in law. For example, one might posit the Divine as the external ground for law, as that source which gives law its validity. Belief in the Divine is transferred to a belief in law, but if one did not already believe that law was valid, one would not accept this foundation (not to mention the fact that one would have to believe in the Divine as well). Again, the point is that belief is necessary for the reasons for belief to be compelling.

Transference is thus inseparable from reason, especially once reason is situated in the contexts that produce it, or especially when one works, as Žižek does, with a Hegelian conception of reason. Žižek follows Hegel's discussion in *Phenomenology of Spirit,* whereby Reason comes to accept law as law.[17] Reason first considers law in terms of universal principles. In so doing, it comes to appreciate the "contingent content and the possible conflictual nature of these laws." Reason's move from universal principles to contingent content is thus a reflective move from law-giving to law-testing. That is, Reason, second, assesses laws with respect to formal criteria of consistency and universality. Finally, Reason realizes that this testing is an empty, formal procedure detached from the concrete ethical spirit that gives content to law. It comes to grasp that law is law "because it is accepted as a constitutive part of our community's historical tradition."[18] Again, as with transference, reason explains our attachment to law with reference to a prior belief or faith in law. We find reasons convincing because we think others would find them convincing; we believe that others believe.

To be sure, law's claim to reason—or our belief in law, which is the same thing—is never complete. There are always excesses and lacks disrupting even what seems to be accepted as tradition. The Real of violence persists to haunt the legal order. Importantly, however, this Real of violence is also a source of our attachment to law. Our investment in law is libidinal, and law's authority stems from this investment. As we shall see, law is law because we enjoy it.

Founding Law

Since Žižek emphasizes law's unavoidable, Real, violence, one might wonder why he thinks belief in law is important. Why should law be law? Why not reject law altogether—or at least recognize it as an inescapable ideological trap? The answer is, again, that there is more to law than violence. Law provides a degree of liberation and disalienation. Differently put, law can be understood psychoanalytically as a solution to some specific problems, even as it creates new ones. Thus, Žižek provides an account of our attachment to law that emphasizes how law both secures desire and is stained by enjoyment.

I begin with desire. Žižek writes,

> ... the advent of Law entails a kind of "disalienation": in so far as the Other itself appears submitted to the "absolute condition" of Law, the subject is no more at the mercy of the Other's whim, its desire is no more totally alienated in the Other's desire ... In contrast to the "post-structuralist" notion of a law checking, canalizing, alienating, oppressing "Oedipianizing" some previous "flux of desire," Law is here conceived as an agency of "disalienation" and "liberation": it opens our access to desire by enabling us to disengage ourselves from the rule of the Other's whim.[19]

Law frees us from the absolute, arbitrary demands of the Other.[20] In *Totem and Taboo*, once the horde kills the father, they are no longer subject to his violent, obscene, monopoly of enjoyment. They have overthrown not just him, but a subjection rooted in exception—the father was exempt from the demands he made. Now authority itself comes under rules: the reign of the band of brothers is a reign of law, of rules regulating access to women, power, and the use of violence. The end of the brothers' subjection to the father is thus the beginning of their subjection to law. As Peter Fitzpatrick writes, "They are now free but that very freedom becomes the mode of their renewed subjection as they bring the power of the father to bear upon themselves."[21] The reign of law internalizes the authority of the Father; as symbolic law, the Other is brought within, as it were, a movement signified as the Name-of-the-Father. Indeed, Freud emphasizes that in death the father was stronger than he had been in life: "what the father's presence had formerly prevented they themselves [the brothers] now prohibited in the psychic situation of 'subsequent obedience.'"[22] What this means for the brothers, and for us, is that subjection to and liberation through law are the same thing.

We might think again of Hobbes. In the state of nature, "every man has a right to everything; even to one another's body."[23] Each is thus necessarily subject to the needs and demands of the Other. With the advent of law, there is an out, something to turn to that relieves the pressure to conform to these demands. One obeys rational rules, not arbitrary whims. Accordingly, one is no longer an instrument and object of the Other. One now has a space for one's own desire. Law liberates, then, through the production of this space for the subject's desire.

There is a twist, though. The liberating aspect of law is both a "symptom" and implicated in yet another set of arbitrary, punishing demands, those of the superego. First, the image of the omnipotent Other to whose whim one is subject is a fantasy.[24] It is a way for the subject to avoid acknowledging that its desire cannot be satisfied, to avoid facing the fact that the Other does not have the ability to give it what it wants. In Hobbes' state of nature, it simply is not the case that one could have everything one desired were it not for the rights of others. As Hobbes acknowledges, desire is itself always in motion, ceaseless, beyond satisfaction. Law intervenes, then, as "a way for the subject to avoid the impasse constitutive of desire by transforming the inherent *impossibility* of its satisfaction into *prohibition*: as if desire would be possible to fulfill if it were not for the prohibition impeding its free reign."[25] For Hobbes, the sovereign guarantees desire not simply by restraining others but by commanding restraint in general. Law lets the subject think it could get what it wants were it not for law's prohibition. Here law lets the subject avoid the impossible Real of its desire. Our attachment to law is a symptom in that it is a way for us to secure our desire (that is to say, the space for it, not the object of it) by avoiding confrontation with the impossibility of fulfilling it.

We should note further, as Žižek does, the peculiarity of Hobbes' position. The Hobbesian solution does not involve a general internalization of restraint. Rather, restraint remains an external command: the command of the sovereign. Hobbes starts out with egoistic individuals struggling to fulfill their impossible desires and "ends up with the Sovereign who has the unlimited power to dispose of my life, the Sovereign whom I experience not as the extension of my own will, as the personification of my ethical substance, but as an arbitrary foreign force."[26] The all-powerful external sovereign, then, follows directly from Hobbes' emphasis on the egoism of particular ethical subjects, an egoism that itself is not changed or transformed but strictly controlled and subjected.

Accordingly, second, as Freud's account of the sons' internalization of the authority of the father after his death illustrates, the advent of the law is accompanied by a punishing superego, by the obscene underpinnings of law that redouble the "public" law (an idea I develop more thoroughly in the following section).[27] The superego is a kind of enforcer, analogous to the Hobbesian sovereign. What liberates us and what punishes and torments us are the two sides of the same split law. The law that guarantees social order confronts us as if we were already guilty, accusing us in ways that make no sense. Disalienation thus comes at the cost of a constitutive alienation (or disalienation at one level is accompanied by alienation at another). Žižek clarifies this point with reference to what he refers to as the basic paradox of Kantian autonomy: "I am a free and autonomous subject, delivered from the constraints of my pathological nature, precisely and only insofar as my feeling of self-esteem is crushed down by the humiliating pressure of the moral Law."[28] I do not have to remain subject to the unbearable (fantasmatic) pressure of the Other—if I come under the unbearable pressure of the law. My freedom and my guilt are inseparable and interdependent.

The final twist in this initial relation between law and superego is that the external law liberates the subject from the pressure of that very superego demand underpinning law. Superego is unrelenting, placing all sorts of contradictory, impossible demands on us. Law enables the subject to escape from its self-torture, from the plague of conscience, by providing regulations and guidelines. "The external law regulates *pleasures* in order to deliver us from the superegotistical imposition of *enjoyment* which threatens to overflow our daily life."[29] With this twist, Žižek reverses the typical understanding of the inner law as more reliable or as what enables a kind of reflective equilibrium through which to evaluate external social laws. For him, the inner law compels us without mercy; external law relieves us of this compulsion. In the following section, I explore this aspect of law and superego in more detail.

Split Law

If stories of law's founding are stories about the persisting Real of violence in law, stories of how law *is*, then how is law? How, in other words, does this violence persist, and what is its relation to split law? I take up these questions by considering violence as a surplus and as a lack. In so doing, I emphasize how violence persists as superego, that is, as the punishing, powerful, obscene, dead father killed by the primal horde.

Surplus

As a nonintegrated surplus, violence gives law the form of an injunction, rendering law as that which is to be obeyed. Law is constitutively senseless: it is obeyed not because it is good, just, or beneficial, but because it is law. We might understand the wide array of competing explanations of law's authority as exemplifying this constitutive senselessness; even as philosophers disagree on the grounds of law, they agree that law is law. As Žižek explains, "The last foundation of the Law's authority lies in its process of enunciation."[30] Law is not only force or brute pressure, but nor is it something we are convinced to obey, something we obey because of a ground outside of law (this would be the transference explanation for law's authority). Rather, we obey the incomprehensible Command. This traumatic, nonintegrated character of law is a positive condition of law.[31]

This traumatic, senseless injunction is also the psychoanalytic notion of the superego. Superego issues unconditional commands, telling us what to do, refusing to take no for an answer, refusing even to consider our specific circumstances, needs, or desires. Moreover, as Bruce Fink explains, the severity of the superego "is actually a vehicle for *jouissance* … The superego commands us to satisfy our drives, oddly—and no doubt to some extent counterintuitively—commanding us to satisfy that sadistic Other within us, the superego."[32] The superego command is thus more than a simple prohibition. It is a prohibition compliance with which produces enjoyment. When we obey the superego, when we give up our own desire and comply or follow orders, a part of us, or, more precisely the Other within us, enjoys. Fink writes, "Whenever we force ourselves to conform to our ideals at the expense of our own satisfaction, we assure the Other's jouissance."[33] Superego thus involves the excess of law, the violence that persists in law's injunction.

More crudely put, obeying the law, "just following orders," can be an excuse for getting off. Frederick Douglass's graphic account of the "savage barbarity" of the overseer of the slaves at Great House Farm, provides a particularly powerful example of the *jouissance* of duty: "when he whipped, he seemed to do from a sense of duty, and feared no consequences."[34]

Because superego involves this absolute injunction, the content of its commands shifts and changes. This makes a perverse sort of sense when we recall that it gets off on making us squirm and feel guilty and horrible for not being able to do what it wants. Important for Žižek is the way that in today's more permissive societies, the superego injunction to enjoy accompanies a duty to be happy. He writes, "The superego is thus the properly obscene reversal of the permissive 'You may!' into the prescriptive 'You must!', the point at which permitted enjoyment turns into ordained enjoyment."[35] We must have great sex lives, fulfilling jobs, interesting hobbies, fantastic vacations. If we do not, we have somehow failed. We are guilty—inadequate. By attending to the superego supplement of law, Žižek thus enables us to grasp how it is the case that what might appear at law's retreat, as law's securing of a larger realm of personal choice and privacy, comes up against a crippling impasse of unfreedom—the command to enjoy that effectively prevents us from enjoying, entwining us in guilt and uncertainty.

Lack

In addition to the violence that appears in the form of law as an injunction, there is a violence that persists as a lack. Žižek considers two lacks in law: incompleteness and inconsistency.[36] Incompleteness involves the way law is never grounded in truth; it is necessary without being true. Hence, there is no fundamental Other who grounds the law or who can shore up the law and integrate or redeem its founding violence. The lack that is inconsistency appears in the way law is a sort of collection that is never fully systematized; the law is not whole or not all insofar as its own structuring principle escapes it. No matter how far it stretches or reaches, there is something beyond it.

Superego, specifically as it manifests itself in the obscene, "nightly," law, fills up these lacks. "Superego emerges where the Law—the public Law, the Law articulated in public discourse—fails; at this point of failure, the public Law is compelled to search for support in an *illegal* enjoyment."[37] Because of law's incompleteness and inconsistency, public rules are not enough. They have to be supplemented by a clandestine unwritten code—by fantasy.

Enough for what? This "enough" seems to refer to problems of *attachment* and *ambiguity*. Superego addresses both problems. In this way, we might think of superego as an aspect of Žižek's account of law in which he sets out some of the imbrications of law and society. That is, Žižek rejects that legal formalism that views law as a sealed system of rules abstracted from society. He rejects as well that legal positivism that finds a meaning to inhere in law apart from the customs, fantasies, and faith that inspire it.[38] Rather, Žižek accepts that law alone cannot hold a community together; cohesion, or attachment, requires a supplement. There needs to be a way to bridge the gap between the rules and principles presenting themselves as law and the behaviors and actions of those subject to law. What induces people to obey, particularly if they have desires and interests that would seem to compel them to disobey?

Žižek's account of the superego supplement to law addresses this classic problem in political theories of obligation. For Žižek, superego "represents the 'spirit of community' at its purest, exerting the strongest pressure on the individual to comply with its mandate of group identification."[39] Communitarian approaches to political obligation typically emphasize shared values as key to understanding group identity. In contrast, Žižek argues that what really binds a community together, what really tells people they are members of the same group, is not their knowing what laws to follow but their knowing what laws to break. Attachment to community comes about through identification with the suspension or transgression of the law—not through identification with positive affirmations of value.[40] Žižek's examples include the "nightly" law of the Ku Klux Klan in the American south, the military's sadistic hazing rituals, and the excess of violence that underlies the precise rules setting out the procedures of the Nazi extermination camps. He includes the torture of Iraqi prisoners by American soldiers at Abu Ghraib prison in this series as well, explaining:

> This is why the assurance from US Army command that no "direct orders" were issued to humiliate and torture the prisoners is ridiculous: of course they were not, since, as everyone who knows army life is aware, this is not how such things are done. There are no formal orders, nothing is written, there is just unofficial pressure, hints and directives are delivered in private, the way one share a dirty secret … in being submitted to humiliating tortures, the Iraqi prisoners were in effect *initiated into American culture*, they got the taste of its obscene underside which forms the necessary supplement to the public values of personal dignity, democracy, and freedom.[41]

Žižek's emphasis on "nightly" thus highlights the way certain practices may be common and well-known, indeed, seen as necessary for the continuation of the community, even as they are not to be exposed to the light of day and even as they are formally disavowed.

Super Cannes, a novel by J.G. Ballard, provides a particularly vivid account of the role of nightly law in the securing of community.[42] Ballard describes a perfect executives' paradise where every need is met so that high-powered scientists and financiers can devote themselves to their work with no distractions. The problem is that the executives start becoming ill, listless, depressed, and distracted. Profits and stock values decline. The solution, introduced by the center's psychiatrist, is crime, violence, and cruelty. Prescribing psychopathology, he organizes the executives into "therapy groups" that go out on weekend rampages in which they brutalize immigrants, prostitutes, and local Arabs. Trying to convince the narrator, Paul, that "a controlled psychopathy is a way of resocializing people and tribalizing them into mutually supportive groups," the psychiatrist, Wilder Penrose, enjoins him to remember childhood: "... like all of us you stole from the local supermarket. It was deeply exciting, and enlarged your moral sense of yourself. But you were sensible, and kept it down to one or two afternoons a week. The same rules apply to society at large .... A voluntary and sensible psychopathy is the only way we can impose a shared moral order."[43] The psychiatrist installs in the community its missing superego injunction to enjoy. He commands—in the contemporary, medical sense of prescribing—the executives to commit the acts inspiring their most violent and sexual fantasies.

This enjoinment to cruelty redoubles that excess of enjoyment that attaches the executives to their community. They get to be cruel and violent because they are instructed to—"just following orders"—and their resulting sense of guilt binds them ever more strongly to the law. On the one hand, they rationalize their behavior, thereby strengthening the element of superego: "In many ways we're carrying out tasks the police would do anyway, and we free them for other duties."[44] On the other, they feel themselves more deeply tied to their community because of their guilt, because of their newly awakened moral sensibility. Crime has enabled them to know themselves as members of a community. As the psychiatrist explains, "Remember that these criminal activities have helped them to rediscover themselves. An atrophied moral sensibility is alive again. Some of my patients even feel guilty, a revelation to them ..."[45]

In *The Plague of Fantasies*, Žižek develops another aspect of the unwritten rules that supplement the public law. This aspect attends to the ambiguity of law. Law is ambiguous. Something always escapes law. Some unforeseen circumstance or condition confronts what seems to be the formal character of law with the fantasies that animate it, which push it one way or another.[46] Žižek views these fantasies in terms of the unwritten rules preventing the actualization of the choices formally allowed by the system.[47] Such rules are transgressive insofar as they violate the explicit rules. At the same time, the unwritten rules are coercive insofar as they prohibit the possibilities that the public law guarantees. The complexities of sexual harassment illustrate this ambiguity. On the one hand, persistently extending unrequited sexual advances to a person in one's workplace is transgressive; it breaks the rules, and one may even enjoy this element of violation. We could even imagine a kind of solidarity emerging among those who, in a given workplace, wallow in their shared willingness to go beyond political correctness. On the other hand, the unrequited sexual advances damage those advanced upon, preventing them from performing in the workplace in accordance with the official rules. Similarly, if we return to the idea that this nightly domain is a domain of fantasy, we can see that if the letter of the law guarantees blacks the right to vote, the superego supplement to the law—the Ku Klux Klan—says no they cannot.

This understanding of the violence of the demanding superego is central to Žižek's reading of Kant (or, more precisely, of his reading of Lacan's reading of Kant). In several places, Žižek revisits the theme of Sade as the truth of Kant already explored by Horkheimer and Adorno in *The Dialectic of Enlightenment*.[48] At stake is an equivalence between the Kantian moral law and the superego: both reject contingent feelings, emphasize pain, and rely on cold, unconditional injunctions that compel the subject to "sacrifice his attachment to all contingent, 'pathological' objects—*Do your duty! Enjoy!*"[49]

To get to the radical dimension of Kant's account of morality, to the way the categorical imperative provides an excessive cut through the attachments and experiences constitutive of everyday life, Žižek emphasizes how Sade makes visible the specific, excessive position of the law's executor. The perverse Sadeian torturer has no regard for people or feelings; his only goal is to push as far as possible, to see whether he can commit an act so abhorrent that it would transgress the laws of nature themselves. The Kantian moral law is similar in that it, too, persists beyond nature, in an other realm indifferent to the laws of the nature. Yet, precisely because the Sadeian torturer carries out his debaucheries in the empirical realm, we can recognize in this figure a position Kant's account occludes: the executor of the law. That is, Kant presents the moral law as a law one gives oneself. The subject authors and obeys the moral law. Indeed, to obey a law one authors is the very notion of autonomy. But how are the positions of author of and subject to law to be mediated? How does one move between one and the other? Kant does not tell us. Žižek, following Lacan, argues that the Sadean sadist-executioner, that is to say, the super-ego, provides the bridge between the dimension of the universal law and the empirical subject.[50] More specifically, Sade introduces the executor, or executioner, as a kind of pathological object into the Kantian subject as its necessary support. The superego commands the subject to follow the law. It is the instrument or object attaching the subject to the law it authors.

Žižek's emphasis on the Sadeian executioner as a stain on the moral law complicates the traditional distinction between obedience to the letter of the law and obedience to a higher law of conscience. Superego provides a "short circuit" insofar as the very allegiance to something higher is stained by enjoyment—claiming this allegiance enables the subject to procure enjoyment, to get that thrill of entering a hidden domain.[51] (I am reminded here of Oliver North during the Iran-Contra hearings and his perverse satisfaction in serving his country covertly.) This very short circuit points to the capriciousness of the Kantian law: insofar as it remains stained by the absolute command, the command that holds no matter what, it is indistinguishable from the perverse vagaries of Sade's torturer.

Nevertheless, Sade is not the whole truth of Kant. In fact, Žižek argues that Sade is less the truth of Kant than he is a symptom of Kant's inability to push his thought to the limit.[52] Admittedly, if one thinks of Kant as providing an apparatus that enables us to figure out what our duty is (is what we want to do universalizable?), then there is no difference between the injunctions to "do your duty" and "enjoy." Why? Because duty can provide an excuse that allows one to get off without taking responsibility: "Oh, I didn't intend to harm or humiliate anyone; I was doing it for the good of the community, for their own good …. I was just doing my duty" (as in the example from Ballard's *Super Cannes*). Procuring enjoyment and obeying the law are the same thing; the law is stained with this obscene supplement. This very stain provides the ground for our obedience—*we must do our duty … no matter what!* Yet if we read Kant as saying simply *that* one should do one's duty, then the subject him or herself must take responsibility for determining what that duty is, for translating the injunction into a concrete obligation. This is where desire itself can meet the criterion of a Kantian ethical act. To act on one's desire then requires the utmost bravery and responsibility. Rather than following the dictates of the superego, rather than relying on it to bridge the gap between the universal law and our empirical place, we make ourselves into an object, acting without the assurance of recourse to duty.

Such bravery and responsibility is rare and difficult. Superego demands obedience and enjoyment, transgression and compliance, staining everything with its obscene excess. If the official rules demand racial tolerance, superego demands our vigilance in the face of irremedial racist guilt. At the same time, the truth of racist guilt, the racism that persists and flourishes through and in the face of official tolerance, creates racist solidarities; our racist jokes become transgressive, permission to break the rules, submission to the injunction "Enjoy!" Accordingly, under conditions of radical indeterminacy and incompleteness, under conditions of cynicism toward and detachment from law, the obscene superego underpinnings of law rise to the fore, taking over or overtaking the letter of the law.

Again, Ballard provides a great example. Paul, the narrator of *Super Cannes*, investigates the wild crimes of the rampaging executives, but what hooks him in are his own sexual fantasies—fantasies of sex with young girls. These fantasies lure him into not simply investigating the crimes, but participating in them, going along for the ride. Paul watches his wife slide into drug addiction and a complex acquiescence to an increasingly degrading sexual relationship with a powerful couple in the executives' complex (they prostitute her and make her available to be raped by a man she loathes). He rides in a car as someone is chased down and killed. Like the psychiatrist, Paul justifies his own violence as the cure for the community's ills.

Enjoying Law

The violence of law persists as superego. It is punishing *and* permissive, disciplinary *and* obscene, telling us to get off even as it constrains us. It appears as surplus and lack. How should all this be understood? In a nutshell, the answer is that the violence of law persists in the hail that interpellates the legal subject.

Discussing Louis Althusser's theory of the subject, Žižek argues that prior to ideological recognition, we have an intermediate moment of obscure, impenetrable interpellation without identification.[53] We might understand this as an answer to the question of how it is that the subject answers the ideological call at all. Why, in other words, does the subject assume a symbolic mandate and recognize itself as the subject of Power? Žižek answers by saying that this assumption alleviates the impasse in which the subject finds itself. For example, the individual's reaction to the policeman's "Hey, you there!" is a mixture of innocence—why me? What does the policeman want with me?—and abstract guilt, a feeling that before Power I am guilty but do not know why or of what and that this very ignorance is no doubt proof of my guilt.[54] The subject, in other words, does not know what the Other wants from him. As Žižek writes,

> So we are again at the tension between the public Law and its obscene superego underside: the ideological recognition in the call of the Other is the act of identification, of identifying oneself as the subject of the public Law, of assuming one's place in the symbolic order; whereas the abstract, indeterminate "guilt" confronts the subject with an impenetrable call that precisely prevents identification, recognition of one's symbolic mandate. The paradox here is that the obscene superego underside is, in one and the same gesture, the necessary support of the public symbolic Law and the traumatic vicious circle, the impasse the subject endeavors to avoid by way of taking refuge in public law—in order to assert itself, public law has to resist its own foundation, to render it invisible.[55]

We feel guilty without knowing why, indeed, precisely because we do not know why (and because of our repressed unconscious desires). To escape from guilt, we identify ourselves as subjects of law. Law delivers us from our guilty feelings, providing us with a way out. The law can tell us what to do so that we do not have to remain tormented by the uncertainties and doubts and unyielding commands of the superego.[56] Ultimately, then, the public law gets its energy—its force, its kick, its investment—from these guilty feelings. Conversely, without the tormenting superego, there would be no law. Put somewhat differently, without the tormenting uncertainties generated by the superego there would be no motivation to respond to the ideological hail and therefore no interpellation of a legal subject. Authority would not be constituted through such a response.

We can summarize the parallax gap in law between the public letter and its superego supplement as follows:

1. Superego is an excessive object inhering in law, the source of the command that mediates between the subject and the author of law. This addresses the issue of the form of law as we see it in the discussion of Kant with Sade.
2. Superego supports public law as the enjoyment that gives people the incentive to do their duty. This addresses the question of our attachment to law, of the enjoyment we can get through doing our duty.
3. Superego supports public law as the obscene, nightly, transgressions that fill in its gaps with fantasy. This addresses the ambiguity in the letter of the law and the way a community is held together through the knowledge of which rules to break.
4. Superego supports public law insofar as the public law provides a release from superego's unyielding demands. This addresses the interpellation of the legal subject.

The question, then, is whether there can be a law that does not rely on its superego supplement. Are we to remain caught within a cycle of superego demanding enjoyment, law providing relief from this demand, yet generating its own transgressive supplements, which then cloud any capacity to know whether we should obey the rules or not—or even what the rules are? As I explain in the following section, for Žižek, this cycle is not all there is. Love provides a way to escape it.

Love With Law

Žižek draws from Saint Paul to consider how it might be possible to "cut into the Gordian knot of the vicious cycle of Law and its founding Transgression."[57] Is there a law and a relation to law that is not mediated by superego? I approach these questions in terms of the four aspects of the superego support of law mentioned above. In place of the superego as the object mediating between the empirical subject and the universal law, Žižek posits *objet petit a*, the nugget of enjoyment supporting and displacing the subject (as we saw in Chapter One). In place of enjoyment in doing one's duty, Žižek offers enjoyment through love. In place of the obscene transgressions of the nightly law, Žižek suggests a community of believers in a cause. In place of the interpellation of the legal subject, Žižek asserts the vitality of the engaged activist. To introduce Žižek's attempt to escape from the dialectic of law and its transgression, I take up his engagement with Giorgio Agamben's reading of Paul's letter to the Romans in *The Time That Remains*.[58]

Agamben focuses his discussion of the letter to the Romans on Paul's account of law in messianic time and on the new collectivity, or "remnant," that Paul theorizes as the messianic Christian community. Briefly put, Agamben argues for the relevance of Paul's account of messianic time insofar as it draws out the indeterminacies and indistinctions that mark law in the state of an exception, a state Agamben finds at work in the Nazi extermination camps and persisting today in legal arguments for the war on terror as a state of emergency. In the state of exception, it is not clear whether law is being transgressed or upheld. The Nazi death camps were both sites from which the rule of law was radically absent, suspended, and sites allowed for and established through law. To use a contemporary example, when an American president authorizes the surveillance of American citizens in the absence of a warrant, is he violating their civil liberties or upholding his constitutional obligation to protect the people? These examples demonstrate how, in the state of exception, one cannot distinguish between the inside and outside of the law. The outside, the exception, is brought in, declared by law to be the state of things. The very suspension of law is declared to be lawful. How then might one determine whether a specific act is within the law or outside it?

Agamben takes the view that these same indeterminacies and indistinctions characterize Paul's account of messianic time. For Paul, the messiah ushers in the future, a future in which the law is fulfilled and in being fulfilled rendered inoperative. Agamben thus interprets the Pauline law of a faith that holds in messianic time as a law that surpasses legal obligations.[59] In this time, law may be available for use, but it is not binding; it has no hold on those bound in and through faith. We might understand this in terms of grace, a grace that exceeds relations of contract and exchange to persist as the potential for a goodness or generosity that is freely extended but never exhausted, never completed, and never encapsulated in an injunction or command.

The remnant is Paul's version of the new messianic community. Agamben argues that Paul confronts the separation between Jew and non-Jew on which Jewish law is premised with a new division, a new cut that divides this division into non-Jew and non–non-Jew. This operation "divides the divisions of the law themselves and renders them inoperative, without ever reaching any final ground. No universal man, no Christian can be found in the depths of the Jew or the Greek, neither as a principle nor as an end; all that is left is a remnant and the impossibility of the Jew or the Greek to coincide with himself."[60] The non–non-Jew figures a new universality, the universality of the remnant. This universality is thus non-all, that of a people that can never be fully identified with themselves or in opposition to another. Finding the remnant politically valuable as a way to think anew about questions of the people and the political subject, Agamben writes, "The people is neither the all nor the part, neither the majority nor the minority. Instead, it is that which can never coincide with itself, as all or as part, that which infinitely remains or resists each division, and, with all due respect to those who govern us, never allows us to be reduced to a majority or minority."[61]

Žižek accepts Agamben's discussion of the remnant, reading it in terms of his own preferred Hegelian logic of "reflexive determination" wherein the remainder is the excessive element giving body to the whole and confronting the whole (or conventional universality) with a more radical universality. For both, the remnant points to the possibility of a universal collectivity that arises as a result of a division.[62] Yet, as I explain below, unlike Agamben, Žižek views this remnant as a fighting, partisan collective bound together through adherence to a cause. Žižek qualifies further Agamben's account of the indeterminacies and indistinctions of law in messianic time and in the state of exception, pointing out that they are better understood as another version of the law's superego underside.[63] As we have seen, superego functions as the obscene supplement to the law that transgresses the letter of the law and in so doing limits law's application. Consequently, Žižek asks whether it makes sense to see the Pauline law of faith as the obverse of the obscene supplement. Is Paul's account of love, his fulfillment and overcoming of the law, really just the other side of the superego coin? Žižek's answer is no and this leads to his argument against Agamben.

Žižek rejects Agamben's version of the Pauline suspension of the law, arguing that the idea of an empty, abstract law of faith that disinterestedly uses available law while remaining itself a kind of pure potentiality is not Paul's. Rather, "In Paul, the distance is not that of a disengaged observer aware of the nullity of worldly passions, but that of a thoroughly engaged fighter who ignores distinctions that are not relevant to the struggle."[64] For Žižek, Paul is a revolutionary, an actor putting his commitment to truth actively to work.[65] Reading Paul as "Christianity-in-becoming," as a vanishing mediator between institutionalized Judaism and institutionalized Christianity, Žižek observes how little attention

Paul pays to Jesus as a living person. What matters to Paul is that Jesus "died on the Cross and rose from the dead—after confirming Jesus's death and resurrection, Paul goes on to his true Leninist business, that of organizing the new party called the Christian community."[66] Pauline engagement means that Paul's law of faith is not simply a suspension that uses law while remaining unbound by it. The love Paul advocates involves active work and struggle. Pauline love, then, does not suspend law per se. It suspends law's superego supplement, the obscene prescriptions that tell us when and how to follow the law, that limit and determine law's applications.[67] These fantasies and the sustaining acts of violence are the real crime of law—as law itself enables us to see.

Žižek also makes this same argument from a different direction. What are the conditions under which law appears as constraint or irrational injunction? Kant has already answered this question: the moral law appears as a constraint from the perspective of a natural or phenomenal realm, from our perspective as embedded in the attachments, in the loves and desires constitutive of who we are in the world we experience. For Žižek, this means law appears to us as an external imposition to the extent that we hold onto an exceptional place beyond law, that is, to the possibility of a special core or precious treasure that law cannot touch, that does not come under the law. Only when this treasure is relinquished, only when we submit it to the rule of law, does law lose its brutal, alienating character. From Žižek's perspective, Agamben's reading of the Pauline suspension remains trapped in an account of law as a barrier to enjoyment, as a violent imposition that remains itself permeated by enjoyment (and hence necessarily unobservable, indeterminate and indistinct).[68] Such a reading proceeds as if law did not itself express or reveal the possibility of a disentanglement from enjoyment or a distance from violence.

To my mind, Žižek's argument becomes clearer if analogized to Jean-Jacques Rousseau's version of the social compact. Rousseau describes an act of association such that each member gives all of his rights to the community, retaining nothing. Describing this "complete alienation," Rousseau writes, "Since each has made surrender of himself without reservation, the resultant conditions are the same for all ... whoso gives himself to all gives himself to none."[69] As they come fully into the community and under the community as sovereign, each associate member becomes subject and free at once. Were they to retain an interest outside the community, they would lose this freedom, confronting instead the violent instability of their natural condition. There is thus no part of the subject that does not come under the law, no space of exception that would suspend the law. To be sure, there are limits to the analogy with Rousseau, the most important of which is that Rousseau is suggesting the model for a limited polity, for a nation or city (actually, he says his idea could really only work on the island of Corsica). In Rousseau's version, then, the citizen mediates between the sovereign and the subject, and precisely because this citizenship is in a state, it relies on an outside, on an external limit. Nevertheless, the analogy helps clarify the idea that a full submission to the law is a way beyond or through law's brutal injunction or the obscenity of the exception. It reminds us as well of precedents for such an argument in political theory.

Žižek argues that Pauline love involves full immersion in the law. It is a stance toward law from within law, from a place that posits no outside into which one might fantasize escape. One fully accepts one's place within the law—opening up the possibility of hope and change from within. Such an immersion transforms law from a field held in place by an exception into a field that is non-all (in the sense that it cannot be totalized or completed). Žižek develops this idea by appealing to Paul's famous treatment of love in the thirteenth chapter of his letter to the Corinthians (also addressed by Lacan in *The Ethics of Psychoanalysis*):

If I speak in the tongues of mortals and of angels, but do not have love, I am a noisy gong or a clanging cymbal. And if I have prophetic powers, and understand all mysteries and all knowledge, and if I have all faith, so as to move mountains, but do not have love, I am nothing ...

Love never ends. But as for prophecies, they will come an end; as for tongues, they will cease; as for knowledge, it will come to an end. For we know only in part, and we prophesy only in part; but when the complete comes, the partial will come to an end ... For now we see in a mirror, dimly, but then we will see face to face. Now I know only in part; then I will fully, even as I have been fully known.[70]

Žižek points out that in these passages knowledge appears as both complete and incomplete. Confronted with love, knowledge of everything is incomplete. Love thus marks an incompleteness or lack in something that otherwise might seem complete. Love is not an exception to knowledge; rather, it is the point where knowledge is non-all.[71] The fulfillment of the law that Paul announces with the coming of the messiah, then, does not involve supplementing law with love and grace, or completing it and in so doing overcoming it, as Agamben suggests. Rather, in Žižek's view this fulfillment involves full surrender to the law, with no exception. This full surrender to law changes one's subjective perspective toward law, rendering law non-all. Law cannot be completed; it cannot cover, direct, or determine everything (indeed, as we saw in the example from Stalin, the very presumption of determining *everything*—including tractor repair—indicates a lack of authority, authority's pathetic, paranoid obverse). Full alienation to the law transforms one's experience of law away from that of a brutal, alien compulsion to that which the subject simply accepts as a condition for getting on with what really matters. That there is no part of me that is not subject to law thus means that I no longer experience law as an "ought" or constraint, again, as Kant has already made clear. Law is part of the condition in which I am. It is incomplete, non-all, available for use and transformation.

Does the account of a revolutionary collective clash with the idea of full immersion in the law? Is Žižek saying that revolutionaries are limited by the law, that they can never go outside the law or break the law, or that law limits their sphere of action? No. These sorts of questions retreat back into a logic of law and its exception. As they posit an outside, they presume a completeness of law at odds with the notion that law is non-all. For Žižek, law may be used by a fighting collective, but such a collective does not ground or base its action in law. It bases its action fully in itself (as I explain in more detail in the concluding chapter). We should also recall here the way that law as non-all reminds us of the multiplicity of and within law: the distinctions between the moral law and legal regulations, between state and canon law, and between the public law and superego. From this perspective, it makes no sense to treat one version of legality (say, state law) as the only one relevant in a situation—a point already well established in traditional liberalism as a right to revolt. Again, it is vital to admit that even here, in the case of such a right, Žižek's position is that working within the law in no way means that law is the ground for an action; to posit such a ground would reintroduce enjoyment into the law in that one uses duty to justify one's act, rather than acting because one must or because one cannot do otherwise.[72]

Žižek sometimes exemplifies this point of an immersion in the law that traverses the superego fantasy with the idea of sticking to the letter of the law. To this end he reads the complexities of Jewish law not as some Christians or anti-Semites would, that is, as a kind of haggling over details in order to escape or avoid the "truth" of God's commandment, but as the proper version of a law that does not rely on a superego supplement; the truth is not hidden behind the law in some esoteric other meaning but fully present in the text of the law (he illustrates this point with reference to the practice of a kibbutz outside Tel Aviv where pigs are raised on a platform three feet off the ground so as not to violate the injunction against raising pigs on the land of Israel).[73] There is no need to agonize over the law or to worry about whether one has the proper spirit when one is observing it. Instead, one simply follows it to the letter, thereby shaking off the sense of brutal compulsion.

Other examples of keeping to the letter of the law might include working to rule. Here, workers stop doing all the "extras" that come attached to their jobs, strictly observing the terms of their contracts. They arrive exactly on time and leave exactly on time—no matter what. One might imagine a bus driver closing the doors in the faces of a line of commuters in order to follow the schedule to the letter or shop clerks painstakingly filling out form after form as customers wait ever so impatiently around them. We could think of teachers and coaches allowing their students' bodily excretions to remain on the floors of classrooms and gyms—they were not hired to clean up. What these examples make clear is the way sticking to the letter opens up a range of activity, a range of freedom. The worker is fully submitted to the law, and this very submission is a way to contest arrangements that, seemingly legal, rely on law's superego supplement.

I will use my kids as one last example. The literalism of children can be maddening—particularly to a harried mother who might say "put the milk in the television" when she means "in the refrigerator." When my son was seven, he would emphasize the literal meaning of everything I said. For him, the results were liberating. So, I would say, "We need to run to the store." His response: "I don't want to run." Me: "I don't mean run, I mean walk." Him: "But you said run and I don't want to run."

This discussion of Žižek's response to and difference from Agamben with respect to Paul, law, and love points to the idea of the remnant and to Žižek's reading of Paul as a kind of revolutionary institutionalizer. It emphasizes the idea that Pauline love fulfills the law as it renders law non-all. I turn now to the four aspects of the superego supplement to law in order to show how Žižek draws on Paul to suggest a way out of the cycle of law and its transgression.

The Object in Law: From Superego to Objet Petit a

As I explained above, Žižek views superego as mediating between the subject as the author of law and the subject as one subjected to law. When nothing is withheld from law, when the subject comes fully under the law, there is no need for this mediating figure. The law does not appear as a brutal imperative. It is simply what one does—as Kant and Rousseau already make clear.

How is it possible for the subject to relinquish everything? One possible model is Bartleby the Scrivener. Žižek defends Bartleby politics as opening up a place in law by subtracting from law its superego supplement. Bartleby's gesture of refusal, his "I would prefer not to," figures the complete displacement or destitution of the subject. Bartleby is nearly inhuman, basically an "inert, insistent, impassive being" rendered into a maddening object.[74] Insofar as Bartleby does not simply negate, insofar as he affirms a non-predicate, his politics is more than resistance. It steps away from dependence on a Master and from a dynamic of compliance, guilt, and transgression. Bartleby politics responds to the parallax gap in law by keeping it open as a minimal difference "between the set of social regulations and the void of their absence."[75] Thus, Žižek describes Bartleby's refusal as "what remains of the supplement to the Law when its place is emptied of all its obscene superego content."[76] The place is emptied, but it remains as a place, a gap. Bartleby's withdrawal, his preference not to, suggests precisely this emptiness.

Žižek also sometime describes the relinquishing of everything (subjective destitution) as "shooting oneself in the foot" or "sacrificing what is in one more than oneself" (ideas I mention briefly in Chapter Three). Žižek's examples include Keyser Soeze in Bryan Singer's 1995 film, *The Usual Suspects*. Played by Kevin Spacey, Soeze is a mysterious criminal figure who, upon finding his wife and child held at gunpoint by rival criminals, first kills his wife and child and then pursues the other criminals and their families to their deaths. By killing his own family, Soeze escapes the false choice (there was no way for him to save them) presented in the situation, gaining the freedom to act. Having lost everything, he has nothing left to lose.

Žižek's more powerful example is Sethe, the former slave who murders her own child to save her from slavery, in Toni Morrison's *Beloved*. The child, Beloved, was the most precious core of Sethe's being. For this precious thing, this part of Sethe that was in her more her than herself, death was preferable to life in slavery. Morrison writes,

> That anybody white could take your whole self for anything that came to mind. Not just work, kill, or maim you, but dirty you. Dirty you so bad you couldn't like yourself anymore. Dirty you so bad you forgot who you were and couldn't think it up. And though she and others lived through and got over it, she could never let it happen to her own. The best thing she was, was her children. Whites might dirty *her* all right, but not her best thing, her beautiful magical best thing—the part of her that was clean.[77]

These examples have their drawbacks. In them, the sacrifice of "what is in one more than oneself" is actually the sacrifice of someone else. These others may well be those closest to or most like one's self, so they fill in as substitutes for that which one sacrifices in oneself, giving it material form. Even less fortunate is the way that in these examples the bodies are feminine and infantile, sacrifices, in a way, of the maternal as well as of the future.

Nevertheless, the examples work as imaginings of acts that momentarily suspend the contours of a given situation, to open it up to the possibility that things might be otherwise, that our very criteria for what counts as fair and right can change. Indeed, Morrison notes in *Beloved* that infanticide came to be rearticulated not in terms of the savagery of slaves but in terms of the brutality of the very institution of slavery.[78] Žižek's point is that radical acts like Sethe's and Keyser Soeze's collapse the gap between the ethical and the political. Rather than holding onto some ethical moment as the limit or exception to the political, the act suspends the limit or exception in a political gesture par excellence.

Crucial to Žižek's account of this suspension is the way the sacrifice of the object (*objet petit a*), that is, of one's special treasure, one's uniqueness, or "own best thing," is a sacrifice through which the subject itself becomes or takes the place of the object. He writes, "It is not so much that, in the act, I 'sublate/integrate' the Other; it is rather that, in the act, I directly 'am' the impossible Other-Thing."[79] The idea is that in the act, I am not responding to an ethical injunction or call from another; I am not trying to make the will of the Other into my own; hence, superego is not involved. I am not confronting the Other as a kind of frightening, Real, Thing, someone unfathomable and barely recognizable as human within the terms of the situation. Instead, through my sacrifice of my own best thing, I become this Thing, this unrecognizable entity, a kind of object splitting the situation, a compulsion (much like Bartleby). It is not that I am compelled, that there is part of me remaining and responding to a set of given conditions; I am compulsion, changing these conditions. To do this, I have to abandon or sacrifice that which makes me who I am. Differently put, the symbolic determinations of my identity simply do not matter.

Recalling Žižek's critique of multiculturalism discussed in the preceding chapter may be of some help here. As I pointed out, Žižek rejects the way identity politics urges that each difference be tolerated, that each particularity be respected and acknowledged. We can connect this position to his account of law. When law is called upon to acknowledge differences rooted in identity, not only does this effect a profound depoliticization but it also presumes that this difference precedes law and hence demands a response from law. I appeal to law to acknowledge my femininity, for example, treating this as my own best thing. To the extent that law fails in recognizing this femininity, particularly in the way I want it to, I will experience law as a violent imposition. So will others who find law's recognition of my femininity an imposition on their beliefs, convictions, ethnicity, or sense of personhood. Thus, Žižek turns to the Pauline idea that in Christ there is neither Greek nor Jew, male nor female. There is instead a new division that cuts through all others. Returning to the example of law and femininity, we might think of this as law becoming not more detailed and determined but more abstract and responsive as it replaces a division like "masculine" and "non-masculine" with "non-masculine" and "non–non-masculine." The sacrifice of specificity, of one's own best thing, then, can be understood in terms of a move away from a vision of law in terms of its exception and toward an understanding of law as non-all.

Attachment to Law: From Enjoyment Through Duty to Enjoyment in Love

As we have seen, superego attaches the subject to law through the enjoyment of doing one's duty. Doing our duty can be a way that we get off. Under communicative capitalism, moreover, subjects confront a duty to enjoy. We are perpetually confronted with the injunction to have it all, consume, be better than we thought we could be, and enjoy! Yet this very injunction turns into its opposite insofar as unconstrained pleasure is a danger: enjoy food! (but be careful about too much fat and sugar); enjoy partying with your friends! (but do not take drugs, do not smoke, and limit your intake of alcohol); enjoy sex! (but make sure you use a condom and have secured full consent for everything); enjoy the diversity of a multicultural society! (but make sure no one offends anyone else and that the practices of each culture respect the individual choices of all persons). Accordingly, Žižek views biopolitics as a necessary corollary to the contemporary capitalist arrangement of expert knowledge. The subject is a kind of biopolitical object, the object of technocratic and administrative advice and regulations, preoccupied with the proper care and maintenance of itself. It perpetually finds itself in a cycle of seeking and renouncing pleasure, of transgressing and instating regulations.

This cycle is another version of the cycle of law and its transgression. Žižek argues that the Pauline model of love provides a way out of this trap as well. Not only does full immersion in the law free us from superego guilt, but the violence of subjective destitution, that is, of the sacrifice of our own best thing, of what makes us who we are, opens up the possibility of an enjoyment or love beyond law. True love is often incompatible with pleasure—with fulfilling our wants and desires. The work of love generally demands innumerable sacrifices. It traumatically disrupts the mindless, everyday course of our lives. Falling in love can be miserable and horrifying—as years of pop tunes remind us and as many young people experience with painful intensity. (I recently saw a character in a television drama describe the intensity of her love as the "I-listen-to-your-awful-music-give-up-the-last-slice-of-pizza-love-you-so-much-I-hate-you kind of love.")

Understood as an element of our collective life, this love exceeds the biopolitical, pointing to that excess of life beyond life, that excess that provides meaning and makes everything worthwhile. Some political conservatives and religious fundamentalists seem to have taken this idea quite seriously, mobilizing people to follow them precisely because they present an alternative to the pleasures and constraints, seductions and dangers of biopoliticized life in communicative capitalism. For the most part, these fundamentalists remain within the cycle of pleasure and renunciation, providing enjoyment through renunciation. They deny the excess of life rather than acknowledging the excess that already adheres in and cuts through, everyday experience. Nonetheless, such conservatives express a political insight that the Left has forgotten: the importance of commitment beyond life. For Žižek, immersion in the law exposes this beyond, this excess that renders law non-all. We can express this idea another way: as an embrace of the commitments that inform our relations within law.

Crucial to the work of love that finds ways to work within law while recognizing law's incompleteness is the acknowledgment of one's neighbor, the Other, as Real (as traumatic Thing and as vulnerable, lacking being)—not as imaginary or symbolic. The imaginary neighbor is the one who looks like me. I respect him because of this similarity, which thus stands in for a notion of Good that I impose on him. He might be worthy of respect because he is a victim (how would I feel if this happened to me?) or a hero (overcoming circumstances that would be the end of me) or because of the significance of his cultural expression (this drumming is his version of Mozart!). These are reasons for me to respect the neighbor—my reasons through which I imagine him. The symbolic neighbor is the abstract subject of rights. Here my respect is ultimately my respect for law, my sense of duty to the law. This connects me to my enjoyment of law as well as the enjoyment I get from transgressing it. A third, Pauline, approach tells us to love our neighbor for herself—not for whom we might imagine her to be or in her position as an abstract human being. We love her as Real. We do not try to change her. We do not look for her essence. We do not make the Other an object through which to enjoy.

Ambiguity in Law: From the Nightly Law
to the Community of Believers

In place of the obscene transgressions of the nightly law, Žižek posits a community of believers in a cause. We saw in the example from Ballard's *Super Cannes* the idea of a community united through its transgressions. One element of this unity emerged out of an enlivened moral sensibility, an invigorated and expanded sense of the self in a moral world. As an alternative to such a community united through experiences of hatred, obscenity, and violence, the community that sustains and supplements the public law, Žižek draws from the Pauline remnant to envision a connection that also enlivens one's experience of the world but that does so by eliminating law's superego support. The Pauline law of faith suspends "the obscene libidinal investment in the Law, the investment on account of which the law generates/solicits its own transgression."[80] Rather than having her relation to law mediated by superego, the Pauline believer alienates everything to the law, withholding nothing and becoming herself an object. The subject is compulsion, testimony to a cause that has transformed it. Thus, Paul posits the new community of faith as following the law but not libidinally invested in it.

Accordingly, a crucial aspect of this community, one Žižek analogizes to a collective of outcasts, is that it has traversed or overcome the fantasy that law is all powerful, all knowing, and always right. As Žižek points out, superego is precisely the object that attempts to conceal the impotence of law and to fill it in with force.[81] The new community accepts that law is non-all, recognizing its limits as opportunities for love. Law will not solve all problems; its abstractions, however, establish a space within which we struggle for solutions.

One might respond by asking whether different communities might understand and enact love in radically contrary ways, ways that do not simply differ from but actively oppose each other. What is to prevent one kind of committed community from seeking to wipe out all others? Nothing. There are no guarantees. As Žižek explains with reference to psychoanalysis, its ultimate goal "is not the confessionary pacification/gentrification of the trauma, but the acceptance of the very fact that our lives involve a tragic kernel beyond redemption, that there is a dimension of our being which forever resists redemption-deliverance."[82] Submitting to the law, then, rests not on being convinced of its reason or rightness; much more simply, it rests on an acknowledgment of where we are and of a working toward something better from where we are. Bluntly put, leftist attempts to leave the law behind are basically provocations that have little to do with actually attempting to exercise political power to effect change. Žižek's treatment of Paul suggests another way, one that attacks the obscene supplement of law and works to traverse the fantasies that attach us to law as it focuses on the task of building radical collectives.

The Interpellation of the Legal Subject: To the Vitality of the Engaged Activist

Žižek finds in Paul "a commitment, an engaged position of struggle, an uncanny 'interpellation' beyond ideological interpellation, an interpellation which suspends the performative force of our 'normal' ideological interpellation that compels us to accept our determinate place within the sociosymbolic edifice."[83] Rather than involving recognition of oneself in the ideological call or the seeing of one's self from what one takes to be the perspective of law, "uncanny" interpellation disconnects the subject from its symbolic identity. This identity simply doesn't matter; it cannot fill in the lack constitutive of the subject. At best it provides a screen onto which are projected the images of whom can be counted or recognized in law, images imbricated in the obscene fantasies that limit the law and images that we perpetually reject for their failure to account for who we "really are." Uncanny interpellation, however, suspends these fantasies and acknowledges the lack: only a lacking subject is capable of love.

Thus, Žižek reads Paul's account of the fulfillment of law in terms of a traumatic event that ruptures law from within; law remains, but without its interpellative force. This trauma, moreover, unites a new collective, one engaged in the radical project of enacting their faith. For this reason, Žižek takes from the Pauline message the political message to "*practice* utopia."[84] The practice of a new collective cannot rely on the old ways—on previously given norms or on the fantasies formerly underpinning law. Instead, its practice is a new beginning out of the rupture with the old. As we have seen with Paul and Lenin, this practice is in between the old and the new; it is a bringing into being of something else. Such a moment will be transitory. Indeed, this very transience appears clearly in the fact that the institutions that might provide a symbolic identity are not yet present. To this extent, Žižek's discussion of love as the fulfillment of law suggests the possibility of building something new from within something old, in the course of a changed, transformed relation to what has been.

Conclusion: Hope in Law

Such a building from within can also be understood as a moment already within law. If we return to the fact that Žižek's account of law is synchronic, we can recognize the way in which, like law's founding, this possibility of a love that ruptures, this incompleteness, can be understood as already present, as persisting in law in its utopian dimensions. There is in law something more than superego enjoyment that attaches us to it; inhering in law, in its very circularity, in the irrationality of its injunction, is belief, or faith. What makes law law is a belief that there is more to law than violence.

In the monstrosity of their acts, Sethe and Keyser Soeze posit this other moment, this utopian alternative that inverts the existing order. In the case of *The Usual Suspects*, the possibility of such an order is hinted at through the retroactive presentation of the murder of wife and daughter. The scene is murky, indistinct, part of the fantastic, originary trauma constituting the mythic Keyser Soeze, who appears throughout the film as the singularly unimpressive, indeed, "crippled" petty criminal, Verbal. The story of Sethe is clearly the more powerful. In *Beloved*, hope in a time and space of African-American freedom is the dream—the tomorrow that persists once Beloved is forgotten.[85] Belief in this dream is what enabled and even inspired Sethe to act.

If we continue this emphasis on the utopian fulfillment of law as persisting within it, we might understand as well Žižek's emphasis on the letter of law. Yes, it is ambiguous and indeterminate, but this opens it up for emancipatory as well as repressive meaning. Thus, when confronting a cynical age, an age when the worst, most corrupt alternatives seem not simply to proliferate but no longer to surprise or outrage, finding a utopian dimension to inhere in law may be truly radical. To this extent, the idea that law is law expresses more than the violence of the injunction; it captures the hope inspiring law as well. Belief in law is a belief that violence is not everything. Just as the founding violence persists in law, so does the founding dream that things might be otherwise, and indeed, this dream tends to be concealed as well, suppressed by injunctions to compromise, to accept the way things are, and to give up naïve belief in something better. Ultimately, then, the revolutionary fulfillment of law is contained within it. The task is thus to find ways to attach ourselves to law through belief in the founding dream rather than through the enjoyment of founding violence.

CONCLUSION
REVOLUTION TODAY

Introduction

Thomas Frank's 2004 book, *What's the Matter with Kansas?*, was an important political touchstone for many progressives and some liberals in the aftermath of the 2004 elections. Frank provided a way to think about the changes in the political landscape that accompanied what seemed to many a rightward shift in American politics.[1] His book is a gripping account of how neoliberals were able to use a neoconservative politics of values to engineer a right-wing takeover of a state that had once been a center of progressive politics.

Frank's book is gripping, but its explanation was not, for me at least, quite satisfying. Why, I wanted to know, were so many poor people in rural areas galvanized by the pro-life, antiabortion message? Why did this particular issue mobilize them against their economic interests? My best answer: this message and these groups were what was available. The fundamentalist churches and the conservative activists were there. They had something to offer: a location for rage and a way to give form to experiences of frustration with devalued life and pains too long unacknowledged.

I begin with Frank because his analysis of the appeal of conservative politics provides, perhaps counterintuitively, the proper setting for thinking about Žižek's discussion of revolution. Žižek's critics and commentators generally focus on his idea of the act—the violent disturbance or breaking through of the given order.[2] These emphases on the act are clearly supported by Žižek's writings. Nevertheless, they remain one-sided insofar as Žižek's account of revolutionary activity relies on more than the miracle of an act. It involves as well an emphasis on the role of the revolutionary-political Party, a point we saw already in the preceding discussion of the Pauline community or collective of believers. Both the act and the Party are crucial to Žižek's theory of revolutionary change; there cannot be one without the other. Thus, I conclude this book by setting out Žižek's notion of revolution. I argue that Žižek's theory of the act replaces the notion of an active subject with one whose reaction to an ideological impasse must be retroactively given form by the political truth of the Party.

Thomas Frank's discussion of the change in Kansas politics relies not simply on what was there, on the ground, reaching the people. Rather, it indicates an institutional absence increasingly filled in by religious fundamentalists and neoconservatives because nothing else is available. This absence should compel us to consider what radical Left politics might be like today if there were something, not to fill this absence, but to express it, to give it organizational form. How, in other words, can radical Left politics demonstrate the ways this institutional deficit enables the brutalities of neoliberal capitalism and the systematic looting of the state? How can we give form to the ways the procedures that claim for themselves the name of democracy continue to function so as to disenfranchise and disempower most of the world's peoples? Voter turnout in the United States as well as the European

Union suggests that elections are not a viable political form; they do not seem capable of representing or galvanizing the voice of the majority. So, what is to be done? With this absence in mind, I defend and explain Žižek's account of revolution. I first consider the general idea of revolution—is it not an outmoded, bourgeois concept, out of tune with new social movements and the networked interactions of the information age? In some ways, the obvious answer is yes, it is outmoded: the conceptions of politics most prominent among political theorists have been formatted through the exclusion of revolutionary possibilities. Nevertheless, utopian aspirations to collectivity, to some sort of commons, remain, and this is what the concept of revolution helps open up. Second, I address problems in older accounts of revolutionary agency in order to demonstrate the utility of Žižek's emphasis on the act. The notion of the act, however, is not sufficient on its own, as we will see. Indeed, Žižek explicitly rejects the "pure politics," the politics without the party, associated with Alain Badiou, Jacques Ranciere, and Etienne Balibar.[3] In the third section, I set out Žižek's vision of the Party as a political form for a split political subject—a subject whose relation to the world and its experiences are not ontologically determined but have to be given form and represented.

Here is the argument in a nutshell: through the Symbolic one can intervene in, touch, and change, the Real.[4] (This point should make sense given Chapter Four's discussion of working within the law.) Žižek views Capital as Real insofar as it is the underlying, meaningless, background to politics, what is excluded in accounts of democratic action, for example, yet what always reappears and distorts even radical democracy. Politics, actions taking place within the Symbolic, can impact the Real. As Žižek frequently emphasizes, miracles do happen.

Revolution

Revolution: why bring back this concept? The most important reason is that the concept has already been brought back; it already circulates within and informs contemporary politics in the United States. The American Right confidently uses the words revolution and revolutionary. Appearing on Fox News on January 20, 2005, Charles Krauthammer, for example, proclaimed George W. Bush's second inaugural address to be "revolutionary."[5] The conservative CATO Institute held a conference in May 2004 entitled "The Republican Revolution Ten Years Later: Smaller Government or Business as Usual?" This conference, with Newt Gingrich as a featured speaker, examined "the successes and failures of the Republican revolution." The far Right does not view its political achievements in terms of their adherence to constitutional law or responsiveness to the living conditions of the majority of Americans. Rather it champions its ability to effect revolutionary change. Thus, Christian Brose writes on the conservative website *National Review Online*:

> In a great bit of irony, a man who is lambasted by his critics for being an archconservative laid out a foreign-policy vision that was nothing shy of revolutionary. But for the administration's truly conservative critics—those who think radical revisions of the status quo to be extremely dangerous and therefore imprudent—one serious question remains with no easy answer in sight. At what point does maintaining a political status quo become so treacherous that revolution becomes the only prudent course of action? Bush believes now is such a time, and his decision, whether right or wrong, will have repercussions beyond the scope of present imagination.[6]

Revolution is not a relic of the distant past. It is a part of the present political moment.

Perhaps oddly, it is those generally associated with the Left who today eschew the term *revolution*, as if it were too dangerous, too outside the mainstream. It is as if broad segments of the Left fail to recognize what the Right takes to be a basic fact: the world, viewed as the terrain of a globalized capitalist economy, is already in the midst of a great revolution. Rather than grasping the openness and indeterminacy of the revolutionary moment, an indeterminacy that the Right recognizes as enabling the production of new realities, Left activists and intellectuals proceed as if the basic coordinates of contemporary politics were already fixed. The Left is left describing and reacting to the reality that the Right creates. On the one side, as we saw in Chapter Three, this fixity assumes the form of democratic fundamentalism wherein democracy is the ultimate horizon of political thought. On the other, as we saw in Chapter Two's discussion of class struggle, this fixity proceeds as if there were no alternative to capitalism.

Thus, most Left critical and political theorists reject the concept of revolution. Postmarxists from the second and third generations of the Frankfurt school (such as Jürgen Habermas and Jean Cohen and Andrew Arato) as well as radical democratic theorists of hegemony (Ernesto Laclau and Chantal Mouffe) reject emphases on the primary role of the economy in political struggle. For the Habermasians, the recognition of the systemic requirements of complex societies entails a self-limiting radicalism and the development of communicative capacities within their own sphere of the lifeworld. For radical democrats, the very notion of an economic sphere capable of determining political identities is false, failing to account for the multiplicity of political identities and the struggles through which they may be articulated together to hegemonize a political field. Thus, both discursive and radical democrats proceed as if democracy is possible on the basis of existing capitalist relations. Capitalist globalization is the presupposed ground of democratic deliberation and struggles for identity.

I read Žižek as rejecting both these positions insofar as they entail an accommodation with capitalism, the acceptance of capitalism as the only game in town, and the equation of class struggle with any other political struggle. And, I value his reintroduction of the concept of revolution into Left thought as vital given the fact that neoliberal capitalism is incompatible with not simply democracy but with human life. Under conditions of post-Fordist informationalized production, ever more workers, ever more people, are redundant, unnecessary obstacles to expansions and intensifications of growth and profit. Accompanying this immiseration, moreover, is the dismantling of the welfare state, that is, the reformatting of its suppositions of the collectivization of risk and a general social solidarity into neoliberal calculations of value and neoconservative judgments of worth. Capitalist excess generates dangerous forms of populist nationalism and right-wing fundamentalism, "a typical post-political mixture of pure publicity spectacle and Moral Majority concerns."[7] What this means for U.S. politics (and arguably politics in the United Kingdom and European Union as well) is that the liberal-democratic compromise of the eighties and nineties, the embrace of neoliberal economics as the proper form of globalization and general shift to the right, has had disastrous results. The long-fought-for achievements of the welfare state have been lost, millions sink into poverty, and the Right continues to fight tooth and nail for more.

In this setting, then, I read Žižek's introduction of revolution as producing an opening, a space in which we might dare to consider the possibility of transforming the fundamental order of constitutional democracy and capitalism. Is such a revolution possible? To consider the possibility of a revolutionary intervention, I turn now to Žižek's discussion of the act.

Agency and the Act

Marxists have had immeasurable problems with the agents of revolution. They never seem to do what Marxists want. The working class was rarely sufficiently radical, preferring raises and job security to the violent overthrow of the state. Other groups of marginalized people seemed ideal candidates for revolutionary activity, but some ended up brutally massacring millions, devolving into corrupt dictatorships, ultimately depending on the larger states and markets Marxists have sought to transform, or justifiably hostile to the racism of western Marxists who wanted to determine their role and keep them in their proper place.

In light of these problems, post-Marxists pluralize struggles, identifying multiple sites of political activity and change. According to these views, agency is not a problem; it is a given, a characteristic of engaged activity. The failure to acknowledge this agency is a failure of theory properly to conceive the sites and practices of politics, a failure to recognize the resistances embedded in everyday activities such as watching television and going to the mall.[8] A more nuanced and influential version of this position can be found in Michael Hardt's and Antonio Negri's concept of the multitude of singularities.[9] The desiring, productive activity of the multitude is politics today, politics as it has become intertwined with post-Fordist informationalized economies and the hybrid resistances and creativities involved in forming an identity.

There is a way, however, that post-Marxist political agency is actually the same as in the traditional Marxist account: in both, agency is given. It is a characteristic of who one is, of one's position as a subject. The only real difference is whether or not one sees the position as activated or as potential. Post-Marxists see politics as happening, as active presence, and as given. Marxists see it as potential, as a result of historical changes.

Žižek rejects both these options. For him the post-Marxist alternative of the agonistic struggle of differing groups avoids the harder core of antagonism, the fundamental delimitation of the political field between adversaries and enemies.[10] Adversaries are permissible opponents in struggle. Enemies are those who threaten our very way of life. We might think of those American conservatives who view all liberals as traitors, as fundamentally anti-American, and as outside the domain of those who count as us.

An additional problem with the post-Marxist radical democratic approach stems from the disparate struggles involved in politics. These struggles remain specific, with their own aims and goals. Radical democrats (as well as many activists) take this specificity to be a virtue—a mark of their unwillingness to speak for another, of their respect for the voice of each. This means specific struggles can be dealt with in their specificity. Technocratic or administrative responses, for example, can deal with problems on a case-by-case basis before the cases pile up or articulate into a global assault on the system. For Žižek, as I explained in Chapter Three, the problem with this politics of affinity groups is its failure to make universal claims, to allow a particular crime, issue, position, or identity to stand in for the problems of the system itself.

The Marxist option of a historically given political subject is not persuasive to Žižek for a number of reasons. First, he recognizes transformations in work, labor, and property today. Digitalization changes the regime of private property as well as distinctions between mental and physical labor. Second, as we saw in Chapter Two, there is no such thing as an "authentic" working class.[11] Third, even if there were, one could in no way assume that such a working class would somehow perceive its interests and act on them.[12] Ian Parker is thus mistaken in his claim that Žižek endorses the logic of capitalism. Parker misreads as an acceptance of capitalism what is actually Žižek's acknowledgment of the problems facing a materialist analysis.[13]

Žižek appeals to the act in order to respond to these problems of agency. In contrast to an account of actions in terms of the intentional activity of a subject or a consciously willed decision, Žižek emphasizes the reactive dimensions of the act. An act intrudes upon or happens to a subject. With respect to revolution, the result is a disconnecting of revolutionary agency from revolutionary will or, more precisely, a shift away from will and toward urge or compulsion. He writes:

> The will to revolutionary change emerges as an urge, as an "I cannot do otherwise," or it is worthless. In the terms of Bernard William's distinction between *ought* and *must*, an authentic revolution is by definition performed as Must—it is not something we "ought to do," as an ideal for which we are striving, but something we cannot but do, since we cannot do otherwise. This is why today's Leftist worry that revolution will not occur, that global capitalism will just go indefinitely, is false insofar as it turns revolution into a moral obligation, into something we ought to do while we fight the inertia of the capitalist present.[14]

In other words, the revolutionary act is not a matter of obligation or choice. It is simply what one must do. Consequently, in place of the economic contradictions that force changes in capitalist relations of production, Žižek emphasizes an ideological impasse or double bind from which escape is only possible through a violent *"passage à l'acte,"* that is, a destructive or self-destructive outburst through which one attempts to break out of a restricted, unbearable situation. I address these points in turn.

At its most basic, an act is a point at which "something emerges out of nothing."[15] It is when something takes place that cannot be explained away as the necessary outcome of a causal change.[16] An act "exceeds calculation."[17] In a sense, Žižek's act resembles Hannah Arendt's idea of action as bringing something new into being. The difference, however, is that Žižek attends more to the destruction and disruption of the act than to what it creates (a point I return to below). Nevertheless, as for Arendt, so for Žižek does an act involve the suspension of strategic and normative considerations as something new is ventured, or risked. Žižek's descriptions of the act include "shooting oneself in the foot," "taking the system at its word," and a "traumatic encounter" with the Other as Real. All these formulations get at the same thing: the suspension of the symbolic order in an opening up to a possibility for change—for action beyond the given matrix of expectations.

Žižek's notion of the act as something that happens to the subject also resembles Nietzsche's insight that there is no "doer behind the deed" and poststructuralist emphases on the ways an act exceeds its conditions of emergence, doubling back into and changing these conditions. Yet the poststructuralist version does not completely disconnect itself from the concept of the will; rather, it simply acknowledges the instabilities of the will, its failure to be what liberalism has claimed it to be. Accordingly, Žižek goes further insofar as he emphasizes not just a will that is never sovereign, knowing, or in control, but the fact that the act disrupts the very frame within which anything like sovereignty, knowledge, or control might be assessed. The act divides the subject, "who can never subjectivize it, assume it as 'his own,' posit himself as its author-agent—the authentic act that I accomplish is always by definition a foreign body, an intruder which simultaneously attracts/fascinates and repels me, so that if and when I come too close to it, this leads to my *aphanisis*, self-erasure."[18] In the act, I cannot believe what I did; I did what I had to, even though I thought I could not.[19]

If an act is not something an agent decides, if it is not the result of the will of an agent, where does it come from? It is a reaction to the situation of a double bind, an ideological impasse.[20] We could say, then, that the act is homologous to a spontaneous revolt occasioned by contradictions between the capitalist mode of production and relations of production, and the difference between the act and such a revolt is that the act arises from an *ideological* impasse. A potential problem here is that Žižek's analysis could be insufficiently materialist, especially insofar as he resolutely identifies himself as a materialist philosopher. A second potential problem with the homology between the act and the revolt is that it fails to say why, exactly, an ideological impasse would result in something like an act—what makes this sort of impasse such a big deal?

Žižek uses enjoyment to answer to both questions. The notion of enjoyment supplies the necessary material kernel of the Real and the account of traumatic rupture. Unfortunately, this turn to enjoyment introduces an additional problem, namely, one of singularity.[21] Žižek takes the view that there is only one point at which a system ruptures—one point that serves as the truth of an ideological formation. Thus, he describes the basic feature of ideology critique as detecting "the element which represents from within its own impossibility."[22] Moreover, he associates the feminine logic of the non-all (discussed in Chapter Four) with "the logic of the singular symptomal element" which gives body to the falsity of the supposition of a complete or closed universality (a universality rooted in a constitutent exception).[23] Finally, he reads radical-revolutionary politics in terms of the discourse of the analyst, where the position of the agent is occupied by *objet petit a*, that is, "the symptomal point, the 'part of no part' of the situation."[24] Why should we accept that there is only one point that functions as the truth of the system? Another way of posing this question is, even if we agree that an individual organizes his or her enjoyment around a specific fundamental fantasy, why should we assume that collectivities are similarly constituted around a singular fundamental fantasy rather than through multiple ones? To consider this problem in proper detail, I summarize the discussion of enjoyment presented in the book thus far.

As we saw in the first chapter, Žižek views enjoyment as an ontological category, as something crucial to the being of the subject.[25] It is the traumatic element of the Real that decenters the subject, that persists as a kernel of intensity—that inexpressible remainder of "more" when one, for example, lists all a person's experiences and attributes but still does not get to who he or she *really* is. Enjoyment is this inert substance. Ideologies, Žižek argues, attach themselves to enjoyment, organizing it in terms of different, often contradictory, fantasmatic elements. Even more importantly, enjoyment is that extra element beyond an ideology's express content that enables it to secure compliance. It is that irrational nugget involved in accepting authority or responding to an ideological hail.[26] This accepting is manifest in actions and practices, in what the subject does apart from what the subject claims to know. It is profoundly excessive and sacrificial. Accepting symbolic identity within an ideological formation requires that one disavow the fundamental fantasy that organizes one's enjoyment. Such disavowal does not disturb the fantasy; indeed, it protects and sustains it.[27]

This account of ideology enables Žižek to analyze the different ways that contradictory or incompatible ideological arrangements of enjoyment create unbearable binds for the subject. At one level, the subject is enjoined to disavow his or her fantasy. At another, this disavowal is a way for the subject to protect or secure it. For example, I might disavow the ways that I find pornography stimulating by criticizing the porn industry for making and distributing stimulating pornography. I might self-effacingly emphasize the unimportance of academic writing, even as I keep writing, support the necessity of publishing for tenure, and avoid confronting the gaping hole that would be left if I simply stopped and said, "I would prefer not to."

As the discussion of the superego injunction to enjoy makes clear, these tensions occur at larger, societal levels: under conditions of communicative capitalism, subjects are commanded to enjoy and to have it all, even as all sorts of regulations and instructions establish constraints on the enjoyment commanded. Indeed, in communicative capitalism the traditional structures organizing enjoyment and regulating libidinal life have disintegrated. Whereas traditional and modern accounts of patriarchy emphasize prohibition, that one should not engage in extramarital sex, for example, current society encourages sexuality. Drugs for erectile disfunction, sex therapists, wife-swapping on reality television—all tell the subject to enjoy sex and that something must be seriously wrong if one is not having frequent, vigorous orgasms. Likewise, whereas families under Fordist economics were expected to save, under post-Fordist consumerist arrangements, we are enjoined to spend, to buy on credit, and to fight terrorism by going shopping.

With respect to both injunctions to enjoy, however, subjects get caught in such a way that their very access to enjoyment is blocked. On the one hand, it is increasingly difficult to arrange sexuality transgressively: those transgressions that remain—sex with children, students, interns, employees—are criminal and unconscionable. They are sexual abuses rather than sexual expressions. On the other hand, directly telling someone, "*Do it! Go for it! Perform! Have an orgasm!*" can make arousal difficult. Similarly, spending and consuming are expected, obligatory, and difficult to avoid. We might think here of mall shopping and tourism, of the search for something to buy, out of boredom or necessity, that, once bought, fails to satisfy. We might think of how much more difficult it is to achieve satisfaction: *there must be something better out there, something that is really what I want, really what will do it; I just haven't found it yet.* Žižek's use of enjoyment as a political category, then, gives us some insight into new experiences of command and frustration, insight into how we remain profoundly unfree even as choices multiply and ever more experiences seem available for the taking.

I have been emphasizing the tensions occasioned by the contradictions and inconsistencies within ideological arrangements of enjoyment, yet these are not the only impasses Žižek emphasizes. He also considers the deadlocks in what is theorized as the risk society (the dilemma of choosing in low-probability, high-risk contexts) as well as in the "passion for the Real" that treats pain and violence as markers of authenticity in the context of the networked spectacles of communicative capitalism.[28] What is interesting is the way these two phenomena are linked: undecideability is accompanied by violence.

As poststructuralists have long emphasized, the gap between knowledge and decision is undecideable. There is no ultimate foundation or recourse to tradition that can guarantee the rightness of a course of action in advance. We have to decide, even though we can never have enough information to know whether our decision was the right one. The present is thus marked by this experience of profound contingency.[29]

In the face of this contingency, assertions are too often backed up by violence and by force. On the one hand, the very absence of authorization renders claims to authority unjustified plays of power.[30] On the other, it renders all interpretation impotent, yet another opinion or perspective.[31] The 2004 presidential campaign in the United States provides (unfortunately) key examples of this point: Republican attacks on Senator Max Cleland as an unpatriotic traitor despite his loss of limbs in Vietnam and the Swiftboat Veterans' ads challenging the medals Senator John Kerry received for his military service. We might think as well of the skepticism and lack of belief that came to greet terror alerts from the Department of Homeland Security after a couple of years of what seemed to many to be politically motivated elevations of the level of threat. Given the way that today nothing is fact, it is not surprising that political theorists might try to support our positions with insights from evolutionary biology, neuroscience, and psychoanalysis insofar as each of these claims a kind of contact with or access to the Real.

The act is a response to deadlocks, an attempt to break out of an ideological impasse. To use one final example, we might think of the double bind of an injunction to tolerance. Contemporary liberals are committed to the view that we should all tolerate others' differences—the ways they organize their own enjoyment. Indeed, we are supposed to secure this tolerance and make sure tolerance is generalized as an attribute of our society. As we saw in Chapter Three, however, this generalized liberal tolerance works in fact as a kind of intolerance, a refusal to tolerate the intolerant, a limitation of tolerance to those who are not fundamentalist, ethnocentric, racist, sexist, or homophobic. What the *passage à l'acte* does is explode against this impasse. Often this explosion merely testifies to a more fundamental impotence, to an inability to change anything at all. Nevertheless, on rare occasions such an act can change the very coordinates out of which it emerges.

Here, then, is the problem of singularity. Why should we assume with Žižek that there is only one point at which the weakness of a system appears—one point that is its symptom? The contemporary political field is rife with multiple deadlocks. That the reaction to an impasse is an explosion or rupture makes sense, but why must there only be one point of fundamental weakness? Žižek claims that "the depoliticized economy is the disavowed fundamental fantasy of postmodern politics."[32] This is an important point—although it is of course contestable. After all, is not economic policy a key topic in much political discussion, an idea that Bill Clinton summarized in his 1992 presidential campaign against George H. W. Bush with the words, "It's the economy, stupid"? More importantly, however, Žižek's claim regarding the depoliticized economy as the disavowed fundamental fantasy does not follow from his account of the arrangement of enjoyment in contemporary ideological formations.

Even if he is right about the urgent need to subject capitalism to political demands (rather than remaining trapped in the inverse situation of constraining politics because of the logic of Capital), the idea that acts will occur at such critical points does not follow—unless, of course, one remains committed to an analysis of ideology as rising directly from an economic base, a view Žižek rejects. In fact, almost none of Žižek's examples of acts are situated at a point where an ideological impasse connects with a postpolitical exclusion of the capitalist economy.[33] The two lines of argumentation do not link up. In the terms I introduced in Chapter Two, what we have is a parallax gap between them. When we approach acts from the standpoint of the economy, that is, from class struggle as the fundamental antagonism, we do not arrive at the same point that we do when we approach acts from the psychoanalytic perspective on contemporary society as permeated by injunctions to enjoy. The move from one perspective to another results in a pronounced parallax: a fundamental shift in how we see the present ideological formation.

There is, however, an answer to this problem of singularity, a way of linking the psychoanalytic account of the act with the critique of post-Marxism and the depoliticization of the economy. It involves Žižek's account of the truth of a situation and the additional component of Žižek's account of revolution: the Party. The claim that there is a singular point of weakness, the symptom or truth of a system, is a *political* claim, not a claim rooted in some kind of empirical facticity. It is not *objective* in the typical sense of the term. The disruption of an act will not be determined by historical forces, behind our backs, apart from our interventions. As I have emphasized throughout this book, one of Žižek's basic points is that there are no guarantees (in Lacan's words, the big Other does not exist). The truth of the singular disruption is a truth that stems from an underlying political commitment, as I now explain by turning to the Party.

The Party

The idea that political theorists should talk about the Party might raise some eyebrows. What is "the" Party anyway? Do we want to accept some old Marxist rhetoric about a revolutionary Party? In a less radical direction, might we not think of the Party as a sort of conventional or mundane concept, part of a mode of political action oriented to winning elections? These questions are important. Nevertheless, the idea of the Party I take Žižek as suggesting can push political theorists in interesting directions. First, it entails thinking more about organized action. In Žižek's words, "Politics without the organizational form of the Party is politics without politics."[34] Rather than critique that is disembodied, detached from an actual position, or critique that is loosely linked to a vision of diffuse radical democrats or a multitude of singularities that actually seem to have no need for critique, or an argument that is simply one of many introduced into a process of collective-will formation, critique that affiliates itself with a Party takes responsibility for power. It associates itself from the beginning with more than resistance, with the actual taking and exercise of power in all its messiness.

Second, the idea of a Party entails thinking about solidarity and sacrifice. The Party is an organizational form for political collectivity, for a logic of the collective. Žižek sometimes describes such a collective in terms of psychoanalytic communities or communities of outcasts. Given Žižek's emphasis on the Party as an organization for collective action, as the standpoint of political collectivity, I disagree, yet again, with Ian Parker. Parker claims that not only does Žižek confine political action "to the individual," but also that "the collective project of class consciousness and revolutionary change envisioned by Marxism is outside the frame of his political analysis."[35] Parker is simply wrong on this score, as Žižek's emphasis on the Party attests.

Turning to the second point regarding the current utility of the idea of the Party, as I have worked in new media and technology contexts, I have been struck by the way many digital activists view solidarity as an outmoded concept. They seem to want a politics oriented exclusively toward a kind of absolute freedom from any kind of restriction, impediment, responsibility, or commitment. They think new technologies enable this. I disagree, but a more thorough elaboration is beyond the scope of this book.[36] My point is that political change and intervention requires collective action, that thinking collectively has become extremely difficult (political theorists are commonly challenged when we use the term *we*), and that the notion of the Party is a way to think about political affiliation that is not naturalized or essentialized into identity categories of sex, race, sexuality, ethnicity, or nationality. With these points in mind, then, I turn to Žižek's account of the Party. I emphasize two aspects of this account: the Party's role in politicizing the act and the Party's relation to Truth.

Žižek explains that the *passage à l'acte* is not the same as an authentic political act. The *passage à l'acte* is a blind outburst that has to be politicized.[37] The disruption or intervention has no politics in itself. Rather, it has to be interpreted, translated, or represented in terms of a politics, and this leads us to the role of the Party. The Party provides the truth of the situation, giving form to the traumatic rupture of the act. As I mentioned earlier, Žižek argues that the Party is necessary "because the working class is never 'fully itself.'"[38] Adequate or revolutionary class consciousness does not emerge spontaneously or on its own; our experience of our position does not itself guarantee a political understanding or interpretation of our experience, particularly a radical one. Class consciousness is the product of a lot of hard work. To return to the example from Thomas Frank with which I began, so is right-wing fundamentalist self-consciousness: it does not come out of nowhere; it is produced through ideological struggle—a struggle that the American Right has fought ferociously over the past thirty or forty years. In turning to the Party, Žižek is emphasizing the role of institutional structures, of a collective form, for universalizing, politicizing, and organizing (ultimately three ways of describing the same thing) experiences and, when they occur, acts. The task of the Party is to question hegemonic ideological coordinates, to challenge and break through prevailing ways of thinking in order to create a space for something new.[39] Thus, the Party does not function as a new Master, providing new names so much as it does as an analyst disturbing the natural course of a situation, serving as a catalytic object. The Party provides the formal position of Truth.

Once we recognize the formal role of the Party, we can understand why Žižek answers the question "what is to be done?" in one word: nothing. His answer is a challenge to intellectuals to think of the coordinates within which our activities are situated and to work to break through and politicize those coordinates. Differently put, his answer is facetious insofar as "nothing" does not mean sit back, go to sleep, or continue shopping and driving around and carrying on with one's daily activities. Rather, the answer "nothing" points to Žižek's rejection of the idea that the revolutionary act is the act of a willing, choosing subject and his provision, in its place, of the Bartleby politics of an object and the Party's role in retroactively determining an act.[40]

I read Žižek as introducing Bartleby as a kind of political myth. Žižek does not undertake a thorough reading of Melville's short story or a nuanced discussion of Bartleby's work as a scrivener. He demonstrates little interest in the Bartleby narrative. Instead, for Žižek Bartleby is "an empty container of a multitude of inconsistent, even mutually contradictory meanings—it is wrong to ask 'but what does the political myth really mean?', since its 'meaning' is precisely to serve as the container for a multitude of meanings."[41] So understood, Bartleby designates a withdrawal from the incessant activity of resistance and resignification in which Leftists remain caught. Instead of such passivity in the guise of activity, Bartleby embodies the activity of the radical, disruptive object who disturbs the order of things. He marks as well an attitude toward law, precisely that attitude discussed in the preceding chapter in terms of the Pauline work of love as that which suspends law's superego supplement and fully immerses in law without exception. How? By foregoing the protest "which parasitizes on what it negates," the simple refusal of an order, neither denies that order nor rejects its authority, but marks a conditional ("would") preference not to do what the order commands. Finally, Bartleby denotes the empty space formerly occupied by the superego, underpinning thereby the active of work of building something new without guarantee and absent the certainty of serving a cause duty to which can provide its own enjoyment.

Bartleby as the figure of a new political myth puts into perspective Žižek's acceptance of revolutionary violence. For Žižek, violence is a necessary excess of any revolutionary situation (and, in this way homologous to the violence necessarily accompanying law). As he explains, "an authentic political revolution cannot be measured by the standard of servicing goods (to what extent 'life got better for the majority' afterward)—it is a goal in itself, an act which changes the very concept of what a 'good life' is, and a different (higher, eventually) standard of living is a by-product of a revolutionary process, not its goal."[42] Nevertheless, this "pure" revolutionary violence is not to be identified with the violent outburst, which itself can easily be a manifestation of impotence that changes nothing. In order for violence actually to change the basic conditions constitutive of a situation, something else has to occur, namely a prior withdrawal which clears a place for transforming violence. Bartleby figures this withdrawal, the withdrawal of pointless activity to create a space for an act capable of changing the very conditions that gave rise to it, capable, in other words, or bringing something new into being.

I see the activity of the Party as the other side of what Žižek terms Bartleby-parallax, the side of collective engagement. The Party provides the meaning of the act; it represents it, seeing in its particularity a moment of universality, retroactively determining the significance of the act. How does it do this? Not with reference to a list of clear criteria; acts are always risky and unpredictable. Instead, the Party gives the act form insofar as it expresses truth. As Žižek says, "What is important about the Party's knowledge is not its content, but the fact that it occupies the place of Truth."[43] The Party provides the additional external element of mediation necessary for an act, that is, for an outburst to have the power to change the coordinates of a given order.

I can make this clearer by saying more about "truth" and "form." In his account of truth, Žižek emphasizes the way that the truth of Marxism and Christianity is discernible only to the believer. There is not a neutral truth that anyone could accept or reject.[44] Truth, for Žižek, is a political perspective: the "truth of an engaged subject."[45] It is the appearance of the universal in the particular (or even singular).[46] The Party occupies the place of *this* truth as a division or cut (a notion we saw elaborated in the discussion of Paul). With respect to the act, then, the Party provides the external position that establishes its truth.[47]

Another way Žižek describes the role of the Party is as providing the "form of knowledge, of a new type of knowledge linked to a collective political subject."[48] Form, he explains, "is not the neutral frame of particular contents, but the very principle of concretion, that is, the 'strange attractor' which distorts, biases, confers a specific color on every element of the totality."[49] Form is not formalistic. It is not neutral or independent of its content. Rather, form refers to the arrangement of content, to how contents are linked together, and to the antagonism that shapes the arrangement. To formalize, then, is to focus on the antagonism that generates or cuts through a given arrangement. From the perspective of the truth of Marxism, "class struggle is the Form of the Social."[50] This means class struggle is what generates the various horizons of meaning within historical formations.

I explained in Chapter Two that Žižek uses the term *class struggle* to designate the antagonism inherent to and constitutive of the social field. What is interesting, though, is that Žižek does not say that from the perspective of the *Party* class struggle is the Form of the Social. He says it is so from the perspective of Marxism. Why? Well, it could have just been an oversight and that he meant to say "from the perspective of the Party," but it seems to me that his account allows for a more abstract, and potentially open, reading, one that emphasizes the "excluded element" (the Pauline remnant) as the Form of the Social. Such a reading is supported both by Žižek's emphasis on the place of the excluded element in the logic of the universal as non-all (insofar as it appears as a constituent exception, the excluded element prevents us from acknowledging the way our social field is non-all) and by his reading of the revolutionary party in terms of the discourse of the analyst.

What does it mean to say that the excluded element is the Form of the Social? It means that the excluded element is that toward which one cannot remain neutral. It links the truth of the Party to this position, a position that is itself an absence when considered in terms of the false or closed universality of a vision of society as a unified whole. This interpretation accords well with Žižek's account of the way that both the law and society are non-all, incapable of totalizing themselves. Indeed, it highlights the fact that the very element that is excluded from an order can be turned against it; it can undermine the alleged universality of the system.

In his interview with Glyn Daly, Žižek emphasizes that the truth of a society can only be formulated from an extreme partial position. His example is Jews in Nazi Germany: "In order to know what Nazi Germany was at its most essential," he says, "you shouldn't balance all discourses; you should identify with the excluded abject."[51] Formalization thus entails identification with the excluded element—a point Žižek also makes when he talks about love and about identifying with the Other as Real, when he emphasizes Palestinians and illegal immigrants, when he draws from Giorgio Agamben's notion of *homo sacer*, and, more recently, when he emphasizes the self-organization of those living in favelas and slums.[52] Taking the position of the excluded disrupts the system that creates their plight; it is an occupation of a position that cannot be acknowledged if the system is to continue and to survive.

For example, slum dwellers provide a key point for an assertion of universality: as the U.N. report on human settlements makes clear, economists today cannot explain how slum dwellers survive.[53] They cannot account for how over 90 million people are able to secure their basic conditions of survival and earn enough to live. Slum dwellers are outside the current order not simply in their poverty, not simply in the fact that they cannot be counted—no one really knows how many people we are dealing with here—but insofar as their very existence cannot be symbolically represented. They are outside the basic coordinates of what passes as economic logic. Identification with slum dwellers, then, is neither empathy with pain nor romantic appropriation of authenticity. Rather, it is a formal exercise in disruption and in transforming the system by emphasizing its symptomatic exclusion, the point that cannot be included or acknowledged if the system is to continue. My point here is that reading the truth of the Party in terms of the excluded element makes sense in terms of Žižek's writing. More importantly, it clarifies the relation between truth and the singular symptom or point of disruption. The form of the social from the perspective of the truth of the Party is the excluded element.

With regard to identification as vital to the Party's politicization of an act, insofar as this identification is with the Real Other rather than the imaginary or Symbolic other, it is disruptive and shattering; it breaks the contours within which we make sense of ourselves and our world. As Žižek explains,

We cannot go *directly* from capitalist to revolutionary subjectivity: the abstraction, the foreclosure of others, the blindness to the other's suffering and pain, has first to be broken in a gesture of taking the risk and reaching directly out to the suffering other—a gesture which, since it shatters the very kernel of our identity cannot fail to appear extremely violent."[54]

The politicization of the act, then, is a secular, materialist version of the process we saw in the preceding chapter's discussion of subjective destitution, the work of love, and the fulfillment of the law. Unlike the essentialist idea of a consciousness that arises from our subject position, for Žižek, politics requires the breaking down and out of one's subject position through avowal of and identification with abjection. Insofar as in this process our own position is shattered, insofar as we are coming to grips with the conditions under which we have been attached to a particular order, we do not repeat the colonizing gesture of speaking for or interpreting the enjoyment or pain of the Other. Rather, the Other disrupts who and what we are: can "we" be those who allow so many millions to suffer and die? Can we acknowledge the necessity and contingency of our enjoyment as well as the Other's? Like the analyst, then, the Party participates in breaking down the subject so that it can find a way out of the deadlock within which it remains trapped.

Conclusion

I have ended this book by emphasizing revolution. Two aspects of Žižek's discussion make the concept a vital one for engaged, leftist political thought: the act and the Party. There is no automatic connection between an act and the structure within which it occurs. Seeing an act as a restructuring happens retroactively; it is a project of the Party as it formalizes the act in accordance with the truth, that is, in accordance with that exclusion that gives form to society. Unlike political theorists who emphasize resistance and provocation, Žižek urges an approach to politics that acknowledges the contemporary deadlock even as it accepts responsibility for the hard work of building a new, better order. Whereas some might find his emphasis on "no guarantees" and the fact that subjective destitution and the violence of the act can involve a choice for the worst, for Žižek this absence of guarantees is the very space of our freedom.

NOTES

Introduction

1. Ernesto Laclau, preface to Slavoj Žižek, *The Sublime Object of Ideology* (London: Verso, 1989), p. xii.
2. Another possible explanation for Žižek's initial popularity in the United States and United Kingdom might be time: his initial books appeared in English at the time of the break up of Yugoslavia and consequent war in the Balkans. For more biographical information about Žižek, see Ian Parker *Slavoj Žižek: A Critical Introduction* (London: Pluto Press, 2004), Chapter 1; Rebecca Mead, "The Marx Brother: How a Philosopher From Slovenia Became an International Star," the *New Yorker* 79, 10 (May 5, 2003): 38 ff. Available online at http://www.lacan.com/ziny. htm. See Robert Boynton, "Enjoy your Žižek!" *Lingua Franca* 7, 7 (October 1998). Available online at http://www.robertboynton.com/index. php?p=70&ch=profiles.
3. Thus, Sarah Kay's insightful reading of Žižek focuses on the notion of the Real and finds its traces in the excesses of style. See her *Žižek: A Critical Introduction* (Cambridge, UK: Polity Press, 2003). Finding Žižek "dauntingly prolific and dazzling versatile," Terry Eagleton refers to Žižek's "flamboyant parade of topics," "Enjoy!" *Paragraph: A Journal of Modern Critical Theory* 24, 2 (July 2001): 40. Geoffrey Galt Harpham emphasizes Žižek's style, seeing it as alien, strange, and other and declaring that Žižek "doesn't seem to believe that books should be *about* something." "Doing the impossible: Slavoj Žižek and the end of knowledge," *Critical Inquiry* 29 (Spring 2003): 454–455. For one of the most quick and egregious dismissals of Žižek's thought on the basis of his style, see John Holbo, "On Žižek and Trilling," *Philosophy and Literature* 28, 16 (2004): pp. 230–240.
4. Parker, p. 115.

Notes

5. Available at the Žižek Watch archive, http://www.mclemee.com/id117.html.
6. Slavoj Žižek, *For They Know Not What They Do* (London: Verso, 1991), p. 2.
7. Slavoj Žižek, *The Parallax View* (Cambridge, MA: The MIT Press, 2006), p. 90.
8. Slavoj Žižek, "Lenin's Choice," afterward to *Revolution at the Gates: A Selection of Writings from February to October 1917, V. I. Lenin,* ed. Slavoj Žižek (London: Verso, 2002).
9. "Lenin's Choice," p. 188.
10. *Parallax View,* pp. 342–343, pp. 382–385.
11. This is the crux of the criticism leveled by Andrew Robinson and Simon Tormey, "A Ticklish Subject? Žižek and the Future of Left Radicalism," *Thesis Eleven* 80, 1 (February 2005): pp. 94–107.
12. As he says in *For They Know Not What They Do,* p. 3.
13. Tony Myers takes a similarly systematic approach to Žižek, focusing on the theory of the subject that informs Žižek's thought. See Tony Myers, *Slavoj Žižek* (London: Routledge, 2003).
14. Slavoj Žižek, *Organs Without Bodies* (New York: Routledge, 2004), pp. ix–x.

Chapter 1

1. Slavoj Žižek and Glyn Daly, *Conversations with Žižek* (Cambridge, U.K.: Polity, 2004), p. 114.
2. Slavoj Žižek, *The Parallax View* (Cambridge, MA: The MIT Press, 2006), p. 309.
3. Slavoj Žižek, *The Ticklish Subject* (London: Verso, 1999), p. 341; Slavoj Žižek, *The Plague of Fantasies* (London: Verso, 1997), p. 86.
4. For the notion of communicative capitalism, see Jodi Dean, *Publicity's Secret* (Ithaca, NY: Cornell University Press, 2002).
5. See Jodi Dean, "Communicative Capitalism: Circulation and the Foreclosure of Politics," *Cultural Politics* 1, 1 (2005): pp. 51–74.
6. William E. Connolly, *The Ethos of Pluralization* (Minneapolis: University of Minnesota Press, 1995), p. xii.
7. Lacan writes, "Jouissance is what serves no purpose." *The Seminar of Jacques Lacan, Book XX, 1972–1973, Encore, On Feminine Sexuality, The Limits of Love and Knowledge,* ed. Jacques-Alain Miller, trans. Bruce Fink (New York: W.W. Norton, 1998), p. 3.
8. Although noting that this absolute *jouissance* is a myth existing "only as a negative point of reference with regard to which every actually experienced *jouissance* falls short," Žižek reads recent developments in neuroscience as pointing to the possibility of real, non-schematized intensity, *The Parallax View,* p. 188.

9. Bruce Fink, *The Lacanian Subject* (Princeton, NJ: Princeton University Press, 1995), p. 59.

10. In *Parallax View*, Žižek discusses the intense enjoyment possible through mere words, that is, Lacan's notion of the *jouissance* of the Other, pp. 188–190.

11. Slavoj Žižek, *The Sublime Object of Ideology* (London: Verso, 1989), p. 122.

12. *Sublime Object*, p. 3.

13. *Sublime Object*, p. 93.

14. *Ticklish Subject*, p. 296; Slavoj Žižek, *The Plague of Fantasies* (London: Verso, 1997), p. 32.

15. *Ticklish Subject*, p. 297; *Plague of Fantasies*, p. 33; *Parallax View*, pp. 62–64.

16. Slavoj Žižek, *On Belief* (London and New York: Routledge, 2001), pp. 29–31.

17. For an excellent discussion of Žižek's contribution to a theory of ideology that brings to the fore his relation to Laclau's theory of ideology, see Jason Glynos, "The Grip of Ideology: A Lacanian Approach to the Theory of Ideology," *Journal of Political Ideologies* (2001) 6, 2, 191–214.

18. *Sublime Object*, pp. 124–125; Slavoj Žižek, *Tarrying with the Negative* (Durham, NC: Duke University Press, 1993), p. 213.

19. For a thorough account of debates on the concept of ideology, see Michele Barrett, *The Politics of Truth: From Marx to Foucault* (Palo Alto, CA: Stanford University Press, 1992). For a selection of different positions within this debate, see Slavoj Žižek, ed., *Mapping Ideology* (London: Verso, 1995).

20. See my discussion in *Publicity's Secret*, pp. 4–8.

21. *Sublime Object*, pp. 43–44.

22. Žižek explains, "In short, the intimate link between *subject* and *failure* lies not in the fact that 'external' material social rituals and/or practices forever fail to reach the subject's innermost kernel, to represent it adequately—that some internality, some internal object irreducible to the externality of social practices … always remains—but, on the contrary, in the fact that the 'subject' itself is *nothing but* the failure of symbolization, of its own symbolic representation—the subject is nothing 'beyond' this failure, it emerges through this failure … ." *Contingency, Hegemony, Universality*, Judith Butler, Ernesto Laclau, and Slavoj Žižek (London: Verso, 2000), pp. 119–120.

23. *Contingency, Hegemony, Universality*, p. 117.

24. My use of the term *imagine* here does not mean that the ego-ideal is imaginary in the Lacanian sense. On the contrary, the ego ideal is a point of symbolic identification.

25. *Sublime Object*, p. 118.

26. *Plague of Fantasies*, p. 55.

27. See Kwame Anthony Appiah, *In My Father's House* (Oxford: Oxford University Press, 1993).
28. *Tarrying with the Negative*, p. 201.
29. *Tarrying with the Negative*, p. 202.
30. *Parallax View*, p. 300.
31. *Tarrying with the Negative*, p. 206.
32. Žižek writes, "What we conceal by imputing to the Other the theft of enjoyment is the traumatic fact that *we never possessed what was allegedly stolen from us*: the lack ('castration') is originary, enjoyment constitutes itself as 'stolen' … ." *Tarrying with the Negative*, pp. 203–204.
33. *Sublime Object*, pp. 69, 72.
34. Žižek writes, "There is a subject only in so far as there is some material/stain leftover that *resists* subjectivization, a surplus in which, precisely, the subject *cannot* recognize itself." Slavoj Žižek, *The Fragile Absolute* (London: Verso, 2000), p. 28.
35. *Plague of Fantasies*, p. 49.
36. *Sublime Object*, p. 50; *Fragile Absolute*, pp. 22–24; see also Fink, pp. 96–97.
37. *Sublime Object*, p. 53.
38. *Parallax View*, pp. 59–60.
39. *Fragile Absolute*, p. 17-18; *Parallax View*, p. 266. In *Parallax View*, Žižek critiques Michael Hardt and Antonio Negri on precisely this point. Like Marx, they fail to recognize the way that "the ultimate limit of capitalism (of capitalist self-propelling productivity) is Capital itself," p. 266.
40. *Plague of Fantasies*, p. 48.
41. Slavoj Žižek, *The Indivisible Remainder* (London: Verso, 1996), p. 211.
42. *Parallax View*, p. 92.
43. *Indivisible Remainder*, p. 212.
44. Slavoj Žižek, *Welcome to the Desert of the Real* (London: Verso, 2002), p. 96. Žižek writes, "The 'totalitarian' notion of the 'administered world,' in which the very experience of subjective freedom is the form of appearance of subjection to disciplinary mechanisms, is ultimately the obscene fantasmatic underside of the 'official' public ideology (and practice) of individual autonomy and freedom: the first has to accompany the second, supplementing it as its obscene shadowy double … ."
45. *Parallax View*, pp. 381–383.
46. *Parallax View*, p. 17.
47. *Parallax View*, p. 17.
48. *Plague of Fantasies*, p. 105.
49. *Plague of Fantasies*, p. 115.
50. *Plague of Fantasies*, p. 116.
51. *Plague of Fantasies*, p. 116.
52. *Plague of Fantasies*, p. 10.
53. *Plague of Fantasies*, p. 51.

54. Slavoj Žižek, *The Metastases of Enjoyment* (London: Verso, 1995), p. 75.
55. Compare with Žižek's discussions of liberal intellectual fascination with nationalism: they "refuse it, mock it, laugh at it, yet at the same time stare at it with powerless fascination. The intellectual pleasure procured by denouncing nationalism is uncannily close to the satisfaction of successfully explaining one's own impotence and failure." *Tarrying with the Negative*, p. 211.
56. Hence, Žižek holds the view that the "threat today is not passivity but pseudo-activity, the urge to 'be active,' to 'participate,' to mask the Nothingness of what goes on," *Parallax View*, p. 334.
57. Žižek writes, "Freud himself pointed out that the superego feeds on the forces of the id, which it suppresses and from which it acquires its obscene, malevolent, sneering quality—as if the enjoyment of which the subject is deprived were accumulated in the very place from which the superego's prohibition is enunciated .... The superego is, so to speak, an agency of the law exempted from its authority: it does what it prohibits us from doing," Slavoj Žižek, *Looking Awry* (Cambridge, MA: MIT Press, 1991), p. 159.
58. *Fragile Absolute*, p. 132.
59. *Ticklish Subject*, p. 380.
60. Žižek writes, "The superego obscene supplement is precisely the support of the public ideological text which, in order to be operative, has to remain publicly disavowed: its public avowal is self-defeating." *Ticklish Subject*, p. 235.
61. In *Ticklish Subject*, Žižek claims that the superego injunction to enjoy is ultimately supported by a figure of the totalitarian master, p. 390.
62. *Plague of Fantasies*, p. 114.
63. *Metastases of Enjoyment*, pp. 56–57.
64. In Lacan's words, "The superego is the imperative of jouissance—Enjoy!" *The Seminar of Jacques Lacan*, p. 3.
65. *Plague of Fantasies*, p. 73.
66. *Ticklish Subject*, p. 234.
67. Quoted by Sheila Samples, "Suddenly This Summer," *Dissident Voice* (August 24, 2005). Available at http://www.dissidentvoice.org/Aug05/Samples0824.htm.
68. *Plague of Fantasies*, p. 56. See also Chapter 4.
69. Slavoj Žižek, *The Puppet and the Dwarf* (Cambridge, MA: MIT Press, 2003), p. 56; *On Belief*, p. 20.
70. For a thorough and more properly complex account of the relation of the figures of consumer and citizen, see Lizabeth Cohen's excellent history, *A Consumer's Republic* (New York: Knopf, 2003).
71. See Žižek's discussion in "Lenin's Choice," his afterward to *Revolution at the Gates: A Selection of Writings from February to October 1917, V.I. Lenin*, edited by Slavoj Žižek (London: Verso, 2002), p. 277.

72. *Parallax View*, p. 310.
73. *Puppet and the Dwarf*, p. 56; *Ticklish Subject*, p. 390.
74. *Puppet and the Dwarf*, p. 56.
75. The quoted terms are from Coulter's blog, www.anncoulter.com.
76. "Lenin's Choice," p. 174.
77. *Puppet and the Dwarf*, p. 96; *Welcome to the Desert of the Real*, p. 11.
78. *Ticklish Subject*, pp. 322–334. See also my discussion in *Publicity's Secret*, pp. 131–138.
79. *Ticklish Subject*, p. 368.
80. See the discussion in *Puppet and the Dwarf*, pp. 166–168.
81. *Ticklish Subject*, pp. 360, 344.
82. See Paul A. Passavant, "The Strong Neoliberal State: Crime, Consumption," Governance," *Theory and Event* 8.3 (2005). See also Connolly's discussion of the desire to punish, pp. 41–74.
83. Connolly, p. xvii.
84. William E. Connolly, *Neuropolitics* (Minneapolis: University of Minnesota Press, 2002), p. 106.

Chapter 2

1. Slavoj Žižek, *The Plague of Fantasies* (London: Verso, 1997), p. 50.
2. Slavoj Žižek, *Did Somebody Say Totalitarianism?* (London Verso, 2001), p. 149.
3. For a short popular presentation of the argument see, Slavoj Žižek, "The Two Totalitarianisms," *The London Review of Books* 27, 6 (March 17, 2005). Available at http://www.lrb.co.uk/v27/n06/print/zize01_.html.
4. This claim refines and corrects his earlier, broad use of *totalitarianism* in *Tarrying with the Negative* (Durham, NC: Duke University Press, 1993), where he states, "At the level of libidinal economy, totalitarianism is defined by a perverse self-objectivization (self-instrumentalization) of the subject," p. 193. His later works make it clear that in Žižek's early discussions, *totalitarianism* is a synonym for real existing socialism. These discussions thus should not be understood as endorsing *totalitarian* as an analytical category.
5. *Did Somebody Say Totalitarianism?*, pp. 2–3.
6. Slavoj Žižek, *Organs Without Bodies* (New York: Routledge, 2004), p. 207.
7. For an example of such an argument, see Assaf Sagiv, "The Magician of Ljubljana," *Azure* no. 22 (Autumn 2005). Available at http://www.azure.org.il/magazine/magazine.asp?id=275.
8. Slavoj Žižek, *The Ticklish Subject* (London: Verso, 1999), p. 139.

9. For a thorough elaboration and defense of this view, see Stephen K. White, *Sustaining Affirmation: The Strengths of Weak Ontology in Political Theory* (Princeton, NJ: Princeton University Press, 2000).

10. For a similar argument, see my "The Politics of Avoidance: The Limits of Weak Ontology," *Hedgehog Review* 7, 2 (Summer 2005): pp. 55–64.

11. Slavoj Žižek, *Welcome to the Desert of the Real* (London: Verso, 2002), p. 117; Slavoj Žižek, *The Puppet and the Dwarf* (Cambridge, The MIT Press, 2003), p. 167.

12. *Did Somebody Say Totalitarianism?*, p. 133.

13. *Organs Without Bodies*, p. 207.

14. *Did Somebody Say Totalitarianism?*, p. 131.

15. He argues likewise in *The Parallax View* (Cambridge, MA: The MIT Press, 2006), "What the anti-Communist dissidents tend as a rule to overlook is that the very space from which they themselves criticized and denounced the daily terror and misery was opened and sustained by the Communist breakthrough, by its attempt to escape the logic of Capital," p. 292.

16. *Did Somebody Say Totalitarianism?*, p. 44.

17. Slavoj Žižek, "Afterword: Lenin's Choice," in *Revolution at the Gates: Selected Writings of Lenin from 1917* (London: Verso, 2002), p. 248. Giorgio Agamben, *Homo Sacer: Sovereign Power and Bare Life*, trans. Daniel Heller-Roazen (Stanford, CA: Stanford University Press, 1998).

18. Žižek provides two different formulae when describing Stalinist bureaucracy. In *For They Know Not What They Do* (London: Verso, 1991), pp. 235–236, he treats Stalinism in terms of totalitarianism and reads the totalitarian subject in terms of one side of the discourse of the Master, S2 over a. Yet in *Iraq: The Borrowed Kettle* (London: Verso, 2004), pp. 155–156, he associates Stalinist bureaucracy with the discourse of the university and uses that formal structure to explain it. I attribute this difference to his tasks in the two works. In the former, his intention is to understand totalitarianism as arising within the space created by the challenge to authority in the course of the democratic invention. In the latter, his interest is in reading Stalinism as the symptom of capitalism. I should add, moreover, that his description of Stalinist discourse remains basically the same. Because of this continuity, then, I follow academic convention in treating his most recent formulation of Stalinism in terms of university discourse as indicative of his position.

19. Author's preface, "The Inhuman," in *Interrogating the Real*, ed. Rex Butler and Scott Stephens (London: Continuum, 2005), pp. 9–10. Žižek attributes his use of the concept of the parallax to Kojin Karatani, *Transcritique: On Kant and Marx* (Cambridge, The MIT Press, 2003). Karatani's discussion of parallax is based on a reading of Kant's *Critique of Pure Reason* through Kant's earlier essay "Dreams of a Visionary." Karatani argues that the essay makes the innovation in Kant's approach

to reflective reason explicit. He quotes Kant: [Formerly] "I viewed human common sense only from the standpoint of my own; now I put myself into the position of another's reason outside myself, and observe my judgments, together with their secret causes, from the point of view of others. It is true that the comparison of both observations results in pronounced parallax, but it is the only means of preventing the optical delusion, and of putting the concept of the power of knowledge in human nature into its true place." *Transcritique*, p. 46.

20. "The Inhuman," p. 9.
21. *Parallax View*, p. 281; *Puppet and the Dwarf*, p. 79.
22. *Parallax View*, p. 4.
23. *Parallax View*, p. 26; *Puppet and the Dwarf*, p. 77.
24. *Parallax View*, p. 26.
25. *Ticklish Subject*, p. 77.
26. *Parallax View*, pp. 28–30.
27. For a careful elaboration of the differences between his view and Laclau and Mouffe's, see Linda Zerilli, "This universalism which is not one," in *Laclau: A Critical Reader*, edited by Simon Critchley and Oliver Marchart (New York: Routledge, 2004): pp. 88–109. The difference hinges on whether antagonism is internal to the subject (such that external division from another is simply an externalization of an internal division) or whether it emerges in the form of opposing positions in a social conflict.
28. Slavoj Žižek, *The Sublime Object of Ideology* (London: Verso, 1989), pp. 5–6.
29. Ernesto Laclau and Chantal Mouffe, *Hegemony and Social Strategy* (London: Verso, 1985).
30. *Sublime Object*, p. 5.
31. See *Sublime Object*, pp. 6–7. Crucial to Žižek's overall approach is a reading of Hegel that breaks with a traditional emphasis on the process of the realization of the Idea and emphasizes instead the movement of negativity, the "non-all" character of any moment. Žižek writes, "What we find in Hegel is the strongest affirmation yet of difference and contingency— 'absolute knowledge' itself is nothing but a name for the acknowledgement of a certain radical loss" (p. 7.)
32. "Lenin's Choice," p. 210.
33. Judith Butler, Ernesto Laclau, and Slavoj Žižek, *Contingency, Hegemony, Universality* (London: Verso, 2000), p. 132, note 32. See also p. 320: "There are no 'objective' relations of production that can *then* involve or not involve the resistance of the individuals caught up in them: the very absence of struggle and resistance—the fact that both sides involved in relations accept them without resistance—*is already the index of the victory of one side in the struggle*" (emphasis in original). See also *Parallax View*, p. 349.

34. *Ticklish Subject*, pp. 186–187.
35. *Parallax View*, pp. 362.
36. *Contingency, Hegemony, Universality*, p. 320.
37. *Contingency, Hegemony, Universality*, p. 319.
38. For a discussion of communicative capitalism, see my *Publicity's Secret: How Technoculture Capitalizes on Democracy* (Ithaca: Cornell University Press, 2002).
39. *Organs Without Bodies*, p. 185.
40. Which explains why in *Parallax View*, Žižek says that "political parallax" is another way to designate class struggle, p. 10.
41. "Lenin's Choice," p. 271; *Parallax View*, p. 320.
42. *Parallax View*, p. 320.
43. *Organs Without Bodies*, p. 99.
44. Slavoj Žižek, *The Fragile Absolute* (London: Verso, 2000), p. 19.
45. See also Slavoj Žižek, *On Belief* (London: Routledge, 2001), p. 82 where Žižek discusses three modalities of the Real, that is, the way that the imaginary, symbolic, and the Real appear within the order of the Real.
46. *For They Know Not What They Do*, p. 186.
47. *Tarrying with the Negative*, p. 210.
48. For a more detailed introduction, see Bruce Fink, *The Lacanian Subject* (Princeton, NJ: Princeton University Press, 1995), pp. 129–136.
49. See *Iraq: The Borrowed Kettle*, pp. 131–134; *The Seminar of Jacques Lacan, Book XX, 1972–1932, Encore, On Feminine Sexuality, The Limits of Love and Knowledge*, ed. Jacques-Alain Miller, trans. Bruce Fink (W.W. Norton, 1998), pp. 16–17. The formulae are from Lacan, p. 17.
50. *Iraq: The Borrowed Kettle*, p. 138.
51. *Iraq: The Borrowed Kettle*, p. 135.
52. *Plague of Fantasies*, p. 55.
53. *Plague of Fantasies*, p. 55.
54. *Plague of Fantasies*, p. 57.
55. *Plague of Fantasies*, pp. 55–56.
56. *Did Somebody Say Totalitarianism?*, p. 193.
57. *Plague of Fantasies*, p. 21.
58. *Plague of Fantasies*, p. 21.
59. *Ticklish Subject*, pp. 184–185.
60. *Plague of Fantasies*, p. 22.
61. *Ticklish Subject*, p. 186.
62. *Did Somebody Say Totalitarianism?*, p. 73.
63. As Žižek writes in *Parallax View*, the Holocaust, "from the economic or technological standpoint of total mobilization of resources … was clearly 'irrational'—representatives of industry and the Army protested to the SS all the time that the Holocaust was a gigantic waste of precious human, economic, and military resources …," p. 285.
64. *Did Somebody Say Totalitarianism?*, pp. 76–81.

65. *Plague of Fantasies,* p. 60; *Did Somebody Say Totalitarianism?,* pp. 129–131.
66. Žižek draws from a substantial scholarly literature on the Soviet Union. Among his sources are Sheila Fitzpatrick, *Everyday Stalinism* (Oxford: Oxford University Press, 1999), J. Arch Getty and Oleg V. Naumov, *The Road to Terror: Stalin and the Self-Destruction of the Bolsheviks* (New Haven: Yale University Press, 1999), and Colin Thubron, *In Siberia* (New York: HarperCollins, 2000).
67. "Lenin's Choice," p. 267.
68. *On Belief,* p. 38.
69. *Did Somebody Say Totalitarianism?,* p. 74.
70. *Did Somebody Say Totalitarianism?,* p. 74.
71. Giorgio Agamben, *The Time That Remains,* trans. Patricia Dailey (Stanford: Stanford University Press, 2005), p. 105. See also Giorgio Agamben, *Homo Sacer: Sovereign Power and Bare Life,* trans. Daniel Heller-Roazen (Stanford: Stanford University Press, 1998).
72. *Did Somebody Say Totalitarianism?,* p. 87.
73. *Did Somebody Say Totalitarianism?,* p. 97.
74. Nikolai Bukharin was one of the leading Bolsheviks. He served as a member of the Central Committee, the Politburo, and as editor of *Pravda* and, briefly, *Izvestia.* He became president of the Comintern (Communist International) in 1926. He was arrested in 1937 during the purges and shot in 1938.
75. *Did Somebody Say Totalitarianism?,* p. 107.
76. *Did Somebody Say Totalitarianism?,* p. 105.
77. *Did Somebody Say Totalitarianism?,* pp. 107–108.
78. *Did Somebody Say Totalitarianism?,* p. 108.
79. In *Parallax View,* Žižek presents a different account of the show trial. He writes: "in Stalinist show trials, for example, the accused has to confess his crimes publicly and give an account of how he came to commit them—in stark contrast to Nazism, in which it would be meaningless to demand from a Jew a confession that he was involved in a plot against the German nation. This difference is symptomatic of different attitudes toward the Enlightenment. Stalinism still conceived itself as part of the Enlightenment tradition, within which truth is accessible to any rational man ... which is why he is subjectively responsible for his crimes," p. 289. That "guilt" under the Nazis was determined racially or biopolitically is a constant in Žižek's analysis. The difference here comes with the emphasis on truth and the Enlightenment tradition. In this passage, Žižek neglects the perverse element of the show trial, an element that clearly overrode any Enlightenment view of truth insofar as it is the truth of the Party that the victim of the show trial is required to avow, whether he is convinced of it or not. In fact, this very partisan truth is understood as such, as a spe-

cific truth not commensurate with, say, bourgeois truth—as the Stalinist effort to build a specifically Soviet science attests.
80. *Iraq: The Borrowed Kettle*, p. 142; *Parallax View*, p. 304.
81. *Did Somebody Say Totalitarianism?*, p. 118.
82. *Did Somebody Say Totalitarianism?*, p. 119.
83. *For They Know Not What They Do*, p. 236.
84. *Did Somebody Say Totalitarianism?*, p. 120.
85. *Plague of Fantasies*, p. 60.
86. *Organs Without Bodies*, p. 205.
87. Yet in *Did Somebody Say Totalitarianism?* Žižek offers a later date for the "Thermidor," namely, with the Brezhnev years of stagnation (p. 130); see also *Parallax View*, p. 287.
88. *Organs Without Bodies*, pp. 205–206; *Parallax View*, pp. 287–288.
89. *Did Somebody Say Totalitarianism?*, p. 127.
90. "Lenin's Choice," p. 262.
91. "Lenin's Choice," p. 261.
92. *Parallax View*, p. 287.
93. *Parallax View*, p. 287.
94. *Iraq: The Borrowed Kettle*, p. 156.
95. *Iraq: The Borrowed Kettle*, p. 156.
96. *Iraq: The Borrowed Kettle*, p. 149; see also *Homo Sacer*.
97. *Iraq: The Borrowed Kettle*, p. 139.
98. For a discussion of this literature, see Chapter Three of my *Publicity's Secret*.
99. Žižek refers to Lenin's emphasis on scientists and expert authority, to a "happy time when politics will recede into the background ... and engineers and agronomists will do most of the talking." "Lenin's Choice," p. 292.
100. *Iraq: The Borrowed Kettle*, p. 145.
101. On moral bankrupty, see *Did Somebody Say Totalitarianism?*, p. 91; on cynicism see *Sublime Object*, pp. 197–198.
102. *Sublime Object*, p. 197.
103. *Iraq: The Borrowed Kettle*, p. 149.
104. "Lenin's Choice," p. 295.
105. *Sublime Object*, p. 26.
106. See, for example, David Harvey, *A History of Neoliberalism* (Oxford: Oxford University Press, 2005). Emphasizing the shift from production to finance, Harvey writes, "Neoliberalization has meant, in short, the financialization of everything," p. 33.
107. Harvey, p. 33.
108. "Lenin's Choice," p. 295.
109. *Parallax View*, p. 303.
110. *Iraq: The Borrowed Kettle*, p. 142.
111. *Ticklish Subject*, pp. 265–268.

112. "Introduction: Between the Two Revolutions," in *Revolution at the Gates*, p. 4.
113. "Introduction: Between the Two Revolutions," p. 5.
114. *Did Somebody Say Totalitarianism?*, p. 112.
115. "Lenin's Choice," p. 188.
116. "Lenin's Choice," p. 192.

Chapter 3

1. For a critique of communicative capitalism in terms of the shift in the structure of communication away from the message in need of response and toward the contribution that circulates, see my "Communicative Capitalism: Circulation and the Foreclosure of Politics," *Cultural Politics* 1, 1 (2005): pp. 51–74.

2. Žižek writes, "The usual notion of the relationship between surplus-enjoyment and symbolic identification is that symbolic identity is what we get in exchange for being deprived of enjoyment; what happens in contemporary society, with the decline of the Master-Signifier and the rise of consumerism, is the exact obverse: the basic fact is the loss of symbolic identity ... and in exchange for this loss we are bombarded from all sides with forms and gadgets of enjoyment." Slavoj Žižek, *Iraq: The Borrowed Kettle* (London: Verso, 2004), p. 145.

3. *Iraq: The Borrowed Kettle*, p. 155.

4. Slavoj Žižek, *The Fragile Absolute* (London: Verso, 2000), p. 100; Slavoj Žižek, "Against Human Rights," *New Left Review* 34 (July–August 2005).

5. Slavoj Žižek, *The Parallax View* (MIT Press, 2006) p. 340.

6. "Against Human Rights," see also *Parallax View*, p. 341.

7. Judith Butler, Ernesto Laclau, and Slavoj Žižek, *Contingency, Hegemony, Universality* (London: Verso, 2000), p. 289.

8 Slavoj Žižek, *For They Know Not What They Do* (London: Verso, 1991), p. 270.

9. *Parallax View*, p. 320.

10. Slavoj Žižek, *The Sublime Object of Ideology* (London: Verso, 1989), p. 148. Žižek remains ambivalently supportive of democracy in *Sublime Object*. He writes, "So although 'in reality' there are only 'exceptions' and 'deformations,' the universal notion of 'democracy' is none the less a 'necessary fiction,' a symbolic fact in the absence of which effective democracy, in all the plurality of its forms, could not reproduce itself" (pp. 148–149). I read Žižek as ambivalently supportive here insofar as his point can be read as primarily conceptual. In all his later work, Žižek challenges the presumption that democracy remains our ultimate political horizon.

11. Slavoj Žižek, "Georg Lukacs as the philosopher of Leninism," in Georg Lukacs, *A Defense of History and Class Consciousness*, trans. John Rees (London: Verso, 2000), p. 176. Elsewhere Žižek rejects "liberal fundamentalism." See his "Afterword: Lenin's Choice" in *Revolution at the Gates: Selected Writings of Lenin from 1917*, ed. Slavoj Žižek (Verso: London, 2002), p. 168.

12. Žižek claims, "The fact that global capitalism is a totality means that it is the dialectical unity of itself and of its other, of the forces which resist it on 'fundamentalist' ideological grounds." Slavok Žižek, *Welcome to the Desert of the Real* (London: Verso, 2002), p. 151.

13. See also *Parallax View*, p. 348.

14. Žižek's position here should be contrasted to the one he takes in *Sublime Object*, where he notes that the extraordinary feature of formal democracy is precisely the willingness to suspend the social order in periodic elections.

15. Slavoj Žižek, *Tarrying with the Negative* (Durham, NC: Duke University Press, 1993), p. 221. Žižek claims that the question of liberal democracy is the only question confronting political philosophy. Yet he also writes that "the only true dilemma today is whether or not the late-capitalist Spinozaism is our ultimate horizon" (p. 219). One could read these pronouncements on fundamental questions as hyperbolic. I read them as an indication of a certain merging of two opponents in Žižek's thought. As Žižek's criticisms of democracy in late capitalism increase in momentum at the end of the nineties and the beginning of the new century, he often blurs together liberal democracy and Spinozaism in his opposition to both. Insofar as neither provides a critical edge against capitalism, both support it.

16. Žižek hints at this option in *The Sublime Object of Ideology* and *Looking Awry*; in the rest of his work, however, he rejects it because of its support for capitalism. Žižek writes, "The democratic attitude is always based on a certain fetishistic split: *I know very well* (that the democratic form is just a form spoiled by stains of 'pathological' imbalance), *but just the same* I act as if democracy were possible. Far from indicating its fatal flaw, this split is the very source of the strength of democracy: democracy is able to take cognizance of the fact that its limit lies in itself, in its internal 'antagonism.'" *Looking Awry* (Cambridge, MA: MIT Press, 1992), p. 168.

17. *For They Know Not What They Do*, p. 260.

18. In Lacan's version, the paternal Law emerges in the place of the renounced incestuous object, the supremely good Mother. As Žižek explains in a contribution to *Contingency, Hegemony, Universality*, "Lacan's 'primordial repression' of *das Ding* (of the pre-symbolic incestuous Real Thing) is precisely that which creates universality as an empty place; and the 'trace of the disavowed in the formal structure that emerges' is what Lacan calls *objet petit a*, the remainder of *joussiance* within the symbolic order," p. 257.

19. *For They Know Not What They Do*, p. 231.
20. *For They Know Not What They Do*, p. 240.
21. *Looking Awry*, p. 167.
22. *For They Know Not What They Do*, p. 234.
23. Žižek suggests that the Hegelian monarch provides a way out of this impasse: the monarch materializes the distance between the empty place of power and the one who, contingently, occupies that place.
24. *For They Know Not What They Do*, p. 262.
25. For an account of the People in the American context, see Paul A. Passavant, *No Escape: Freedom of Speech and the Paradox of Rights* (New York: New York University Press, 2002).
26. See also *Looking Awry*, pp. 165–169.
27. A more thorough discussion here would include Žižek's rejection of new social movements as undermining the foundations of formal democracy (*Looking Awry*, p. 164) and his claim in *Ticklish Subject* that identity politics is really no politics at all (p. 354). The significant concept here is "concrete democracy" and the way new social movements "would absorb the diversity of the lifeworld." New social movements reject the struggle for power and instead want to change ordinary patterns of life. In the process, the very space of the struggle for power collapses: everything is already political. In *Ticklish Subject*, Žižek describes this absorption in terms of the third way and risk society politics and links it to the collapse of the symbolic.
28. This is a paraphrase of *Looking Awry*, p. 168.
29. *Tarrying with the Negative*, pp. 182, 186.
30. *Tarrying with the Negative*, p. 185.
31. *Tarrying with the Negative*, p. 202.
32. *Tarrying with the Negative*, p. 203.
33. *Tarrying with the Negative*, p. 206.
34. Žižek writes, "It is on account of fantasy that an ideology cannot be reduced to a network of elements whose value wholly depends on their respective differential positions within the symbolic structure." *Tarrying with the Negative*, p. 213.
35. *Tarrying with the Negative*, p. 211.
36. *Tarrying with the Negative*, pp. 226–228. For a discussion of the role of radical art and music during and after the breakup of the former Yugoslavia, see Alexei Monroe, *Interrogation Machine: Laibach and NSK* (Cambridge, MA: The MIT Press, 2005).
37. *Contingency, Hegemony, Universality*, p. 325.
38. Gilles Deleuze and Felix Guattari, *A Thousand Plateaus,* trans. Brian Massumi (Minneapolis: University of Minnesota Press); William Connolly, *The Ethos of Pluralization* (Minneapolis: University of Minnesota Press, 1995), *Why I'm Not a Secularist* (Minneapolis: University of Minnesota Press, 1999), and *Neuropolitics: Thinking, Culture, Speed*

(Minneapolis: University of Minnesota Press, 2002); Michael Hardt and Antonio Negri, *Empire* (Cambridge: Harvard University Press, 2000). See also Slavoj Žižek, *Organs without Bodies* (New York: Routledge, 2004).

39. *Contingency, Hegemony, Universality*, p. 95.
40. Slavoj Žižek, *The Ticklish Subject* (London: Verso, 1999), p. 353.
41. *Ticklish Subject*, p. 356. See also *Parallax View*, p. 361.
42. Slavoj Žižek, *The Fragile Absolute* (London: Verso, 2000), pp. 13, 25.
43. Joshua Gamson, "Gay Media, Inc.: Media Structures, the New Gay Conglomerates, and Collective Sexual Identities," in *Cyberactivism: Online Activism in Theory and Practice*, ed. Martha McCaughey and Michael D. Ayers (New York: Routledge, 2003), p. 259.
44. *Ticklish Subject*, pp. 215–218.
45. "Lenin's Choice," p. 225.
46. See *Ticklish Subject*, p. 219.
47. See "Against Human Rights."
48. *Welcome to the Desert of the Real*, p. 11.
49. *Welcome to the Desert of the Real*, pp. 64–66; Slavoj Žižek, "The Ideology of the Empire and Its Traps," in *Empire's New Clothes*, ed. Paul A. Passavant and Jodi Dean (New York: Routledge, 2004), pp. 257–258.
50. *Welcome to the Desert of the Real*, p. 65.
51. *Ticklish Subject*, pp. 208–209.
52. See "Against Rights."
53. *Ticklish Subject*, p. 204.
54. *Organs Without Bodies*, pp. 183–193.
55. See, for example, Connolly's description of fundamentalism as "a political formula of self-aggrandizement through the translation of stresses and disturbances in your doctrine of identity into resources for its stabilization and aggrandizement. It converts stresses and strains in itself into evidence of deviation and immorality in the other; and it conceals the political dynamic of this strategy of self-protection by enclosing it in a vocabulary of God, nature, reason, nation, or normality elevated above the possibility of critical reflection. It is marked by the stringency of its exclusionary form and its insistence upon treating the putative sources of exclusion into certain, unquestionable dogmas" (*Ethos of Pluralization*, p. 106). It is important to note here that Connolly does not confine his notion of fundamentalism to religious or other conservatives but recognizes its impulses in myriad institutions and doctrines in American political life.
56. *Welcome to the Desert of the Real*, p. 69. Žižek's argument here is indebted to Alain Badiou. See Alain Badiou, *Ethics: An Essay on the Understanding of Evil*, translated by Peter Hallward (London: Verso, 2001) pp. 24–25.
57. *Welcome to the Desert of the Real*, p. 68.
58. *Organs Without Bodies*, p. 67. See also Ernesto Laclau, "Can Immanence Explain Social Struggles?" in *Empire's New Clothes*, pp. 21–30.

59. *Organs without Bodies*, pp. 34–35.
60. *Ticklish Subject*, p. 176.
61. *Empire*, p. 354.
62. *Contingency, Hegemony, Universality*, p. 217.
63. *Ticklish Subject*, p. 224.
64. *Ticklish Subject*, p. 176.
65. "Against Rights."
66. *Ticklish Subject*, p. 208.
67. *Empire*, pp. 385–386.
68. *Ticklish Subject*, p. 201.
69. For a thorough discussion of this problem see Paul A. Passavant and Jodi Dean, "Representation and the Event," in *Empire's New Clothes*, pp. 315–328.
70. Žižek writes, "The moment we introduce the 'thinking multitude' what we are in fact asserting is its exact opposite, the underlying all-pervasive sameness—the notion of a radical antagonistic gap that affects the entire social body is obliterated." Slavoj Žižek, *Did Somebody Say Totalitarianism?* (London: Verso, 2001), p. 238.
71. Žižek explains that "leftist universalism proper does not involve any kind of return to some neutral universal content (a common notion of humanity, etc); rather, it refers to a universal which comes to exist ... only in a particular element which is structurally displaced, 'out of joint:' within a given social Whole, it is precisely the element which is prevented from actualizing its full particular identity that stands for its universal dimension." *Ticklish Subject*, p. 224. See also *Parallax View*, p. 30. Žižek writes, "Universality is not the neutral container of particular formations, their common measure, the passive (back)ground on which the particulars fight their battles, but this battle itself, the struggle leading from one particular formation to another,"
72. *Ticklish Subject*, p. 210.
73. *Ticklish Subject*, p. 227.
74. *Parallax View*, p. 150.
75. "Lenin's Choice," p. 186.
76. *Contingency, Hegemony, Universality*, p. 125.
77. *Parallax View*, p. 364.
78. *Ticklish Subject*, p. 191.
79. *Ticklish Subject*, p. 225.
80. "Lenin's Choice," p. 176.
81. This is one of the strangest elements of Hardt's and Negri's position: the multitude provides the crises that Empire needs to realize itself as Empire.
82. *Welcome to the Desert of the Real*, p. 101.
83. In *The Ticklish Subject*, Žižek raises this point against Judith Butler, pointing out that "she overestimates the subversive potential of disturb-

ing the functioning of the big Other through the practices of performative reconfiguration/displacement: such practices ultimately support what they intend to subvert, since the very field of such 'transgressions' is already taken into account, even engendered by the hegemonic form of the big Other—what Lacan calls the 'big Other' are symbolic norms and their codified transgressions," p. 264.

84. *Ticklish Subject*, p. 376; *Welcome to the Desert of the Real*, p. 152; *Contingency, Hegemony, Universality*, pp. 124–127. For a detailed discussion of the act from the perspective of Lacan's notion of *passage à l'acte*, see Sarah Kay's *Žižek: A Critical Introduction* (Cambridge, U.K.: Polity Press, 2003).

85. There is thus a similarity between Žižek's account of the act and Hannah Arendt's idea of action: for both, acts are risky interventions whose meaning is always retroactively determined from the new circumstances that acts bring into being. A key difference between their accounts, however, consists in the relation between speech and acts. For Žižek, following Lacan, real acts lack the support of the symbolic order necessary for speech; they are Real. *Ticklish Subject*, p. 374.

86. *Welcome to the Desert of the Real*, p. 152.

87. *Ticklish Subject*, p. 375.

88. *Contingency, Hegemony, Universality*, p. 125.

89. *Ticklish Subject*, p. 377.

90. *Parallax View*, p. 383.

91. *Fragile Absolute*, pp. 143–160.

92. Slavoj Žižek, *The Plague of Fantasies* (London: Verso, 1997), p. 29.

93. Stanley Hoffman, "America Goes Backward," *The New York Review of Books* (June 12, 2003): pp. 74–80.

94. *Contingency, Hegemony, Universality*, p. 255.

Chapter 4

1. Slavoj Žižek, *The Parallax View* (Cambridge, MA: The MIT Press, 2006), p. 10.

2. Paul A. Passavant, plenary address, Critical Legal Conference, University of Kent School of Law, Canterbury, U.K., September 2001. In his remarks, Passavant considers recent work by Judith Butler, Stanley Fish, and Michael Hardt and Antonio Negri. For a detailed analysis of Butler's *Excitable Speech* that makes a similar argument, see Paul A. Passavant and Jodi Dean, "Laws and Societies," *Constellations* 8, 3 (2001): pp. 376–389.

3. Slavoj Žižek, *The Fragile Absolute* (London: Verso, 2000), p. 93.

4. Slavoj Žižek, *For They Know Not What They Do* (London: Verso, 1991), p. 204.

5. As Costas Douzinas points out, this claim is one of the key tenets of psychoanalytic approaches to law: "Psychoanalysis presents the birth of law as a crime story." *The End of Human Rights* (Oxford: Hart Publishers, 2000), p. 298.
6. I am indebted to Paul Passavant for this example.
7. See *Notes of Debates in the Federal Convention of 1787 Reported by James Madison* (New York: Norton, 1987), p. 657. I am grateful to DeWayne Lucas for bringing this to my attention. For a history of the contentious debates around the Constitution, see Jackson Turner Main, *The Anti-federalists: Critics of the Constitution 1781–1788* (New York: Norton, 1974).
8. *Notes of Debates in the Federal Convention of 1787*, p. 612.
9. James Madison, Number 40, *The Federalist Papers*, ed. Clinton Rossiter (New York: Mentor, 1961), p. 251.
10. Madison, pp. 254–255.
11. *The Antifederalist Papers*, Number 49, "On Constitutional Conventions," available at http://www.thisnation.com/library/antifederalist/print/49/html. Again, I am indebted to DeWayne Lucas for bringing this to my attention.
12. Sigmund Freud, *Totem and Taboo*, trans. A.A. Brill (Mineola, NY: Dover Publications, 1998 [1918]), p. 123.
13. For a thorough elucidation of this impossible temporality, see Peter Fitzpatrick, *Modernism and the Grounds of Law* (Cambridge: Cambridge University Press, 2001), Chapters 1–2.
14. In his discussion of Hegel's notion of truth, Žižek explains that "Notion is the *form of thought*, form in the strict dialectical sense of the 'formal aspect' *qua* truth of the content: the 'unthought' of a thought is not some transcendent content eluding its grasp but its form itself. The encounter between an object and its Notion is for that reason necessarily a *failed* one: the object can never fully correspond to its Notion *since its very existence, its ontological consistency, hangs on this non-correspondence*." *For They Know Not What They Do*, p. 164. The originary parricide, then, explains the notion of law. It tells us—those of us who share this notion—what law means, how law is thought. The legal order cannot correspond to the Notion of law. Rather, the Notion of law marks the place occupied by law, a place from which law can be absent. Thus, the Notion involves the division of law within itself, law's coincidence with crime.
15. Žižek makes this point through a discussion of Kant's prohibition on inquiry into the origins of law: "we cannot assume the historical origins of the law in some lawless violence and remain its subjects. As soon as the law is reduced to its lawless origins, its full validity is suspended." *For They Know Not What They Do*, p. 205.
16. *Sublime Object*, p. 38.

17. Slavoj Žižek, *Tarrying with the Negative* (Durham, NC: Duke University Press, 1993), p. 51.
18. *Tarrying with the Negative*, p. 51.
19. *For They Know Not What They Do*, p. 265.
20. Žižek distinguishes his position here from the customary psychoanalytic account wherein the symbolic law of the father appears as an intervention in the relationship between the mother and the child. Žižek's point is that the symbolic law is more complex. It also liberates the subject from the unbearable demands of the father, from the father in his obscenity. Žižek writes, "... one should not identify this Real Thing [this Other] too hastily with the incestuous object of desire rendered inaccessible by symbolic prohibition (i.e. the maternal Thing); this Thing is rather, *Father himself*, namely, the obscene Father-*jouissance* prior to his murder and subsequent elevation into agency of symbolic authority (Name-of-the-Father)." *The Ticklish Subject*, p. 314.
21. Fitzpatrick, p. 32.
22. Freud, p. 23.
23. Thomas Hobbes, *Leviathan*, ed. Richard E. Flathman and David Johnston (New York: Norton Critical Edition, 1997), Chapter 14, para. 64, p. 72.
24. As Peter Goodrich explains in his introduction to *Law and the Unconscious: A Legendre Reader* (London: Macmillan Press, 1997), the image figures critically in Pierre Legendre's psychoanalytic theory of law. Goodrich writes, "The image is cognate with the imaginary and it is through the image that law is most directly linked to the mechanisms of subjective attachment or to the direction of individual desire," p. 36. Clearly, Žižek is more concerned with the symbolic and Real elements of law.
25. *For They Know Not What They Do*, pp. 266–267.
26. Slavoj Žižek, *On Belief* (London: Routledge, 2001), p. 136.
27. Slavoj Žižek, *Metastases of Enjoyment* (London: Verso, 1995) p. 54.
28. *Tarrying with the Negative*, p. 47.
29. *For They Know Not What They Do*, p. 240.
30. Slavoj Žižek, "How Did Marx Invent the Symptom?" in *Mapping Ideology*, ed. Slavoj Žižek (Verso: London, 1994), p. 318.
31. "How Did Marx Invent the Symptom?," p. 319.
32. Bruce Fink, *A Clinical Introduction to Lacanian Psychoanalysis* (Cambridge: Harvard University Press, 1997), p. 129.
33. Fink, p. 129.
34. Frederick Douglass, *Narrative of the Life of Frederick Douglass, An American Slave, Written by Himself*, ed. David W. Blight (New York: Bedford Books, 1993), p. 51.
35. *The Fragile Absolute*, p. 133.
36. Slavoj Žižek, *Looking Awry* (Cambridge: MIT Press, 1992), p. 151.
37. *Metastases of Enjoyment*, p. 54.

38. For a more systematic exposition of the presumption of the relationship of critical legal studies to legal formalism and legal positivism see, Paul A. Passavant, "Critical Legal Studies," in *Legal Systems of the World*, Volume I. ed. Herbert Kritzer (Santa Barbara: ABC-Clio, 2002).
39. *Metastases of Enjoyment*, p. 54; *Parallax View*, p. 369
40. *Metastases of Enjoyment*, p. 55.
41. *Parallax View*, p. 370.
42. J.G. Ballard, *Super Cannes* (London: Flamingo, 2000).
43. Ballard, pp. 265, 264.
44. Ballard, p. 261.
45. Ballard, p. 262.
46. Paul A. Passavant is developing a powerful account of the faith that animates law. See, "Positivism is Hell or Faith in Law," paper presented at the annual meeting of the Law and Society Association, Vancouver, BC, May 2001.
47. Slavoj Žižek, *The Plague of Fantasies* (London: Verso, 1997), p. 28.
48. See, for example, Slavoj Žižek, "Kant with (or against) Sade," in *The Žižek Reader*, ed. Elizabeth Wright and Edmond Wright (Oxford: Blackwell, 1999), pp. 285–301; *On Belief*, pp. 138–140; Slavoj Žižek, *Iraq: The Borrowed Kettle* (London: Verso, 2004), pp. 174–176.
49. "Kant with (or against) Sade," p. 295.
50. *On Belief*, p. 139.
51. *For They Know Not What They Do*, p. 239.
52. *Iraq: The Borrowed Kettle*, p. 175; *Parallax View*, p. 94.
53. *Metastases of Enjoyment*, p. 61.
54. *Metastases of Enjoyment*, p. 60.
55. *Metastases of Enjoyment*, p. 61.
56. Žižek develops this point in *The Ticklish Subject* (London: Verso, 1999) p. 365. Reading Kant's account of the empty form of the Law as the "promise of an absent content (never) to come," he writes, "This form is not the neutral-universal mould of the plurality of different empirical contents; it bears witness to the persisting uncertainty about the content of our acts—we never know if the determinate content that accounts for the specificity of our acts is the right one, that is, if we have actually acted in accordance with *the* Law and have not been guided by some hidden pathological motives ... a gap forever separates the Law from its positive incarnations. The subject is thus a priori, in his very existence, guilty: guilty without knowing what he is guilty of (and guilty for that very reason), infringing the law without knowing its exact regulations."
57. *The Fragile Absolute*, p. 100. This section should be read as a corrective to my reading of "Žižek on Law," in *Law* and *Critique* 15 (2004): 1–24. The primary difference in my reading, one stemming from Žižek's continued development of his position in *On Belief and The Puppet and*

the Dwarf, consists in seeing love as a relation within rather than beyond law.

58. Giorgio Agamben, *The Time That Remains*, trans. Patricia Daily (Stanford: Stanford University Press, 2005).

59. Agamben writes, "The messianic is therefore the historical process whereby the archaic link between law and religion ... reaches a crisis and the element of *pistis*, of faith in the pact, tends paradoxically to emancipate itself from any obligatory conduct and from positive law (from works fulfilled in carrying out the pact)" (p. 119). Moreover, he writes, "It is obvious that for Paul grace cannot constitute a separate realm that is alongside that of obligation and law. Rather, grace entails nothing more than the ability to use the sphere of social determinations and services in its totality" (pp. 119, 124).

60. Agamben, pp. 52–53.

61. Agamben, p. 57.

62. Slavoj Žižek, *The Puppet and the Dwarf* (Cambridge: MIT Press 2003), pp. 108–109.

63. *The Puppet and the Dwarf*, p. 110.

64. *The Puppet and the Dwarf*, p. 112.

65. Žižek's reading of Paul is indebted to Badiou. See Alain Badiou, *Saint Paul: The Foundation of Universalism* (Stanford, CA: Stanford University Press, 2003).

66. *The Puppet and the Dwarf*, p. 9.

67. *The Puppet and the Dwarf*, p. 113.

68. Agamben writes, "The juridicizing of all human relations in their entirety, the confusion between what we may believe, hope, and love, and what we are supposed to do and not supposed to do, what we are supposed to know and not know, not only signal the crisis of religion but also, and above all, the crisis of law" (p. 135). Agamben thus presents the problem of law in terms of "too much law," an excess of law over and above what should not be within its domain. For Žižek, the question is not one of securing a domain free from law but of recognizing that even as something comes under the law, law remains non-all, incomplete.

69. Jean-Jacques Rousseau, "The Social Contract," in *Social Contract*, ed. Sir Ernest Barker (Oxford: Oxford University Press, 1968), pp. 180–181.

70. Quoted in *The Puppet and the Dwarf*, pp. 114–115.

71. Žižek's analysis relies on Lacan's "formulae of sexuation." See *The Seminar of Jacques Lacan: On Feminine Sexuality, The Limits of Love and Knowledge, Book XX, Encore: 1972–1973*, ed. Jacques-Alain Miller, trans. Bruce Fink (New York: Norton, 1998), pp. 78–83. See also Bruce Fink, *The Lacanian Subject* (Princeton, NJ: Princeton University Press, 1999), pp. 108–113. Žižek draws heavily from Joan Copjec's elaboration of Lacan's formulae in terms of Kant's discussion of the structural differences between mathematical and dynamical antinomies. See Joan Copjec,

Read My Desire (Cambridge: MIT Press, 1993). Following Copjec, Žižek holds that Lacan's "masculine" formulae should be understood as dynamical antinomies insofar as they describe the paradox of a universality constituted through exception, that is, of a noumenal field of reason produced through the exclusion of phenomena; the "feminine formulae" involve mathematical antinomies, that is, antinomies of the phenomenal world. He writes, "The difference in the structure of mathematical and dynamical antinomies hinges on the double negation which defines the status of phenomena: noumenon is a non-phenomenon, a limitation of phenomena, and furthermore, the field of phenomena itself is never complete or whole. Mathematical antinomies are antinomies of the 'non-all' of the phenomenal field: they result from the paradox that, although there is no object given to us in intuition which does not belong to the phenomenal field, this field is never 'all,' never complete. Dynamical antinomies, on the contrary, are antinomies of universality: logical connection of the phenomena in the universal causal nexus necessarily involves an exception, the noumenal act of freedom which 'sticks out,' suspending the causal nexus and starting a new causal series 'spontaneously' out of itself." Slavoj Žižek, *Tarrying with the Negative* (Durham, NC: Duke University Press 1993), p. 55.

72. Slavoj Žižek, *Iraq: The Borrowed Kettle* (London: Verso, 2004), pp. 119–122.
73. *Iraq: The Borrowed Kettle*, p. 161.
74. *Parallax View*, p. 385.
75. *Parallax View*, p. 382.
76. *Parallax View*, p. 382.
77. Toni Morrison, *Beloved* (New York: Penguin, 1988), p. 251.
78. *Beloved*, p. 260.
79. Slavoj Žižek, *Did Somebody Say Totalitarianism?* (London: Verso, 2001), p. 160.
80. *The Puppet and the Dwarf*, p. 113 (italics deleted).
81. *On Belief*, p. 120.
82. *The Fragile Absolute*, p. 98.
83. *The Puppet and the Dwarf*, p. 112.
84. *Iraq: The Borrowed Kettle*, p. 179.
85. Or, as Morrison puts it, "Disremembered and unaccounted for, she cannot be lost because no one is looking for her and even if they were, how can they call her if they don't know her name? Although she has claim, she is not claimed" (*Beloved*, p. 274).

Conclusion

1. See, for example, the contributions to the symposium on elections edited by Jodi Dean and Thomas L. Dumm, *Theory and Event* 8.2 (2005).
2. A thoughtful version of this argument comes from Romand Coles, "The Wild Patience of Radical Democracy: Beyond Žižek's Lack," in *Radical Democracy: Politics Between Abundance and Lack*, ed. Lars Tonder and Lasse Thomassen (Manchester: Manchester University Press, 2006).
3. Slavoj Žižek and Glyn Daly, *Conversations with Žižek* (Cambridge: Polity Press, 2004), p. 145; Slavoj Žižek, "Afterward: Lenin's Choice," in *Revolution at the Gates*, ed. Slavoj Žižek (London: Verso, 2002), p. 271.
4. *Conversations with Žižek*, p. 250.
5. Norman Solomon, "The P.U.-litzer Prizes for 2005," *Truthout* (December 20, 2005). Available at http://www.truthout.org/docs_2005/122105D. shtml.
6. Christian D. Brose, "The Bush Revolution: A Clear White House Message," *National Review Online* (November 7, 2003). Available at http://www.nationalreview.com/comment/brose200311071129.asp.
7. "Lenin's Choice," p. 304.
8. For an overview of how cultural studies attempted to pluralize the sites of politics see Jodi Dean, "Political Theory and Cultural Studies," in *The Oxford Handbook of Political Theory*, ed. John S. Dryzek, Bonnie Honig, and Anne Philips (Oxford: Oxford University Press, 2006).
9. Michael Hardt and Antonio Negri, *Empire* (Cambridge, MA: Harvard University Press, 2000).
10. "Lenin's Choice," p. 269.
11. "Lenin's Choice," p. 308.
12. "Lenin's Choice," pp. 187–189.
13. Ian Parker, *Slavoj Žižek: A Critical Introduction* (London: Pluto Press, 2004), p. 103.
14. Slavoj Žižek, *The Parallax View* (Cambridge, MA: The MIT Press, 2006), p. 334.
15. Slavoj Žižek, *The Fragile Absolute* (London: Verso, 2002), p. 93.
16. Slavoj Žižek, *The Borrowed Kettle* (London: Verso, 2004), pp. 81, 87.
17. *Iraq: The Borrowed Kettle*, p. 81.
18. Slavoj Žižek, *The Ticklish Subject* (London: Verso, 1999), p. 374.
19. See also Slavoj Žižek, *For They Know Not What They Do* (London: Verso, 1991), p. 222. There he discusses how the time of the subject is never "present," He writes, "the subject never 'is,' it only 'will have been': we never *are* free, it is only afterward that we discover how we *have been* free." Freedom is retroactively attributed to an act that could not have gone otherwise, one that seemed to flow automatically is later perceived as the result of a free decision.
20. "Lenin's Choice," p. 225.

21. Romand Coles raises this problem in "The Wild Patience of Radical Democracy."

22. Slavoj Žižek, *The Sublime Object of Ideology* (London: Verso, 1989), p. 127.

23. "Lenin's Choice," p. 268

24. *Iraq: The Borrowed Kettle*, p. 144.

25. *For They Know Not What They Do*, p. 49.

26. As Žižek writes, "... to grasp the functioning of a given ideological field, reference to the symbolic order (the Lacanian 'big Other') and its different mechanisms (overdetermination, condensation, displacement, and so on) is not sufficient. Within this field, there is always at work a remainder of an object which resists symbolization, the remainder which condenses, materializes pure enjoyment, and which, in our case, assumes the form of the King's or Leader's other, sublime, body." *For They Know Not What They Do*, p. 263.

27. *Ticklish Subject*, p. 266.

28. *Ticklish Subject*, pp. 334–347; Slavoj Žižek, *Welcome to the Desert of the Real* (London: Verso, 2002), pp. 5–32.

29. For a more elaborated account of this experience of contingency see, Jodi Dean, *Aliens in America: Conspiracy Cultures from Outerspace to Cyberspace* (Ithaca, NY: Cornell University Press, 1999).

30. *Iraq: The Borrowed Kettle*, p. 118.

31. *Ticklish Subject*, p. 346.

32. *Ticklish Subject*, p. 355.

33. I say "almost" because in *Iraq: The Borrowed Kettle* Žižek provides a powerful example of a political act that touches the economy. He writes, "Whenever a political project takes a radical turn, up pops the inevitable blackmail: 'Of course these goals are desirable in themselves; if we do this, however, international capital will boycott us, the growth rate will fall, and so on.' ... who cares if growth stalls, or even becomes negative? Have we not had enough of the high growth rate whose effects on the social organism were felt mostly in the guise of new forms of poverty and dispossession? What about a negative growth that would translate into a qualitatively better, not higher standard of living for the wider popular strata? That would be a political act today—to break the spell of automatically endorsing the existing political framework, to break out of the debilitating alternative 'either we just directly endorse free-market globalization, or we make impossible promises along the lines of magic formulae about how to have one's cake and eat it, about how to combine globalization with social solidarity'" (p. 74). This is a great example of an act, but it does not solve the problem of why an act would correspond to the singular truth of a situation.

34. "Lenin's Choice," p. 297.

35. Parker, p. 97.

36. But see Jodi Dean, "Communicative Capitalism: Circulation and the Foreclosure of Politics," *Cultural Politics* 1, 1 (2005): pp. 51–74.
37. "Lenin's Choice," p. 225.
38. "Lenin's Choice," p. 189.
39. "Lenin's Choice," p. 170.
40. For a thorough reading of Bartleby that addresses the elimination of the will, see Giorgio Agamben, *Potentialities*, translated by Daniel Heller-Roazen (Stanford, CA: Stanford University Press, 1999). pp. 243–274.
41. *Parallax View*, p. 101.
42. *Parallax View*, p. 381.
43. "Lenin's Choice," p. 188.
44. *Ticklish Subject*, pp. 135–137, p. 144.
45. "Lenin's Choice," p. 186.
46. "Lenin's Choice," p. 177.
47. Ian Parker, once again, is mistaken in his reading of Žižek. Parker says that truth appears only in the act (p. 102). For Žižek, truth is the form of the act, the way the act is formalized.
48. "Lenin's Choice," p. 188.
49. "Lenin's Choice," p. 190.
50. "Lenin's Choice," p. 190.
51. *Conversations with Žižek*, p. 143.
52. *Iraq: The Borrowed Kettle*, p. 91.
53. UN-Habitat, *The Challenge of Slums: Global Report on Human Settlement* (London: Earthscan Publications, 2003).
54. "Lenin's Choice," p. 252.

INDEX

A

Abu Ghraib prison torture, 152
Adorno, T., 154
Agamben, Giorgio, 52, 71, 73–74, 83,
    135, 160–163, 165, 167, 201
Althusser, Louis, 9, 157
American Right, 182, 196
Anarchism, 135
Antagonism concept, 55–60, 87
    class struggle, 57
    racialization of, 69
Antifascism, 50
Antiracism, 2
Anti-Semitism, 66, 88
Arato, Andrew, 183
Arendt, Hannah, 49, 67, 187
Articles of Confederation, 139–141
Autonomy, 21

B

Badiou, Alain, 70, 79, 120, 181
Baldwin, Alec, 26–28, 30
Balibar, Etienne, 181
Ballard, J. G., 152, 156–157, 174
Banality of evil, 67
"Bartleby politics"/"Bartleby the
    Scrivener" (Melville), 22, 29,
    130–131, 168, 170, 197–198
Beloved (Morrison), 169–170, 177
Bentham, Jeremy, 11

Biopolitics, 85, 172–172
"Black ops," 34
Brose, Christian, 182
Brown, Wendy, 115
Bryant, Roy, 35
Bukharin trial (1937), 75–77
Bureaucracy, 97
Bush, George H. W., 193
Bush, George W., 26, 28, 30–31, 99,
    126–128, 131, 182
Butler, Judith, 102

C

Calvinism, 110
Capital, 59–60, 102, 114–115
Capital (Marx), 17
Capitalism, 97, 110
    biopolitics, 85, 172–173
    bureaucratic socialism and, 83
    capitalist production, 18
    class struggle and, 58
    communicative capitalism, 36–37,
        96, 192
    consumer-entertainment economy,
        2, 37
    in Eastern Europe, 111–112
    freedom in, 2–3
    global capitalism, 2, 50–51
    late capitalist subjects, 99
    liberal democracy and, 96
    multiculturalism and, 115

as self-revolutionizing form, 86
speed, flows, and mobility, 16–23,
    36, 42
Stalinism and, 82–83, 86
university discourse in/as, 96–101
CATO Institute, 182
Chavez, Hugo, 34
Christian fundamentalists, 38–39, 50,
    126–127, 179
Clark, Ramsey, 34
Class struggle, 48, 57–58, 87, 95,
    199–200
Capital/capitalist society and,
    59–60
economy and politics, 60
National socialism and, 62
Stalinism and, 82
Cleland, Max, 192
Clinton, Bill, 30, 129, 131, 193
Cohen, Jean, 183
Cold War, 50
Communicative capitalism, 36–37, 96,
    192
Communism, 18, 48–49, 51, 60, 74
Community, 15–16
community of believers, 174–175
Nazi ideal of, 69–71
Connolly, William, 3, 16, 44–45, 115,
    119–120
Conservative politics, 180
Constitutional Congress, 139–142
Consumer culture, 37
Coulter, Ann, 39
Cultural heritage, 14

D

Da Vinci Code, The (Brown), 15
Daly, Glyn, 1, 200
Darwin, Charles, 141
Davis, Gray, 131
Deleuze, Gilles, 115, 119, 135
Democracy; see also Liberal
    democracy

Capital and, 102–103
form of, 105–109
universality, 103, 105
Žižek's critique of, 102–103,
    113–114, 125–133
Democratic fundamentalism, 95, 104
Democratic invention, 106
Democratic Leadership Council, 129
Desire, 12
Dialectic of Enlightenment, The
    (Horkheimer and Adorno),
    154
Did Somebody Say Totalitarianism
    (Žižek), 49, 52
Discourse of the analyst, 88–90, 92
Discourse of the Master, 62–69, 95
Discourse of the pervert, 72–81, 92, 95
Discourse of the university, 82–87,
    95–101
Displacement, 23–29
displaced mediators, 111, 114
fixity vs., 24, 42
Domination, 2, 8, 26, 43
Douglass, Frederick, 149
Drives, 6–7

E

East-European nationalism, 112–113
Ego ideal, 11
Eichmann, Adolf, 67
Empty signifier, 8
Enjoyment
Baldwin/Bush displacement-
    passivity example, 26–31
bureaucratization as source of, 68
community and, 15–16
defined, 4–8
displacement/the Other, 23–29
drives and, 6–7
ethnic nationalism, 14, 23
externalization of, 25
fantasy structures of, 8, 12, 15
fixity vs. displacement, 24, 42

in ideology, 8–16, 48
other as objects, 23
pluralism and, 36–46
as political category, 191
political theory and, 1–3, 31, 43, 47
psychoanalytic account of, 4–5
superego and, 30–36
surplus enjoyment, 19, 37
transgression and, 31, 35
Equality, 101
Ethics of Psychoanalysis, The (Lacan),
 164
Ethnic nationalism, 3, 13–14, 23, 26,
 51, 110, 112
Ethnic violence, 14, 113–114

F

False consciousness, 9
Fantasy, 8, 12, 15–16
Fascism, 48–52, 60–71, 74, 88, 95
Federalist, 140
Fink, Bruce, 5, 149
Fitzpatrick, Peter, 145
Fitzpatrick, Sheila, 79
For They Know Not What They Do
 (Žižek), 1, 103
Form of the Social, 200
Foucault, Michel, 9–10, 76, 83
Founding crime, 137–144
Founding law, 137–138, 145–148
Founding violence, 138, 142
Frank, Thomas, 179–180, 196
Frankfurt School, 51, 183
Freedom, 2–3, 101
Freud, Sigmund, 12, 20, 57, 106,
 141–142, 145–147
Fundamentalism, 38–39, 44–45, 104

G

Gamson, Joshua, 116
Gay marriage, 39
Gay media, 116

Gerry, Elbridge, 140
Gingrich, Newt, 182
Ginsburg, Ruth Bader, 39
Glengarry Glen Ross, 26–28, 30
Global capitalism. *see* Capitalism
Global finance, 87
Guattari, Felix, 115, 119, 135

H

Habermas, Jürgen, 183
Hardt, Michael, 16, 115, 119–121,
 124–125, 185
Hegel, G. W. F., 53–55, 103, 108, 144
Heidegger, Martin, 70
Hobbes, Thomas, 13, 142, 146–147
Hoffman, Stanley, 132–133
Holocaust, 52, 67, 70
Homo sacer, 201
Human rights, 100, 122
Human settlements, 201

I

Identity politics, 57–58, 116, 118–119,
 123
Ideology, 48, 190, 194
 Marxist concept of, 9
Iran-Contra hearings, 155

J

Jacobins, 106–111, 121
Jameson, Fredric, 110
Jewish people, 60–61, 66, 88
Jouissance. see Enjoyment
Justice, 101

K

Kafka, Franz, 143
"Kant avec Sade" (Lacan), 136
Kant, Emmanuel, 21, 54–55, 106–110,
 142, 154–156, 159, 163, 168

Kerry, John, 192
Krauthammer, Charles, 182
Krupskaya, Nadezhda, 90
Ku Klux Klan, 152, 154

L

Lacan, Jacques, 1, 5–7, 11–12, 14, 17,
    30, 48, 52–53, 60, 62–64,
    72, 82, 88–89, 107–108, 126,
    136, 154–155, 194
Laclau, Ernesto, 8, 55–56, 58, 102, 105,
    122, 183
Law
    civil laws, 143
    Constitutional Congress, 139–142
    enjoying law, 157–159
    founding crime and, 137–144
    founding law, 137–138, 145–148
    freedom and disalienation of,
        145–147
    hope in, 176–177
    incompleteness/inconsistency of,
        150
    lawful suspension of, 160–161
    love with, 159–168
    moral law, 106–108, 121, 127,
        154–155, 163
    "nightly law," 33, 136, 152, 159,
        174–175
    object in, 168–171
    origins in trauma, 139, 141–142
    parallax gap in, 159
    public law, 32–34, 136, 153–154,
        158–159
    radical politics and, 135
    Real of violence, 143
    Reason and law as law, 144
    religious law, 136
    split law, 148–150
    superego law, 136–137, 146–150
    surplus/lack and, 148–157
    symbolic law of language/norms,
        136, 146

transference of beliefs to, 143–144
Lazarus, Sylvain, 79
Lefort, Claude, 96, 106, 109
Leftist/liberal politics, 40
Lenin/Leninism, 52, 82, 87–93, 95, 176
"Lenin's Choice" (Žižek), 52
Leviathan (Hobbes), 13
Levy, Primo, 73
Liberal democracy, 50, 96–97, 101,
    122, 132–133
    equality, freedom, justice in, 101
    fundamentalism and, 104, 114–115
Liberal neutrality, 50
Liberal pluralism, 40
Locke, John, 143
Love, Pauline love, 162–168, 172, 176

M

Madison, James, 140
Marx, Karl, 17–18, 20
Marxism, 56, 110, 184–185, 199
Melville, Herman, 21, 130, 197–198
Migration, 3, 16
Milam, J. W., 35
Moral law, 106–108, 121, 127, 154–155,
    163
Morrison, Toni, 169–170
Mouffe, Chantal, 8, 56, 58, 183
Multiculturalism, 40
    depoliticization of economy, 116,
        118
    ethnic other and, 117
    global capitalism and, 115
    Žižek's arguments against, 115–120,
        170–171
Multitude of singularities concept, 185
Muselmann (Muslim), 71–73, 91
Myers, Michael, 68

N

Nation, 109
National myths, 112

National Review Online, 182
National security funding, 34
National Socialism, 52, 61–62, 67–69,
    88, 95
Nationalism, 113–114
Nationalist fundamentalism, 103
Nazism, 48–49, 52, 61–62, 67–69, 95
    experience of community, 70
Negri, Antonio, 16, 115, 119–121,
    124–125, 185
Neoconservative politics, 50, 110, 179
Neoliberal capitalism/neoliberalism,
    103, 110, 113, 179
Netocracy (digital elite), 119
New Economic Policy (Soviet Union),
    52
New social movements, 2, 114
Nietzsche, F. W., 20, 188
"Nightly law," 33, 136, 152, 159,
    174–175
Nomenklatura, 78
Norms, 41
North, Oliver, 155

O

Objet petit a, 5, 10, 12, 16–17, 65, 78–
    79, 83–84, 89–91, 108–110,
    160, 189
Organs without Bodies (Žižek), 49

P

Palestinian suicide bombers, 130
Parallax gap, 52–55, 71, 126, 137, 159
Parallax View, The (Žižek), 1, 130–131
Parker, Ian, 186, 195
Parks, Rosa, 123
The Party, 194–202
Party class struggle, 200
Pascal, Blaise, 143
Passage a l'acte, 196
Passavant, Paul A., 135
Patriarchal family, 2, 16

Pauline love, 162–168, 172, 176, 198
Personhood, 77
Phenomenology of Spirit (Hegel), 144
Plague of Fantasies, The (Žižek), 153
Pluralism/pluralization, 3, 36, 44–45
Political acts, 129–130, 196
Political subjectivization, 116
Political theory, enjoyment as category
    of, 1–3
Politicization, universalization and,
    120–125
Postmodern nationalism, 39
Postmodern relativism, 50
"Practice utopia," 176
Privatization, 110, 113
Property, 87–88, 186
Protestantism/Protestant ethnic,
    110–111
Public law, 32–34, 153–154, 158–159

R

Race/racial identity, 13–14
Racism, 3, 26, 35, 87, 114, 117, 123
Ranciere, Jacques, 34, 123, 181
Reflective determination, 162
Religious fundamentalism, 38–39, 50,
    126–127, 179
Republican Party, 131–132
"Republican Revolution Ten Years
    Later: Smaller Government
    or Business as Usual?," 182
Revolution, 181–184
    agency and act of, 184–194
    Russian Revolution, 79, 81
Revolution at the Gates (Žižek), 52
Revolutionary activity, 180
Revolutionary emancipatory politics,
    90
Revolutionary party, 195
Revolutionary violence, 198
Robertson, Pat, 34
Rousseau, Jean-Jacques, 163–164, 168
Russian Revolution, 79, 81

S

Sacrifice of the object, 170, 195
Sade, Marquis de, 108, 136, 154–156,
    159
St. Paul, 159–167, 171, 175
Schmitt, Carl, 73
Second Treatise (Locke), 143
September 11 attacks, 99, 127
Sexual harassment, 154
Singer, Bryan, 169
Social compact, 163–164
Social justice, 101, 118
Socialism, 50–51, 85–86, 96
Society
    antagonism and, 56
    confrontational change in, 8
Solidarity, 195
Soviet gulag, 72–73
Spielberg, Steven, 118
Stalinism, 48–52, 72–87
    Bukharin trial (1937), 75–77
    bureaucracy and, 82–87
    cult of personality, 79
    discourse of the pervert, 72–81, 92
    discourse of the university, 82–87
    Leninist Party and, 91
    as perversion of revolution, 80, 88
    as post property society, 86
    purges and terror of, 78–82, 88
    as self-revolutionizing form, 86
    show trials of, 72–73, 75, 92
State of the Union address (2003), 28,
    31, 33
Sublime Object of Ideology, The
    (Žižek), 103
Super Cannes (Ballard), 152, 156–157,
    174
Superego
    attachment/ambiguity, 153
    enjoyment and, 30–36
    law and, 136–137, 146–150, 159
    violence of, 152–156
Surplus value, 17, 19

Symbolic efficiency, 99–100
Symbolic identification, 11
Symbolic order of language, 5–6

T

Ten Commandments, 100, 136
Theory of law, 100
Third Reich bureaucracy, 67–68
Ticklish Subject, The (Žižek), 33, 55
Till, Emmett, 35
Time That Remains, The (Agamben),
    160
Torture, 28, 31, 68, 70, 152, 155–156
Totalitarianism, 45, 48–55, 60, 82, 87
Totem and Taboo (Freud), 12, 141, 145
Trial (Kafka), 143
Trotsky, Leon, 79

U

U.S. Constitution, 34, 139–142
Universalization, 120–125
Usual Suspects, The, 169, 177

V

Values, 179
Vanishing mediator, 110–114
Voter turnout, 180–181

W

War on terror, 31, 42, 160
Weber, Max, 110
What's the Matter with Kansas?
    (Frank), 179
Working class, 186

Z

Žižek, Slavoj
    antagonism concept, 55–60

antidemocratic stance of, 102–103,
113–114, 125–133
on capitalist production, 18
class struggle, 57–59
"collapse of the big Other," 40
economy and politics, 60
fantasy of passivity, 22–23
fixity and enjoyment, 17–19, 22,
42
interpassivity, 23
liberal political culture, 21
modern power, 84–85

multiculturalism arguments,
115–120, 170–171
nation's existence, 14
Nazism and parallax Real, 61,
65–66
notion of ideology, 8–9
parallex gap concept, 52–55
politics and economy of enjoyment,
1–3, 20
Ranciere vs., 34–35
regulations vs. symbolic
prohibitions, 38–39
superego and enjoyment, 32, 35

An environmentally friendly book printed and bound in England by www.printondemand-worldwide.com

PEFC Certified

This product is
from sustainably
managed forests
and controlled
sources

www.pefc.org

PEFC/16-33-415

MIX
Paper from
responsible sources

FSC® C004959

www.fsc.org

This book is made entirely of sustainable materials; FSC paper for the cover and PEFC paper for the text pages.

#0035 - 130217 - C0 - 216/138/14 - PB